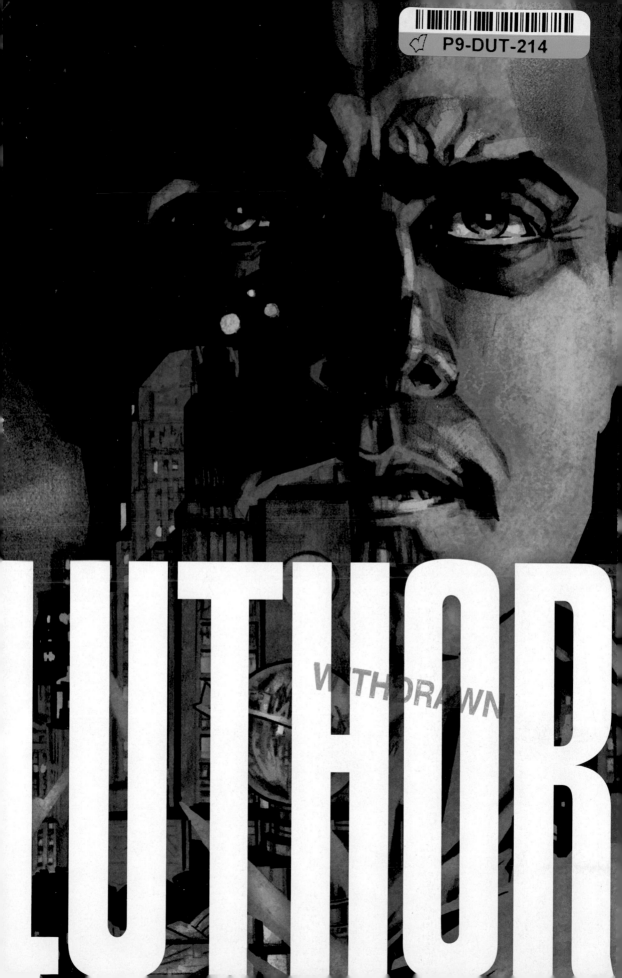

LUTHOR

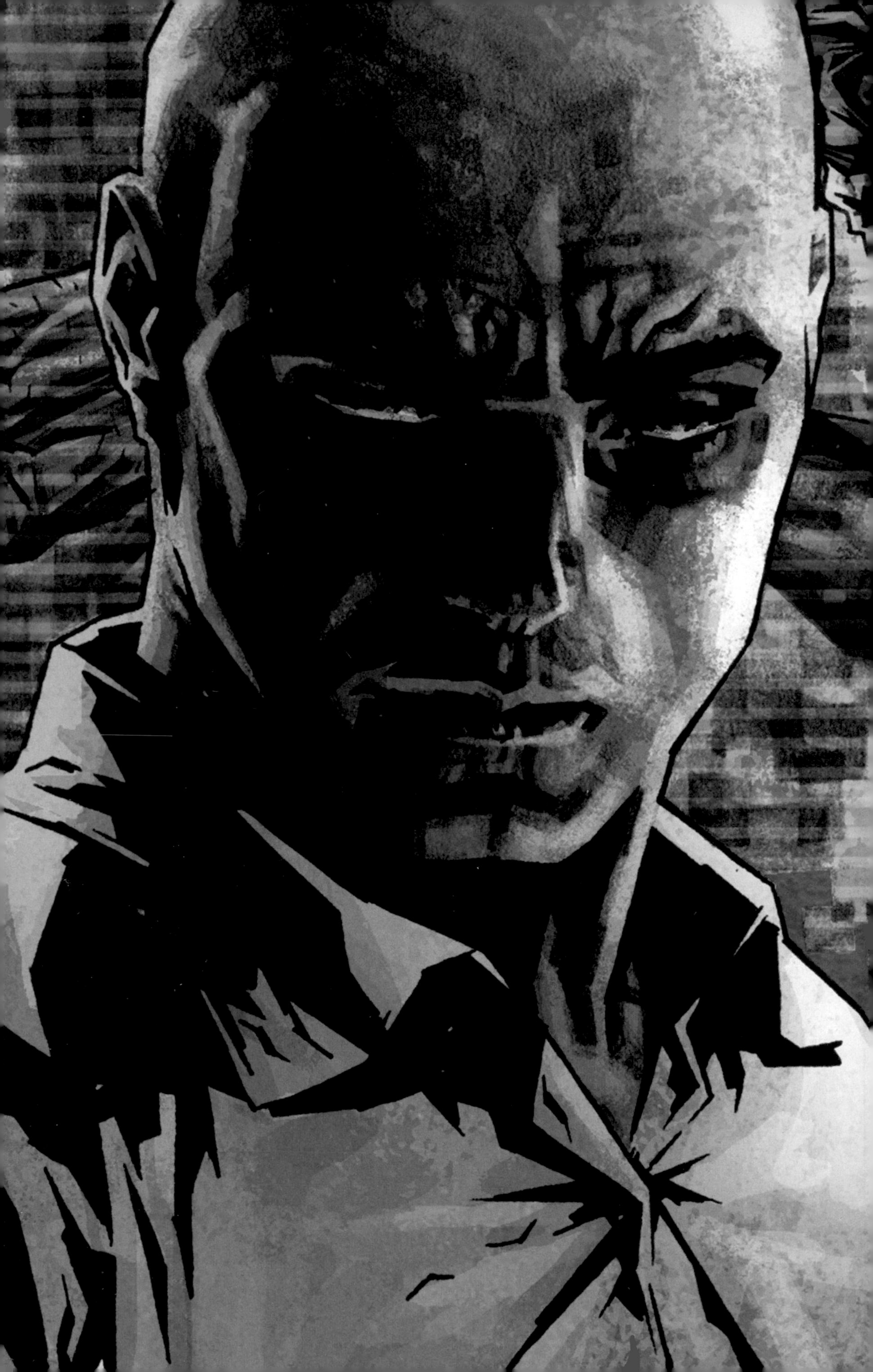

LUTHOR

BRIAN AZZARELLO
WRITER

LEE BERMEJO
ARTIST

MICK GRAY
KARL STORY
JASON MARTIN
ADDITIONAL INKS

DAVE STEWART
JOSÉ VILLARRUBIA
COLORISTS

PHIL BALSMAN
PAT BROSSEAU
ROB LEIGH
NICK NAPOLITANO
LETTERERS

COVER ART AND ORIGINAL SERIES COVERS BY
LEE BERMEJO

RMAN created by JERRY SIEGEL and JOE SHUSTER
By special arrangement with the Jerry Siegel family

BATMAN created by BOB KANE

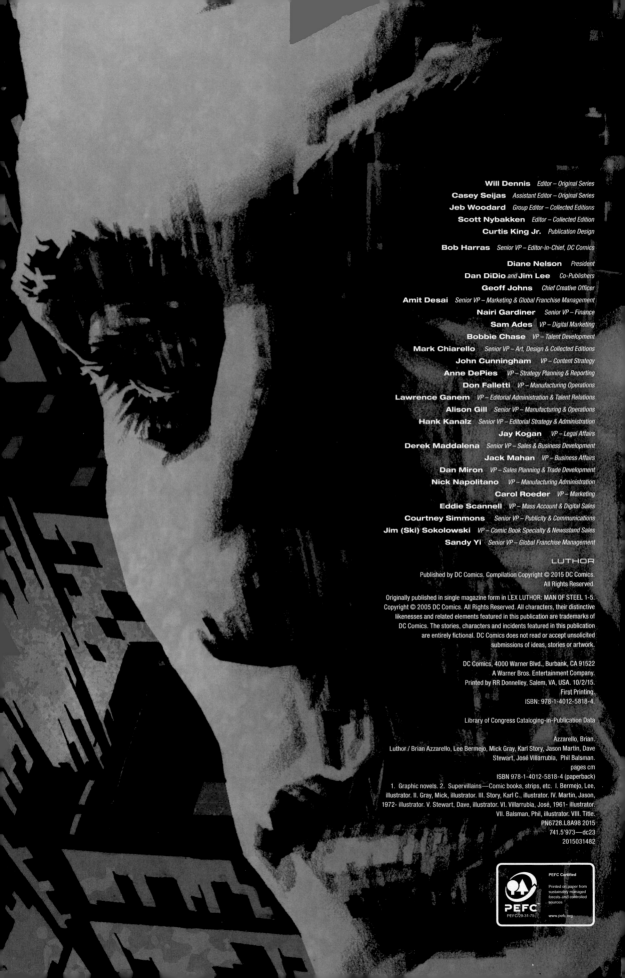

Will Dennis Editor – Original Series
Casey Seijas Assistant Editor – Original Series
Jeb Woodard Group Editor – Collected Editions
Scott Nybakken Editor – Collected Edition
Curtis King Jr. Publication Design
Bob Harras Senior VP – Editor-in-Chief, DC Comics

Diane Nelson President
Dan DiDio and **Jim Lee** Co-Publishers
Geoff Johns Chief Creative Officer
Amit Desai Senior VP – Marketing & Global Franchise Management
Nairi Gardiner Senior VP – Finance
Sam Ades VP – Digital Marketing
Bobbie Chase VP – Talent Development
Mark Chiarello Senior VP – Art, Design & Collected Editions
John Cunningham VP – Content Strategy
Anne DePies VP – Strategy Planning & Reporting
Don Falletti VP – Manufacturing Operations
Lawrence Ganem VP – Editorial Administration & Talent Relations
Alison Gill Senior VP – Manufacturing & Operations
Hank Kanalz Senior VP – Editorial Strategy & Administration
Jay Kogan VP – Legal Affairs
Derek Maddalena Senior VP – Sales & Business Development
Jack Mahan VP – Business Affairs
Dan Miron VP – Sales Planning & Trade Development
Nick Napolitano VP – Manufacturing Administration
Carol Roeder VP – Marketing
Eddie Scannell VP – Mass Account & Digital Sales
Courtney Simmons Senior VP – Publicity & Communications
Jim (Ski) Sokolowski VP – Comic Book Specialty & Newsstand Sales
Sandy Yi Senior VP – Global Franchise Management

LUTHOR

DC Comics, 4000 Warner Blvd., Burbank, CA 91522
A Warner Bros. Entertainment Company.
Printed by RR Donnelley, Salem, VA, USA. 10/2/15.
First Printing.
ISBN: 978-1-4012-5818-4.

Library of Congress Cataloging-in-Publication Data

Azzarello, Brian.
Luthor / Brian Azzarello, Lee Bermejo, Mick Gray, Karl Story, Jason Martin, Dave
Stewart, José Villarrubia, Phil Balsman.
pages cm
ISBN 978-1-4012-5818-4 (paperback)
1. Graphic novels. 2. Supervillains—Comic books, strips, etc. I. Bermejo, Lee,
illustrator. II. Gray, Mick, illustrator. III. Story, Karl C., illustrator. IV. Martin, Jason,
1972- illustrator. V. Stewart, Dave, illustrator. VI. Villarrubia, José, 1961- illustrator.
VII. Balsman, Phil, illustrator. VIII. Title.
PN6728.L8A98 2015
741.5'973—dc23
2015031482

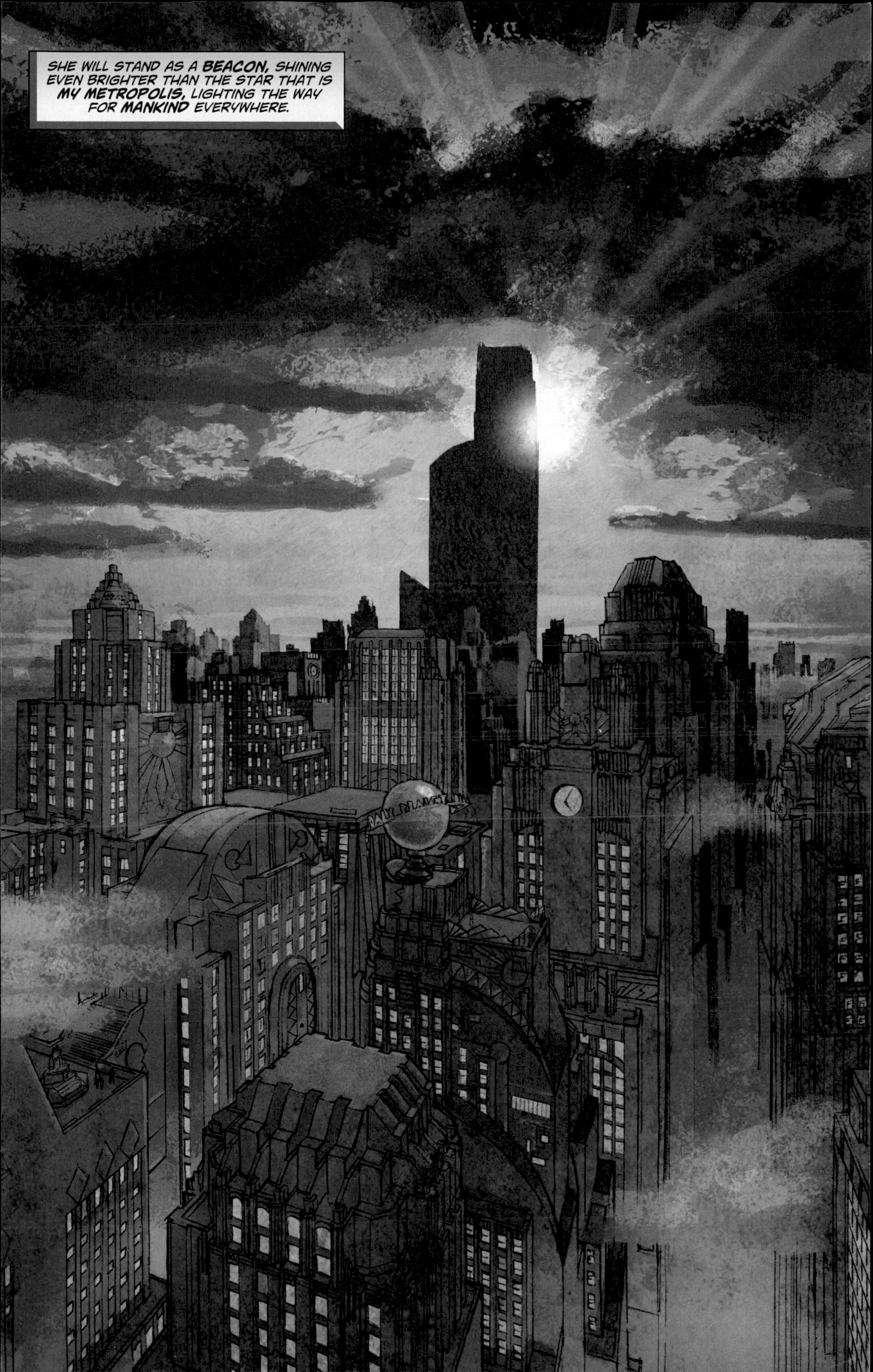
SHE WILL STAND AS A BEACON, SHINING EVEN BRIGHTER THAN THE STAR THAT IS MY METROPOLIS, LIGHTING THE WAY FOR MANKIND EVERYWHERE.

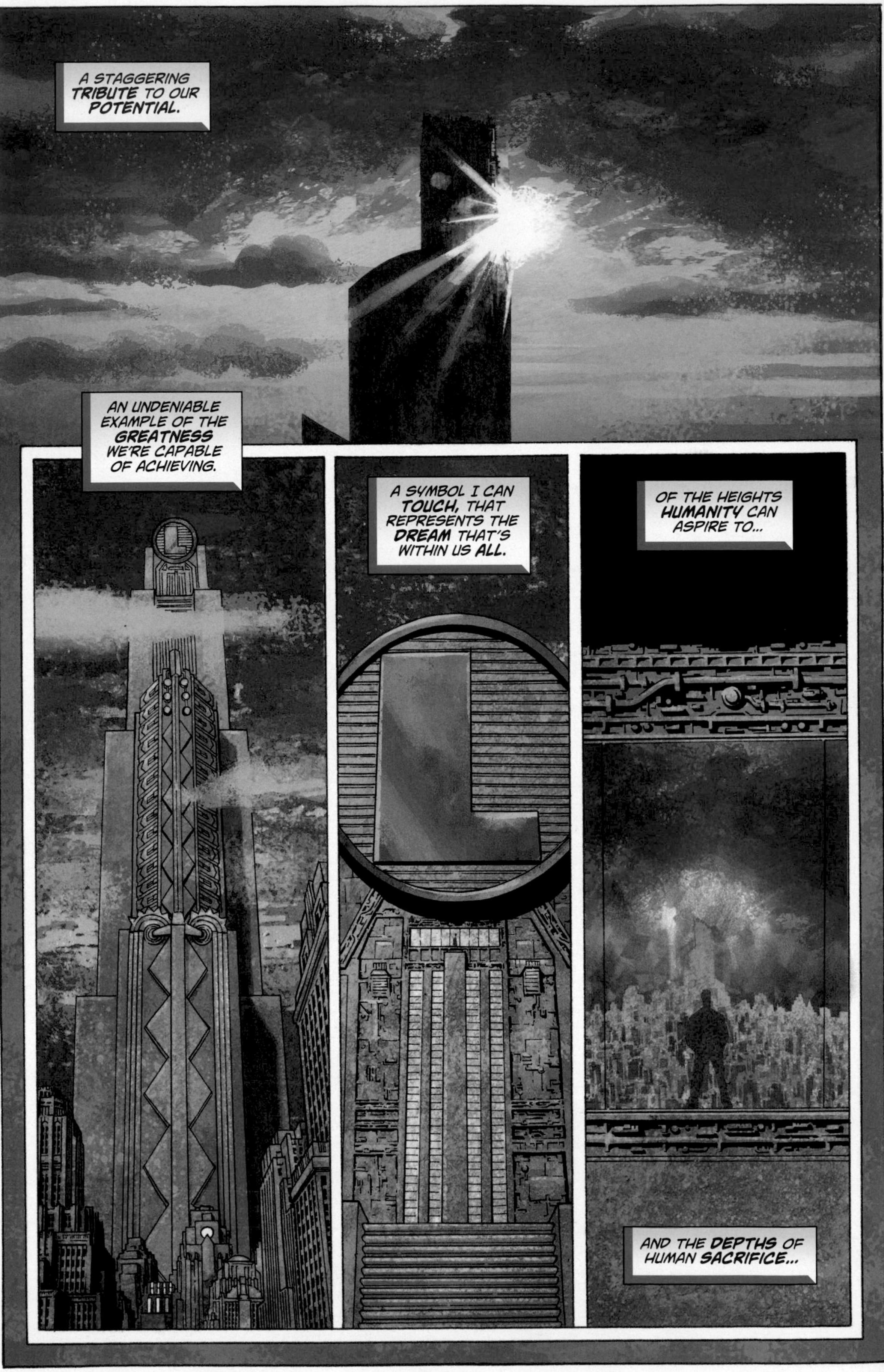
A STAGGERING TRIBUTE TO OUR POTENTIAL.
AN UNDENIABLE EXAMPLE OF THE GREATNESS WE'RE CAPABLE OF ACHIEVING.
A SYMBOL I CAN TOUCH, THAT REPRESENTS THE DREAM THAT'S WITHIN US ALL.
OF THE HEIGHTS HUMANITY CAN ASPIRE TO...
AND THE DEPTHS OF HUMAN SACRIFICE...

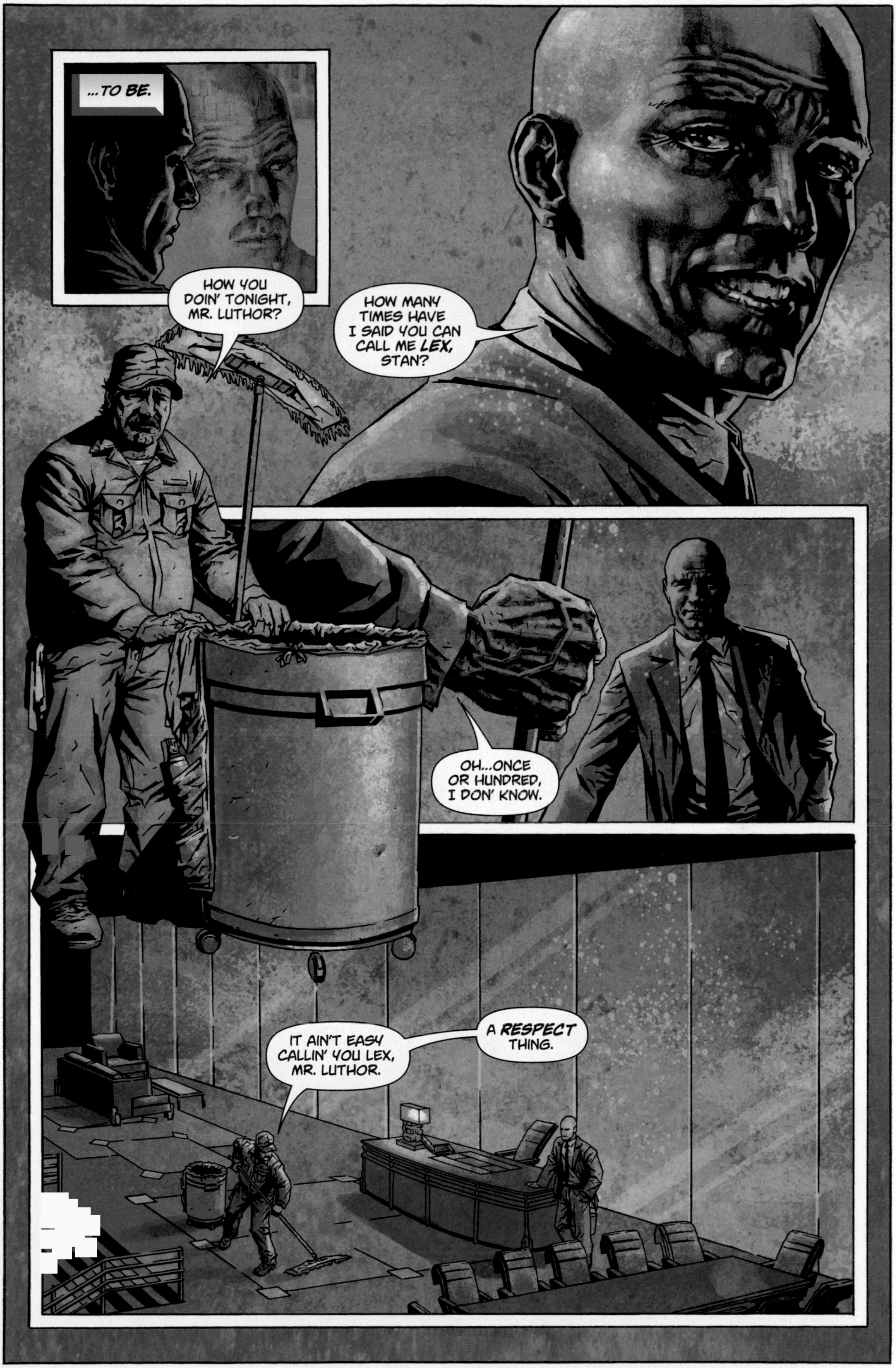
...TO BE.
HOW YOU DOIN' TONIGHT, MR. LUTHOR?
HOW MANY TIMES HAVE I SAID YOU CAN CALL ME LEX, STAN?
OH...ONCE OR HUNDRED, I DON' KNOW.
IT AIN'T EASY CALLIN' YOU LEX, MR. LUTHOR.
A RESPECT THING.

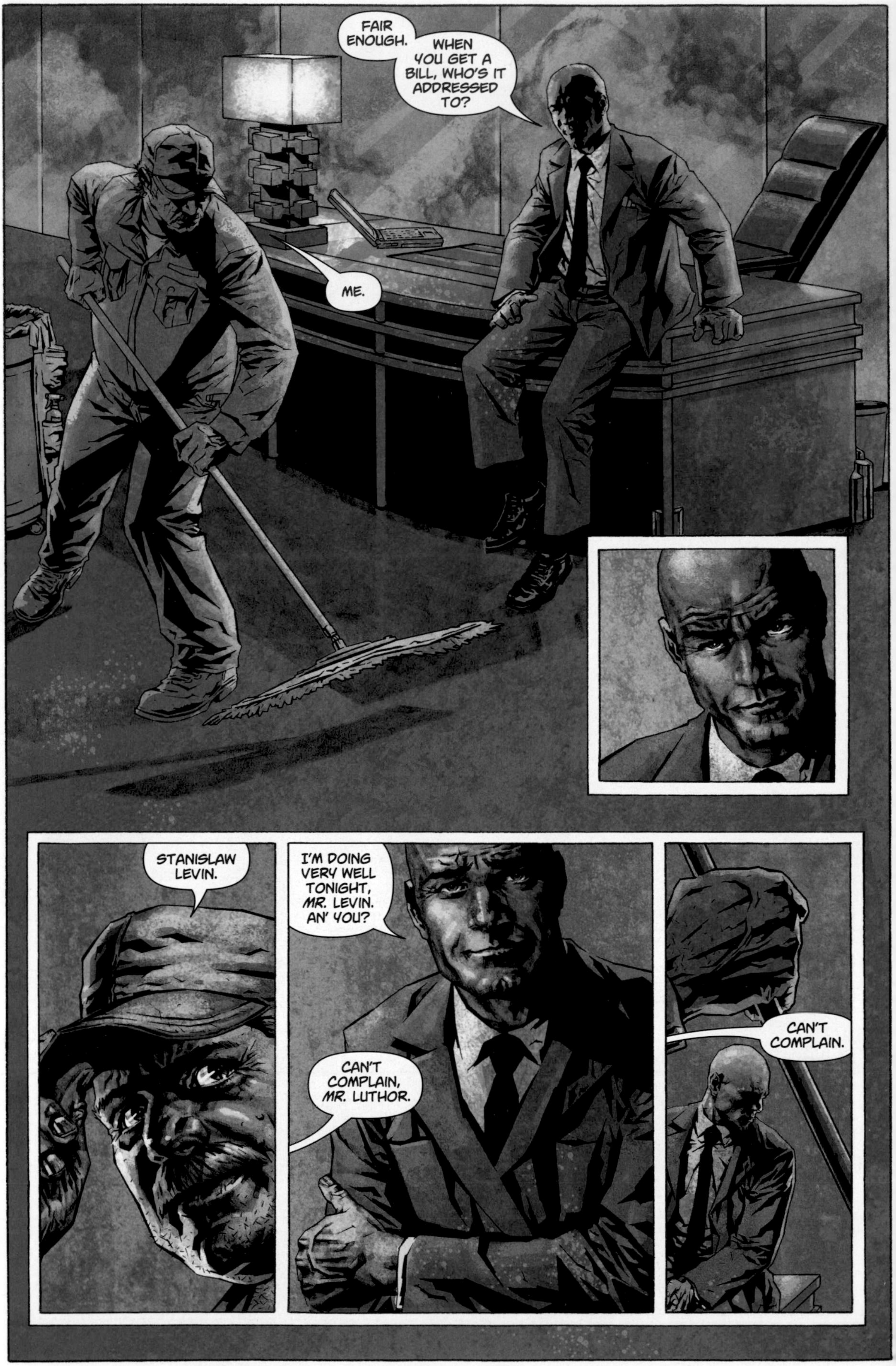
FAIR ENOUGH.
WHEN YOU GET A BILL, WHO'S IT ADDRESSED TO?
ME.
STANISLAW LEVIN.
I'M DOING VERY WELL TONIGHT, MR. LEVIN. AN' YOU?
CAN'T COMPLAIN, MR. LUTHOR.
CAN'T COMPLAIN.

THANKS.

SHE'S SURE GONNA BE *SOMETHIN'*, WHEN SHE'S DONE.

YES, SHE *WILL*.

LOOKIN' FORWARD TO IT, MIGHT EVEN TAKE MY KIDS ON OPENING DAY.

MY BOY--JOEY-- HIS MOTHER TELLS ME HE DOES REALLY GOOD IN SCIENCE AT SCHOOL.

WHEN HE *GOES*.

A LITTLE *INCENTIVE*. IT'S A PERSONAL INVITATION TO BE MY GUEST FOR THE GRAND OPENING OF THE METROPOLIS *SCIENCE SPIRE*-- IF HE GETS AN "A" IN SCIENCE.

YOU DON'T HAVE TO DO THIS, MR. LUTHOR.

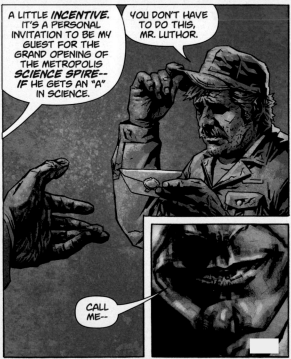

CUTS CLASS?

HE'S THIRTEEN.

HE CUTS CLASS.

GIVE HIM *THIS*.

CALL ME--

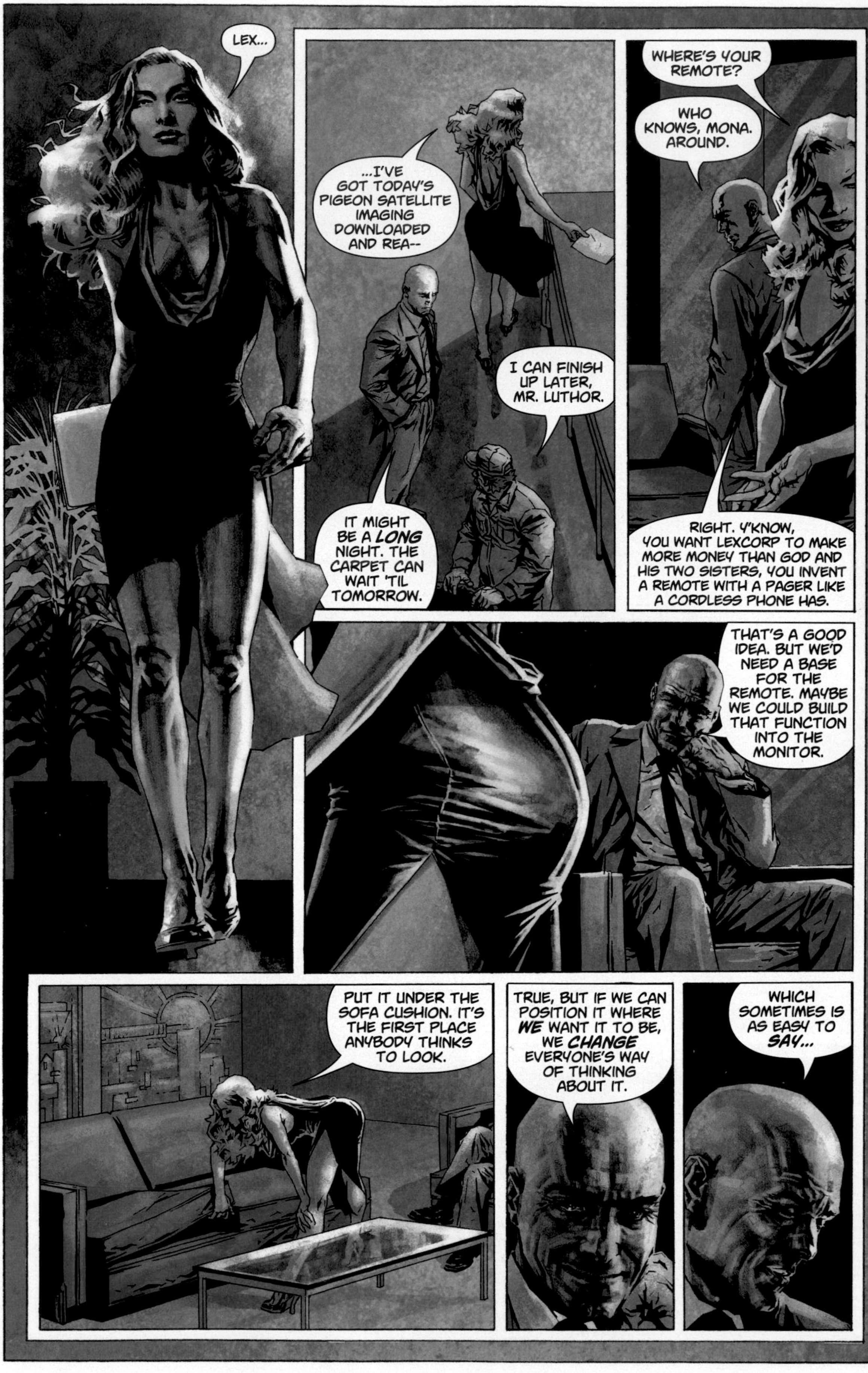
LEX...
...I'VE GOT TODAY'S PIGEON SATELLITE IMAGING DOWNLOADED AND REA--
I CAN FINISH UP LATER, MR. LUTHOR.
IT MIGHT BE A LONG NIGHT. THE CARPET CAN WAIT 'TIL TOMORROW.
WHERE'S YOUR REMOTE?
WHO KNOWS, MONA. AROUND.
RIGHT. Y'KNOW, YOU WANT LEXCORP TO MAKE MORE MONEY THAN GOD AND HIS TWO SISTERS, YOU INVENT A REMOTE WITH A PAGER LIKE A CORDLESS PHONE HAS.
THAT'S A GOOD IDEA. BUT WE'D NEED A BASE FOR THE REMOTE. MAYBE WE COULD BUILD THAT FUNCTION INTO THE MONITOR.
PUT IT UNDER THE SOFA CUSHION. IT'S THE FIRST PLACE ANYBODY THINKS TO LOOK.
TRUE, BUT IF WE CAN POSITION IT WHERE WE WANT IT TO BE, WE CHANGE EVERYONE'S WAY OF THINKING ABOUT IT.
WHICH SOMETIMES IS AS EASY TO SAY...

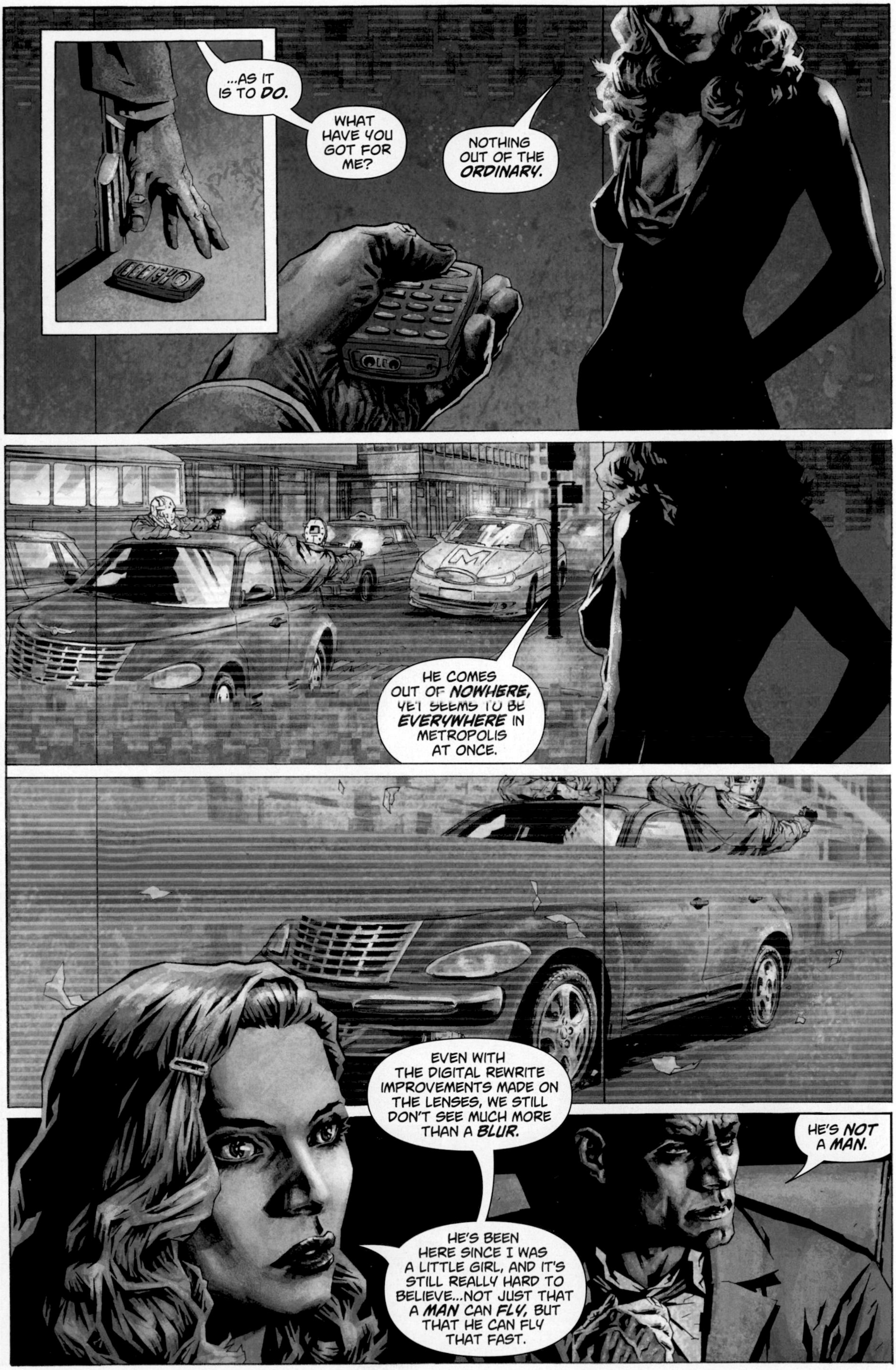
...AS IT IS TO DO.
WHAT HAVE YOU GOT FOR ME?
NOTHING OUT OF THE ORDINARY.
HE COMES OUT OF NOWHERE, YET SEEMS TO BE EVERYWHERE IN METROPOLIS AT ONCE.
EVEN WITH THE DIGITAL REWRITE IMPROVEMENTS MADE ON THE LENSES, WE STILL DON'T SEE MUCH MORE THAN A BLUR.
HE'S BEEN HERE SINCE I WAS A LITTLE GIRL, AND IT'S STILL REALLY HARD TO BELIEVE...NOT JUST THAT A MAN CAN FLY, BUT THAT HE CAN FLY THAT FAST.
HE'S NOT A MAN.

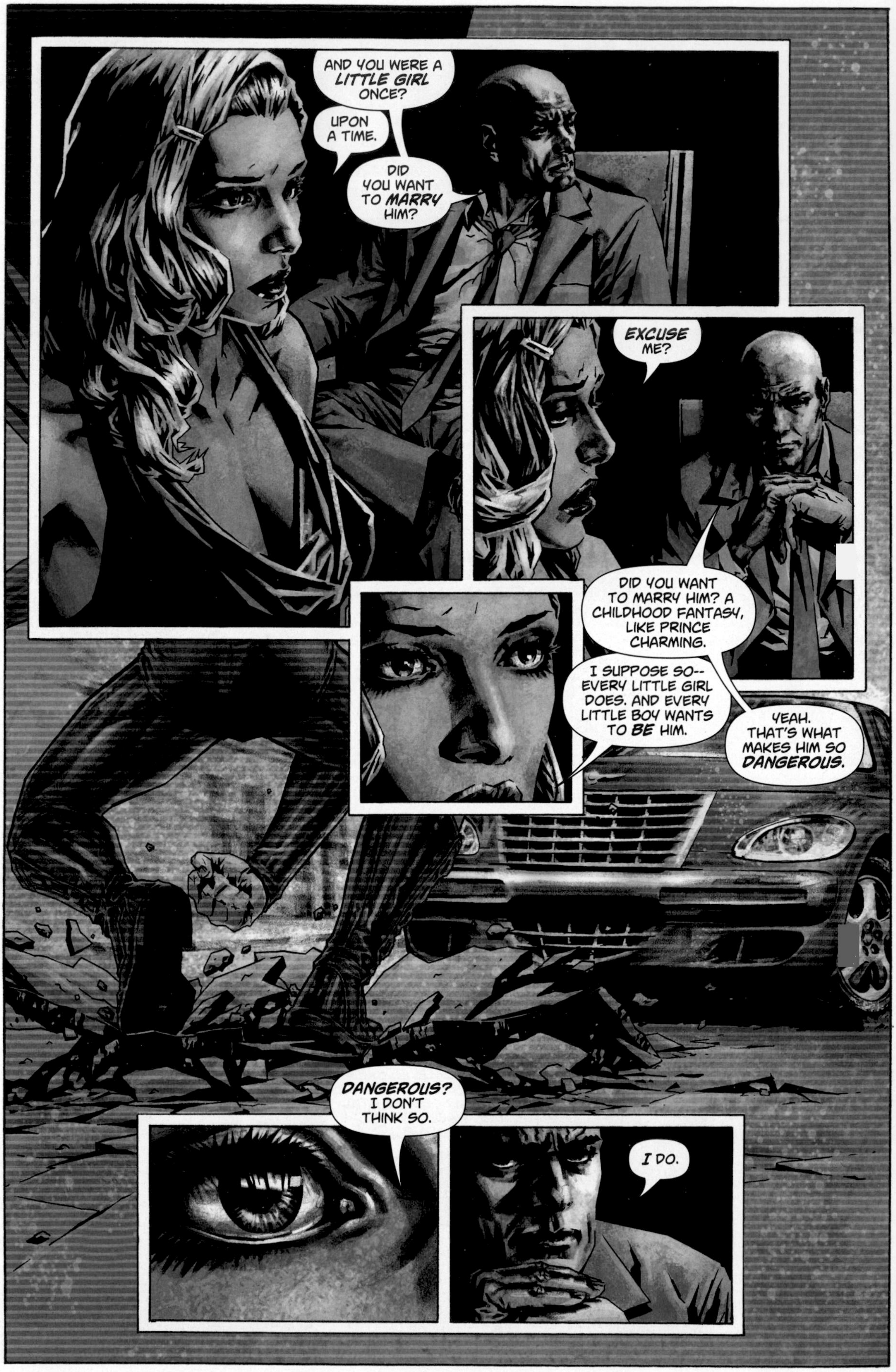
AND YOU WERE A LITTLE GIRL ONCE?
UPON A TIME.
DID YOU WANT TO MARRY HIM?
EXCUSE ME?
DID YOU WANT TO MARRY HIM? A CHILDHOOD FANTASY, LIKE PRINCE CHARMING.
I SUPPOSE SO-- EVERY LITTLE GIRL DOES. AND EVERY LITTLE BOY WANTS TO BE HIM.
YEAH. THAT'S WHAT MAKES HIM SO DANGEROUS.
DANGEROUS? I DON'T THINK SO.
I DO.

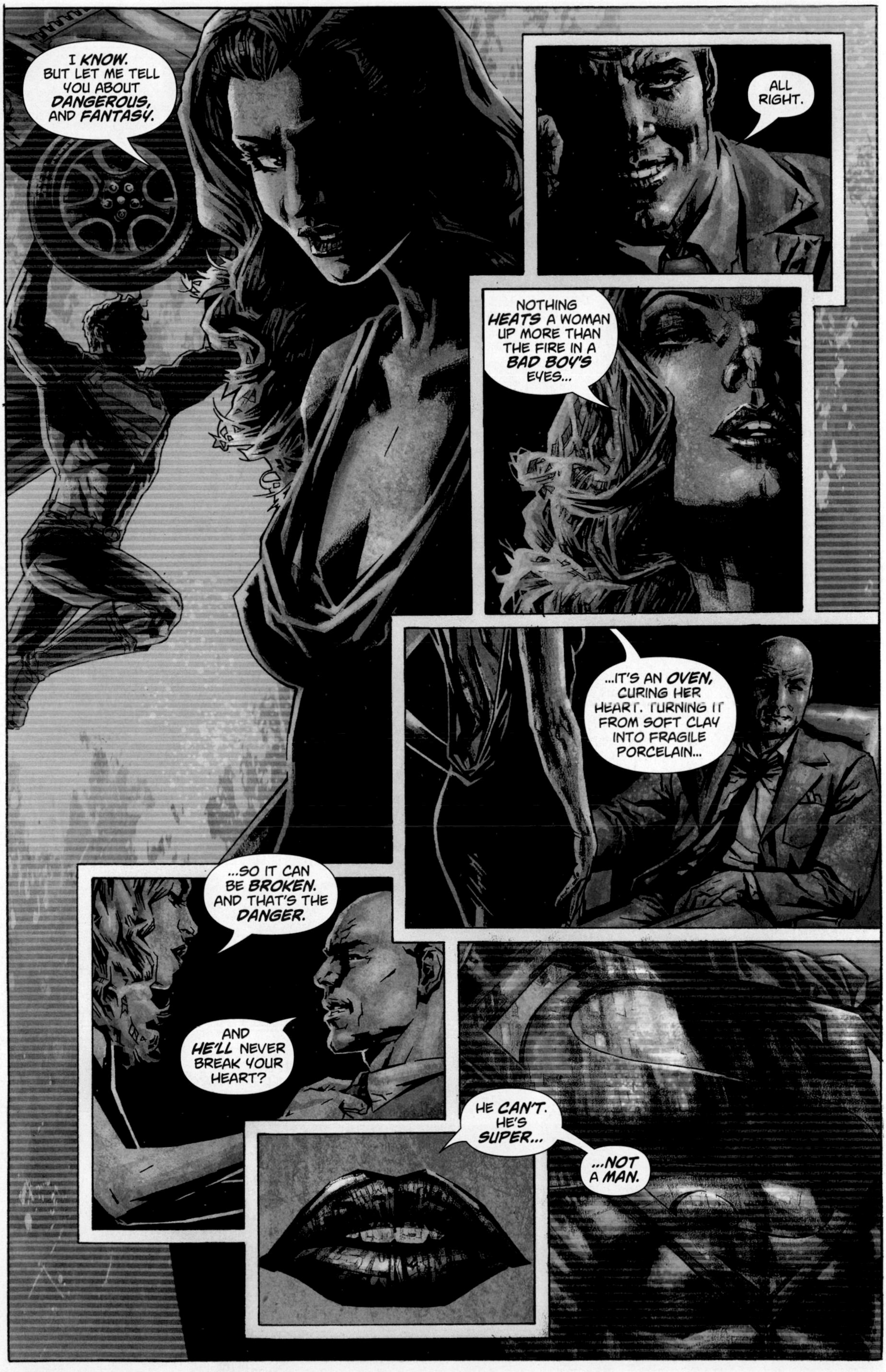

I KNOW. BUT LET ME TELL YOU ABOUT DANGEROUS, AND FANTASY.
ALL RIGHT.
NOTHING HEATS A WOMAN UP MORE THAN THE FIRE IN A BAD BOY'S EYES...
...IT'S AN OVEN, CURING HER HEART. TURNING IT FROM SOFT CLAY INTO FRAGILE PORCELAIN...
...SO IT CAN BE BROKEN. AND THAT'S THE DANGER.
AND HE'LL NEVER BREAK YOUR HEART?
HE CAN'T. HE'S SUPER...
...NOT A MAN.

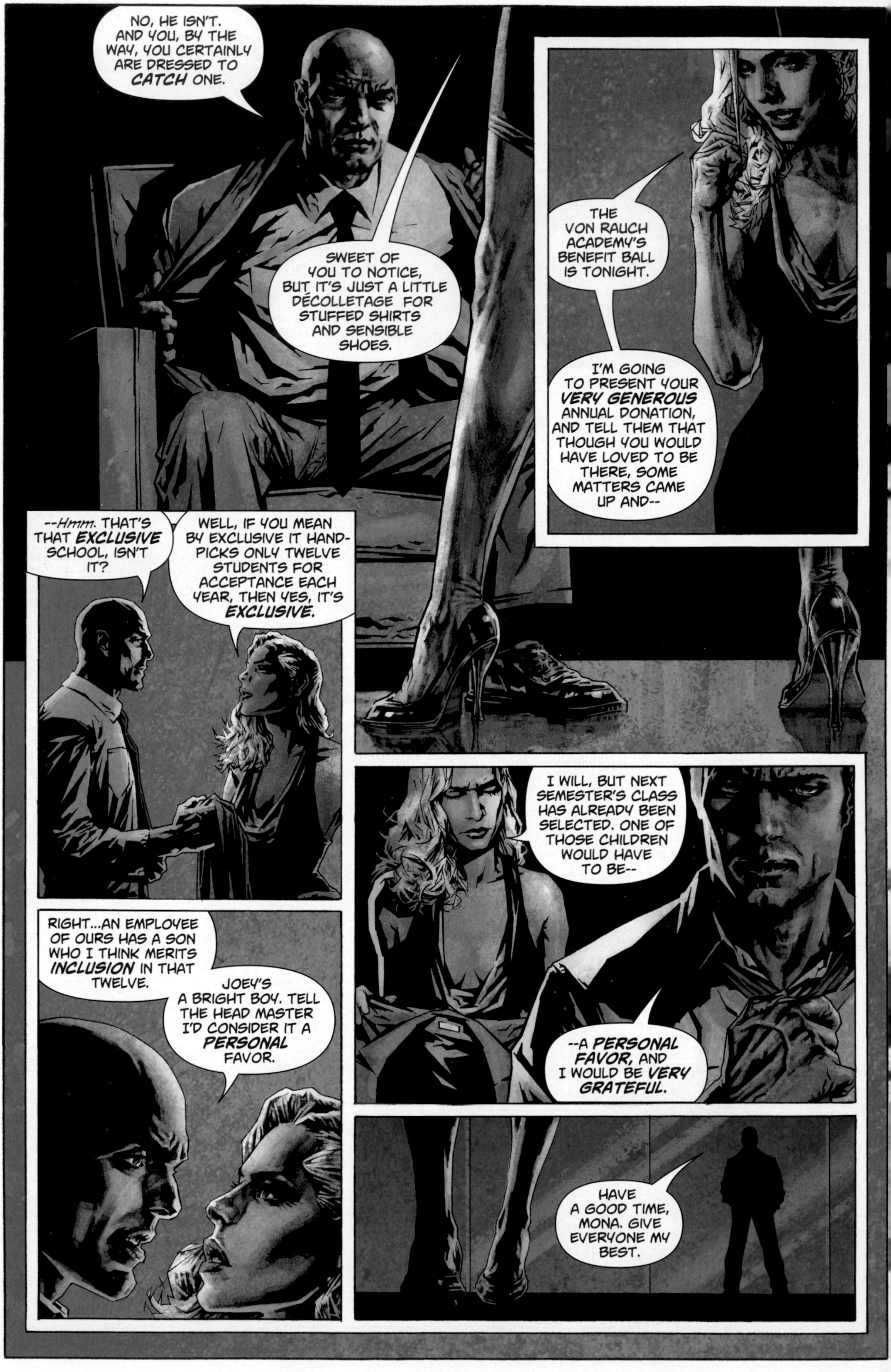
NO, HE ISN'T. AND YOU, BY THE WAY, YOU CERTAINLY ARE DRESSED TO CATCH ONE.
SWEET OF YOU TO NOTICE, BUT IT'S JUST A LITTLE DÉCOLLETAGE FOR STUFFED SHIRTS AND SENSIBLE SHOES.
THE VON RAUCH ACADEMY'S BENEFIT BALL IS TONIGHT.
I'M GOING TO PRESENT YOUR VERY GENEROUS ANNUAL DONATION, AND TELL THEM THAT THOUGH YOU WOULD HAVE LOVED TO BE THERE, SOME MATTERS CAME UP AND--
--Hmm. THAT'S THAT EXCLUSIVE SCHOOL, ISN'T IT?
WELL, IF YOU MEAN BY EXCLUSIVE IT HAND-PICKS ONLY TWELVE STUDENTS FOR ACCEPTANCE EACH YEAR, THEN YES, IT'S EXCLUSIVE.
RIGHT...AN EMPLOYEE OF OURS HAS A SON WHO I THINK MERITS INCLUSION IN THAT TWELVE.
JOEY'S A BRIGHT BOY. TELL THE HEAD MASTER I'D CONSIDER IT A PERSONAL FAVOR.
I WILL, BUT NEXT SEMESTER'S CLASS HAS ALREADY BEEN SELECTED. ONE OF THOSE CHILDREN WOULD HAVE TO BE--
--A PERSONAL FAVOR, AND I WOULD BE VERY GRATEFUL.
HAVE A GOOD TIME, MONA. GIVE EVERYONE MY BEST.

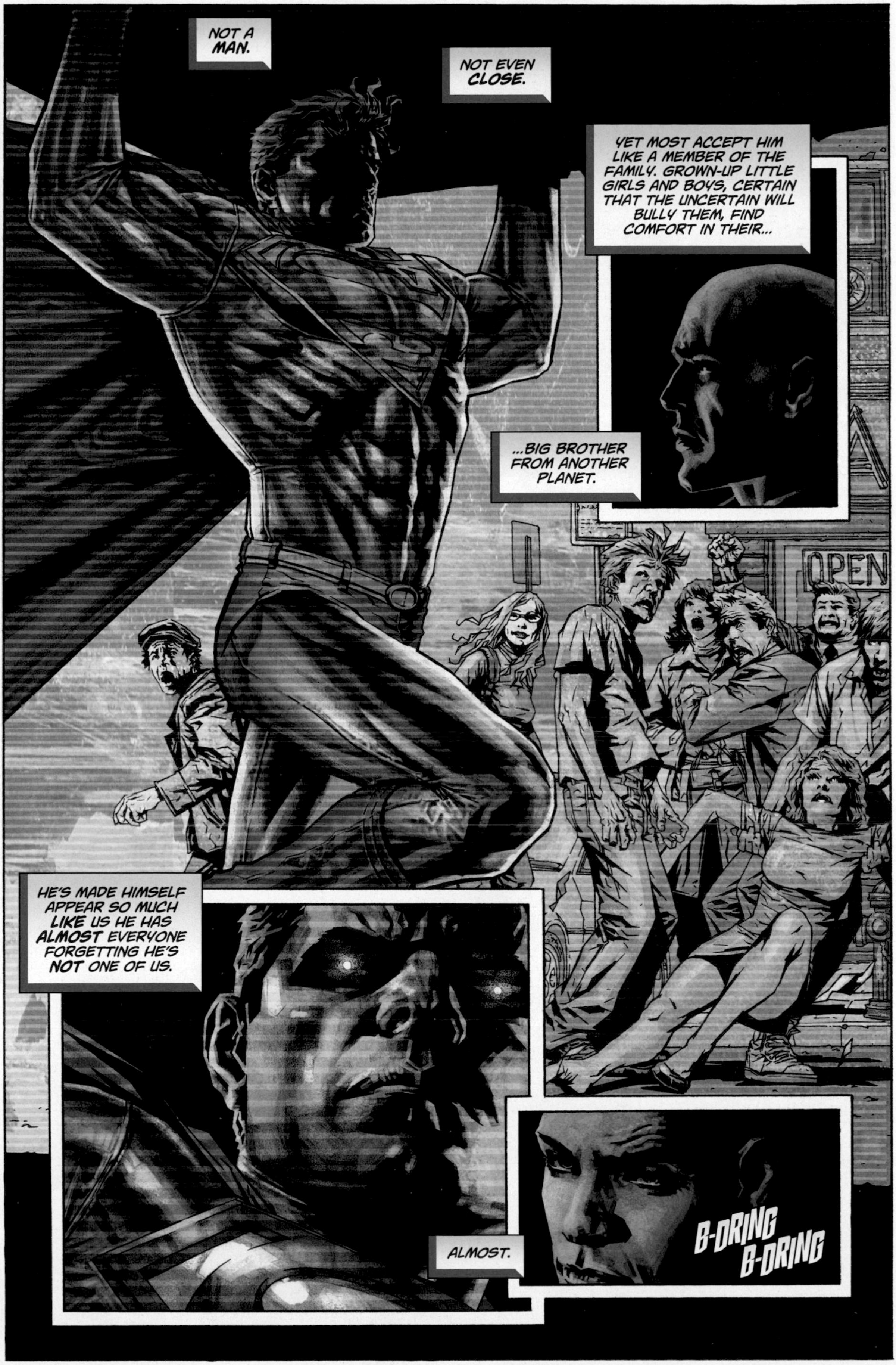
NOT A MAN.
NOT EVEN CLOSE.
YET MOST ACCEPT HIM LIKE A MEMBER OF THE FAMILY. GROWN-UP LITTLE GIRLS AND BOYS, CERTAIN THAT THE UNCERTAIN WILL BULLY THEM, FIND COMFORT IN THEIR...
...BIG BROTHER FROM ANOTHER PLANET.
OPEN
HE'S MADE HIMSELF APPEAR SO MUCH LIKE US HE HAS ALMOST EVERYONE FORGETTING HE'S NOT ONE OF US.
ALMOST.
B-DRING B-DRING

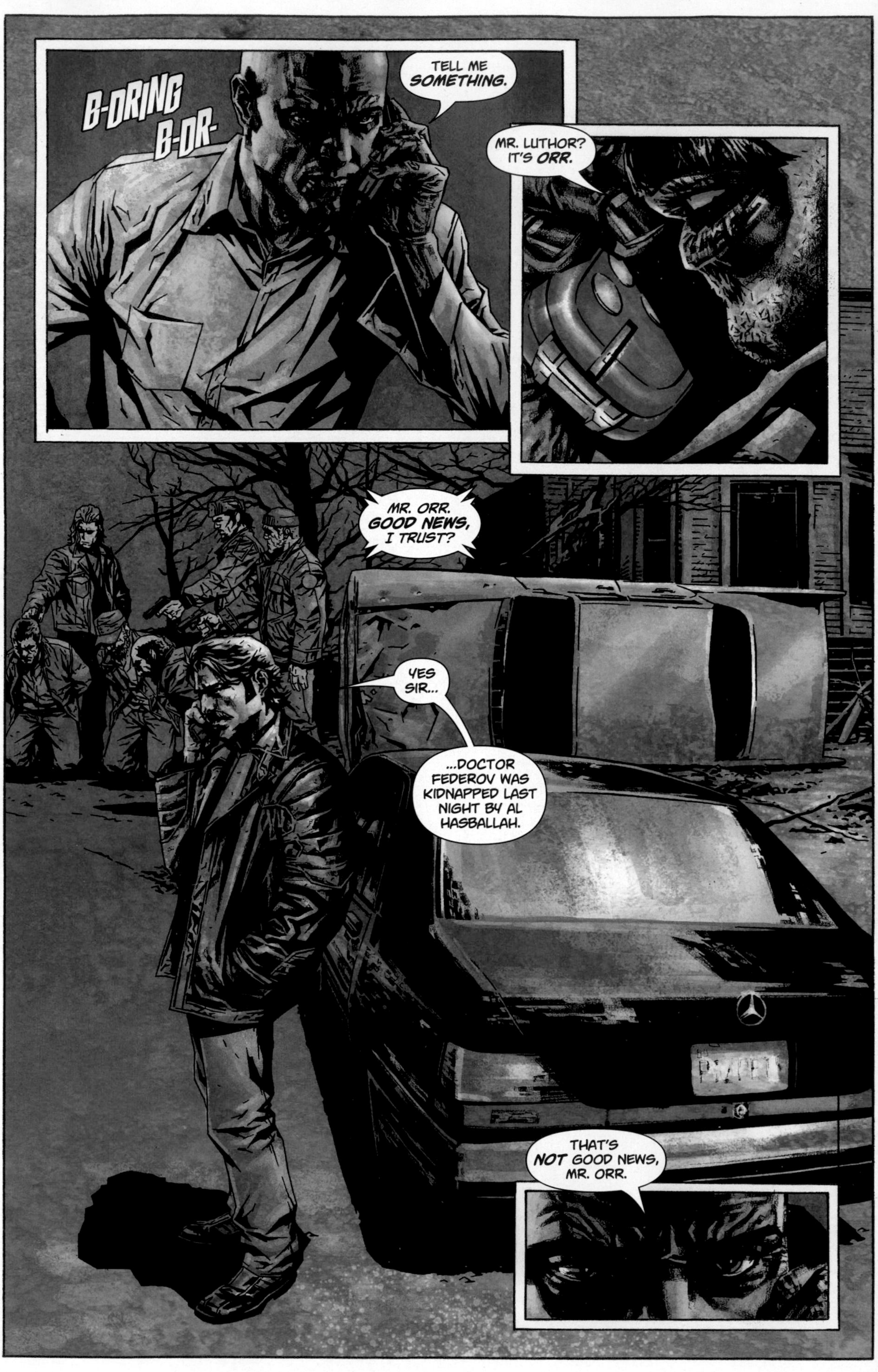
B-DRING B-DR-
TELL ME SOMETHING.
MR. LUTHOR? IT'S ORR.
MR. ORR. GOOD NEWS, I TRUST?
YES SIR...
...DOCTOR FEDEROV WAS KIDNAPPED LAST NIGHT BY AL HASBALLAH.
THAT'S NOT GOOD NEWS, MR. ORR.

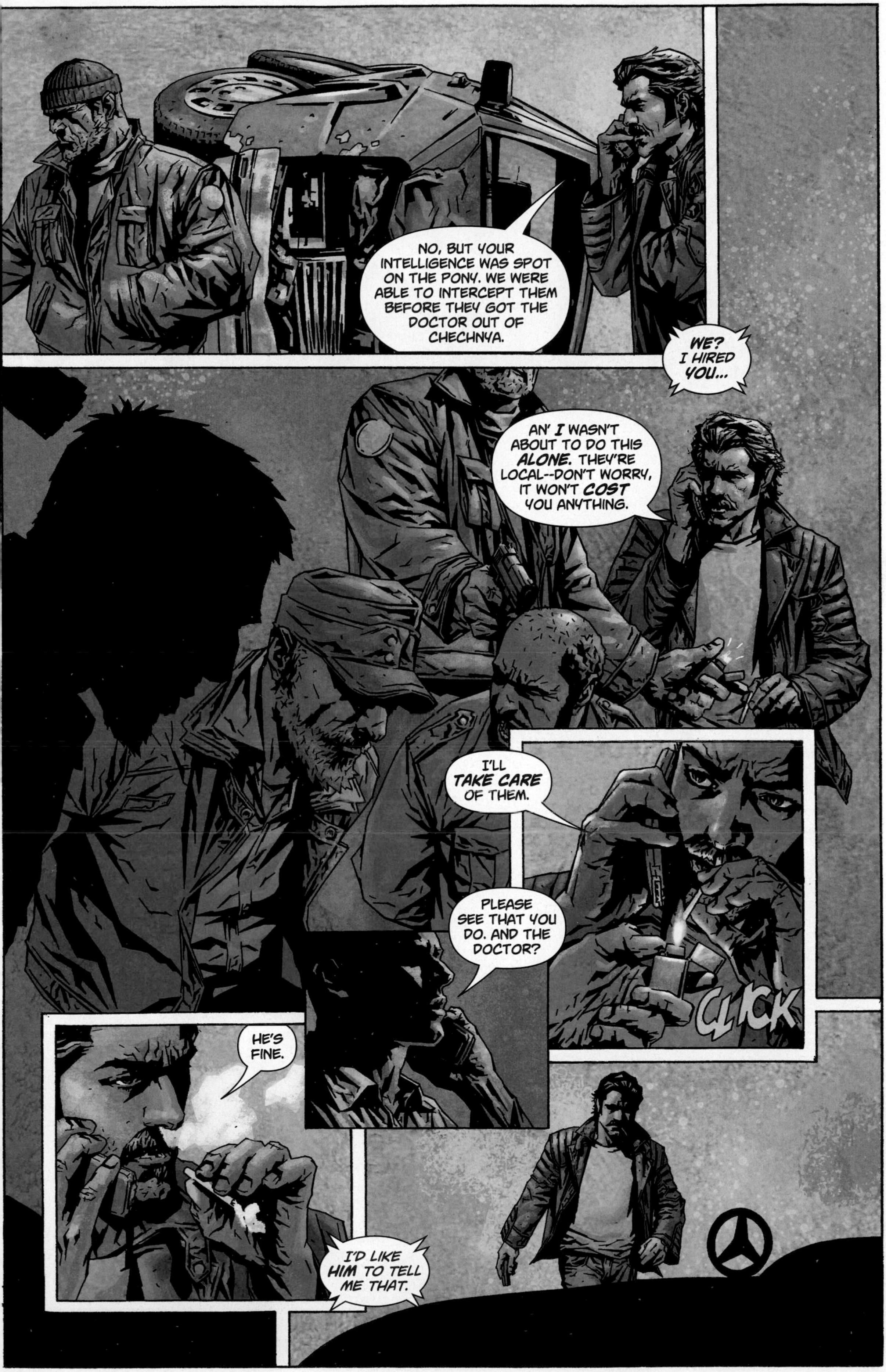

NO, BUT YOUR INTELLIGENCE WAS SPOT ON THE PONY. WE WERE ABLE TO INTERCEPT THEM BEFORE THEY GOT THE DOCTOR OUT OF CHECHNYA.
WE? I HIRED YOU...
AN' I WASN'T ABOUT TO DO THIS ALONE. THEY'RE LOCAL--DON'T WORRY, IT WON'T COST YOU ANYTHING.
I'LL TAKE CARE OF THEM.
PLEASE SEE THAT YOU DO. AND THE DOCTOR?
CLICK
HE'S FINE.
I'D LIKE HIM TO TELL ME THAT.

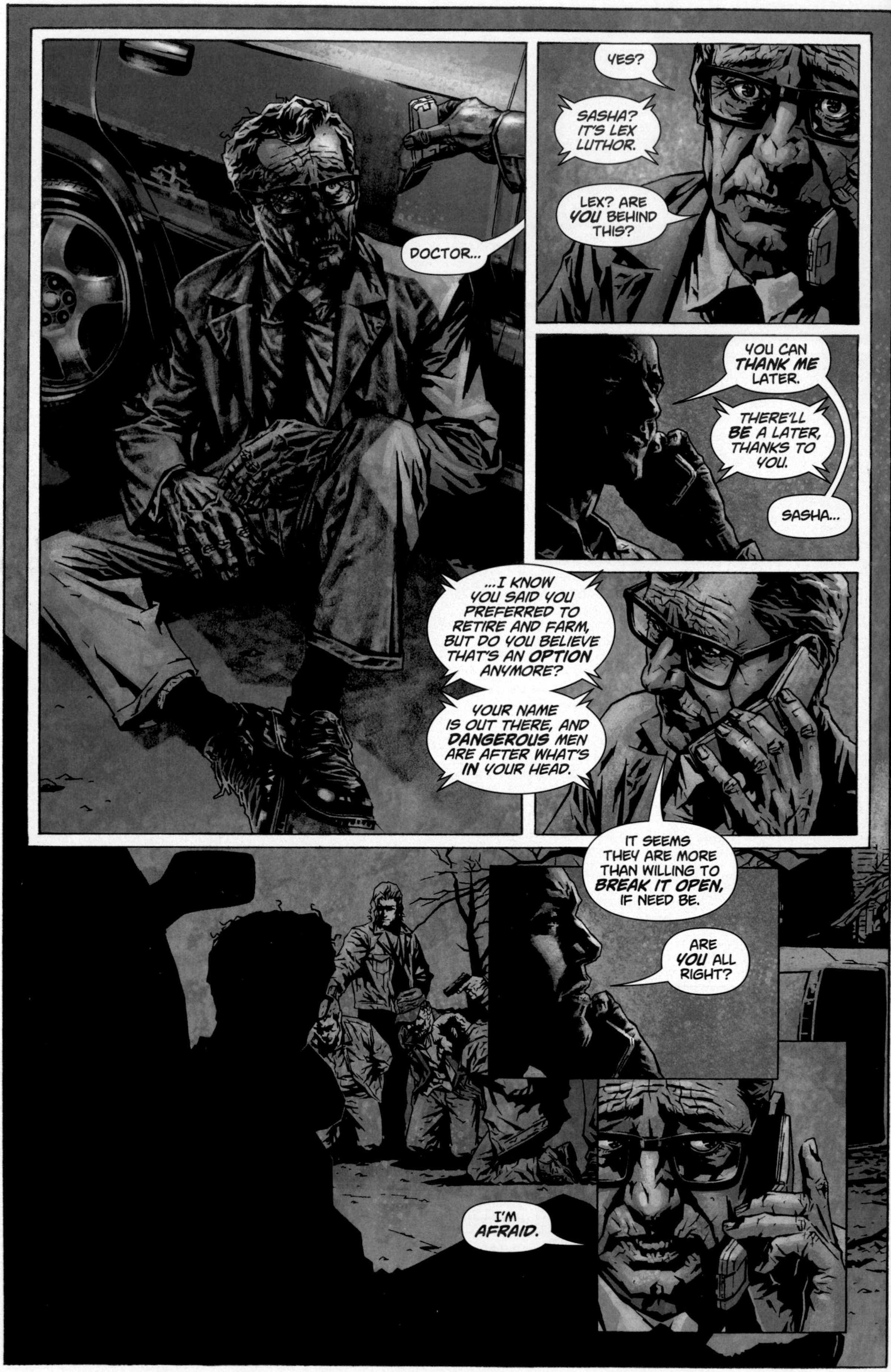

YES?
SASHA? IT'S LEX LUTHOR.
LEX? ARE YOU BEHIND THIS?
DOCTOR...
YOU CAN THANK ME LATER.
THERE'LL BE A LATER, THANKS TO YOU.
SASHA...
...I KNOW YOU SAID YOU PREFERRED TO RETIRE AND FARM, BUT DO YOU BELIEVE THAT'S AN OPTION ANYMORE?
YOUR NAME IS OUT THERE, AND DANGEROUS MEN ARE AFTER WHAT'S IN YOUR HEAD.
IT SEEMS THEY ARE MORE THAN WILLING TO BREAK IT OPEN, IF NEED BE.
ARE YOU ALL RIGHT?
I'M AFRAID.

DON'T BE. MR. ORR IS LIKE YOU--*VERY GOOD* AT HIS JOB. HE'S GOING TO TAKE YOU TO YOUR *HOME*.

BLAM BLAM BLAM

I CAN'T STAY THERE *NOW*.

THEN TELL HIM WHERE YOU WANT TO GO.

WILL I BE SAFE IN METROPOLIS?

YES. AND SO WILL YOUR FAMILY.

YOU HAVE *MY WORD*, SASHA.

OKAY.

LEX?

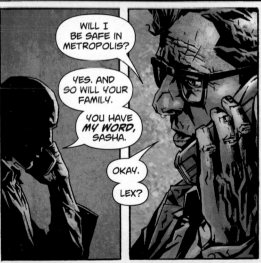

YES?

I WOULD LIKE, FOR A CHANGE, FOR MY RESEARCH TO BE USED FOR THE *BETTERMENT OF* MANKIND.

YOU HAVE *MY WORD* ON *THAT* AS WELL.

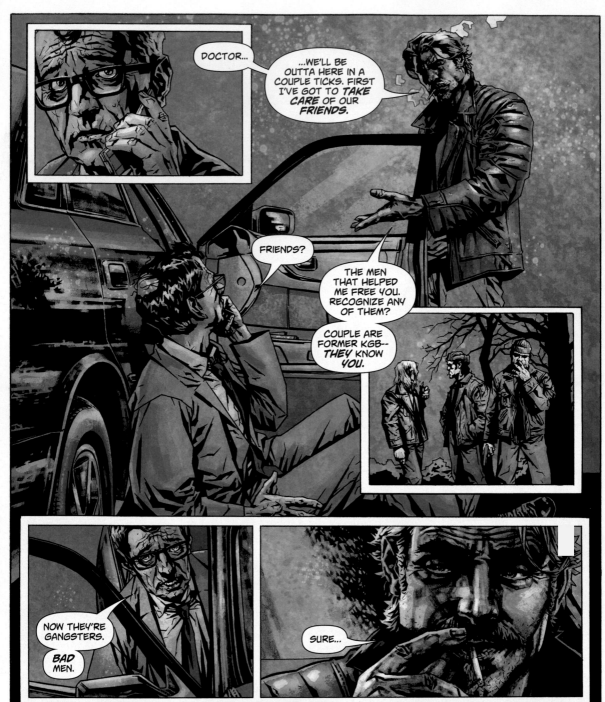

DOCTOR...

...WE'LL BE OUTTA HERE IN A COUPLE TICKS. FIRST I'VE GOT TO *TAKE CARE* OF OUR *FRIENDS.*

FRIENDS?

THE MEN THAT HELPED ME FREE YOU. RECOGNIZE ANY OF THEM?

COUPLE ARE FORMER KGB-- *THEY* KNOW *YOU.*

NOW THEY'RE GANGSTERS.

BAD MEN.

SURE...

...BUT *GOOD* GUYS.

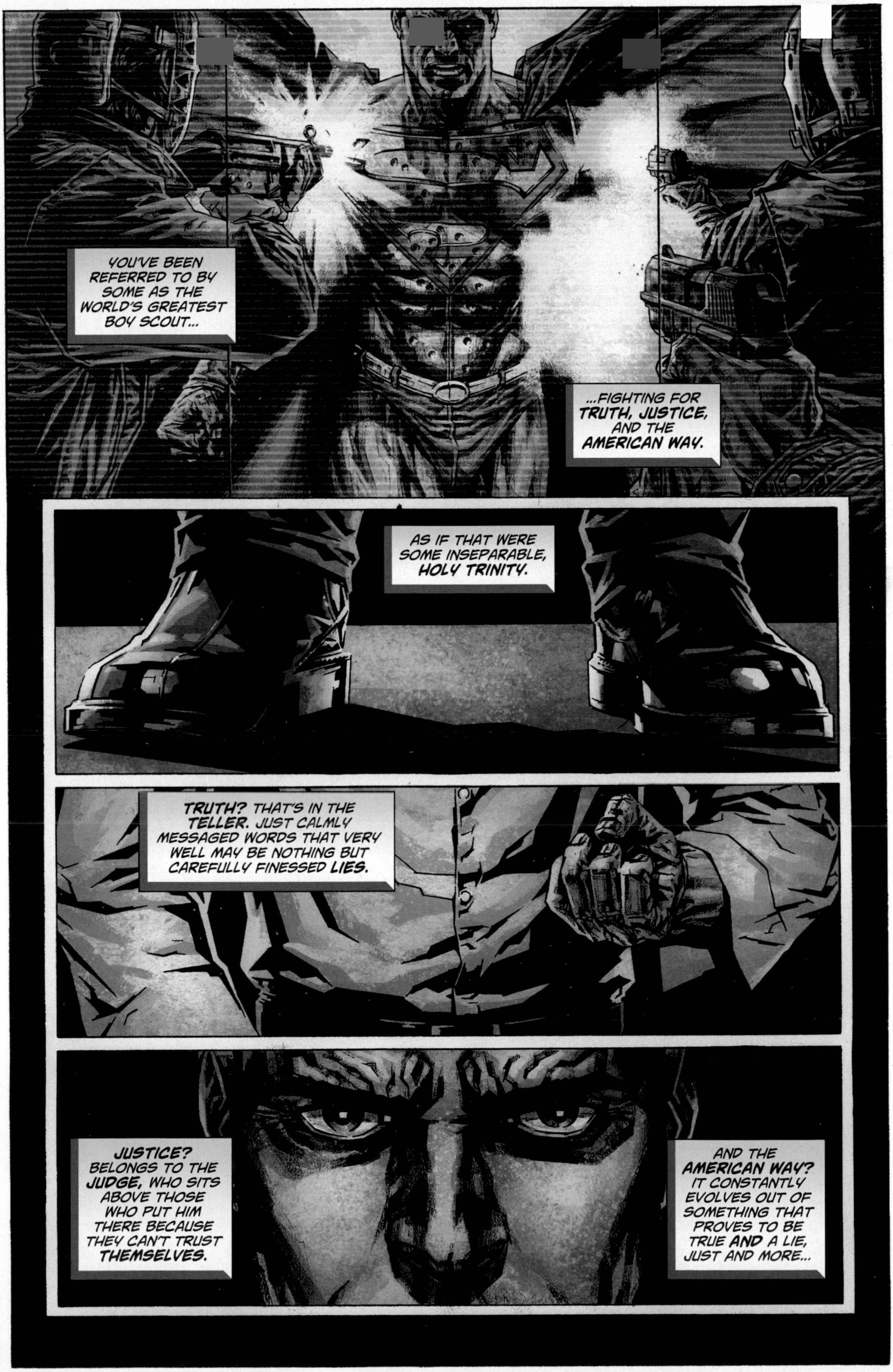
YOU'VE BEEN REFERRED TO BY SOME AS THE WORLD'S GREATEST BOY SCOUT...
...FIGHTING FOR TRUTH, JUSTICE, AND THE AMERICAN WAY.
AS IF THAT WERE SOME INSEPARABLE, HOLY TRINITY.
TRUTH? THAT'S IN THE TELLER. JUST CALMLY MESSAGED WORDS THAT VERY WELL MAY BE NOTHING BUT CAREFULLY FINESSED LIES.
JUSTICE? BELONGS TO THE JUDGE, WHO SITS ABOVE THOSE WHO PUT HIM THERE BECAUSE THEY CAN'T TRUST THEMSELVES.
AND THE AMERICAN WAY? IT CONSTANTLY EVOLVES OUT OF SOMETHING THAT PROVES TO BE TRUE AND A LIE, JUST AND MORE...

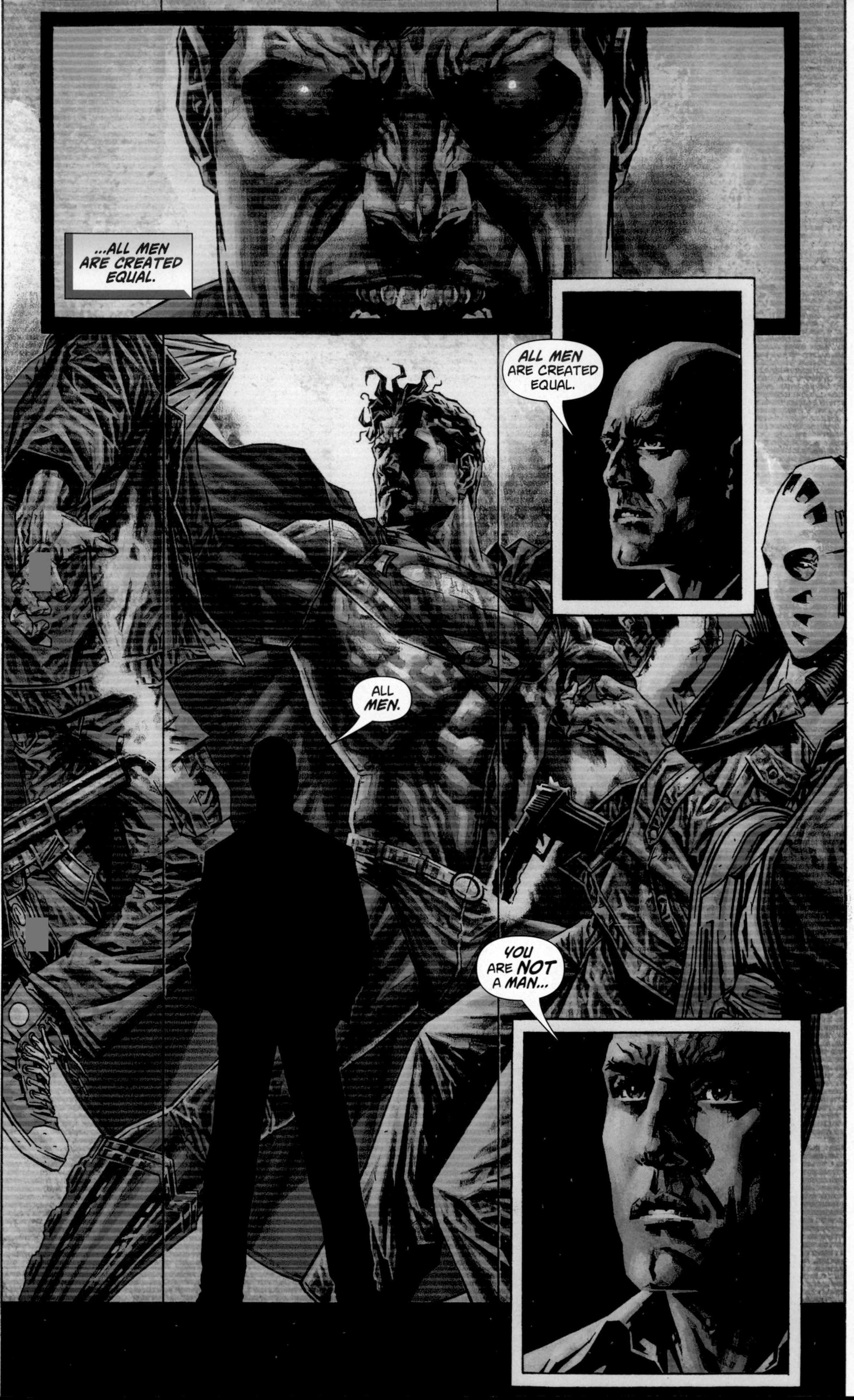
...ALL MEN ARE CREATED EQUAL.
ALL MEN ARE CREATED EQUAL.
ALL MEN.
YOU ARE NOT A MAN...

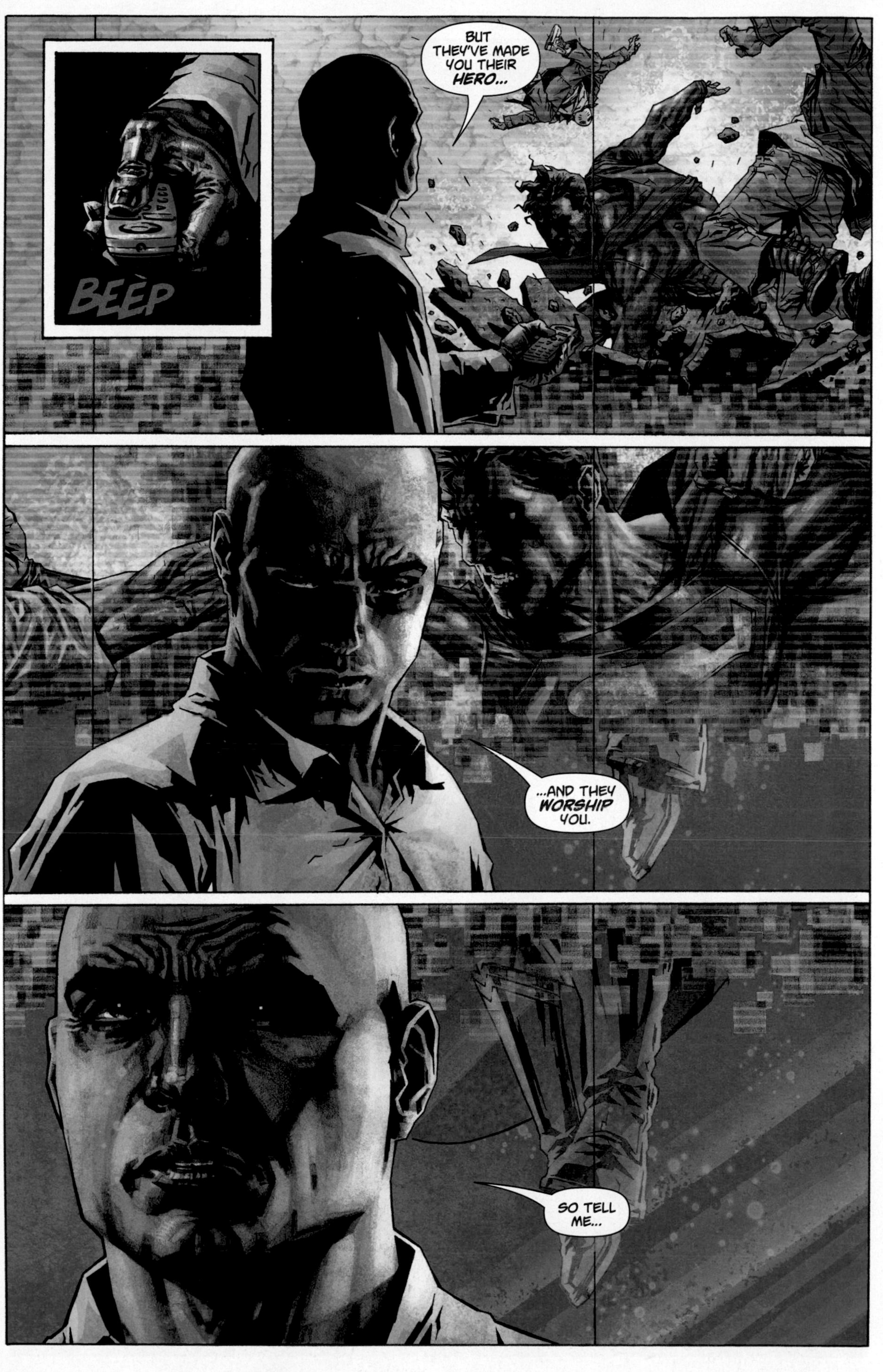
BEEP
BUT THEY'VE MADE YOU THEIR **HERO...**
...AND THEY **WORSHIP** YOU.
SO TELL ME...

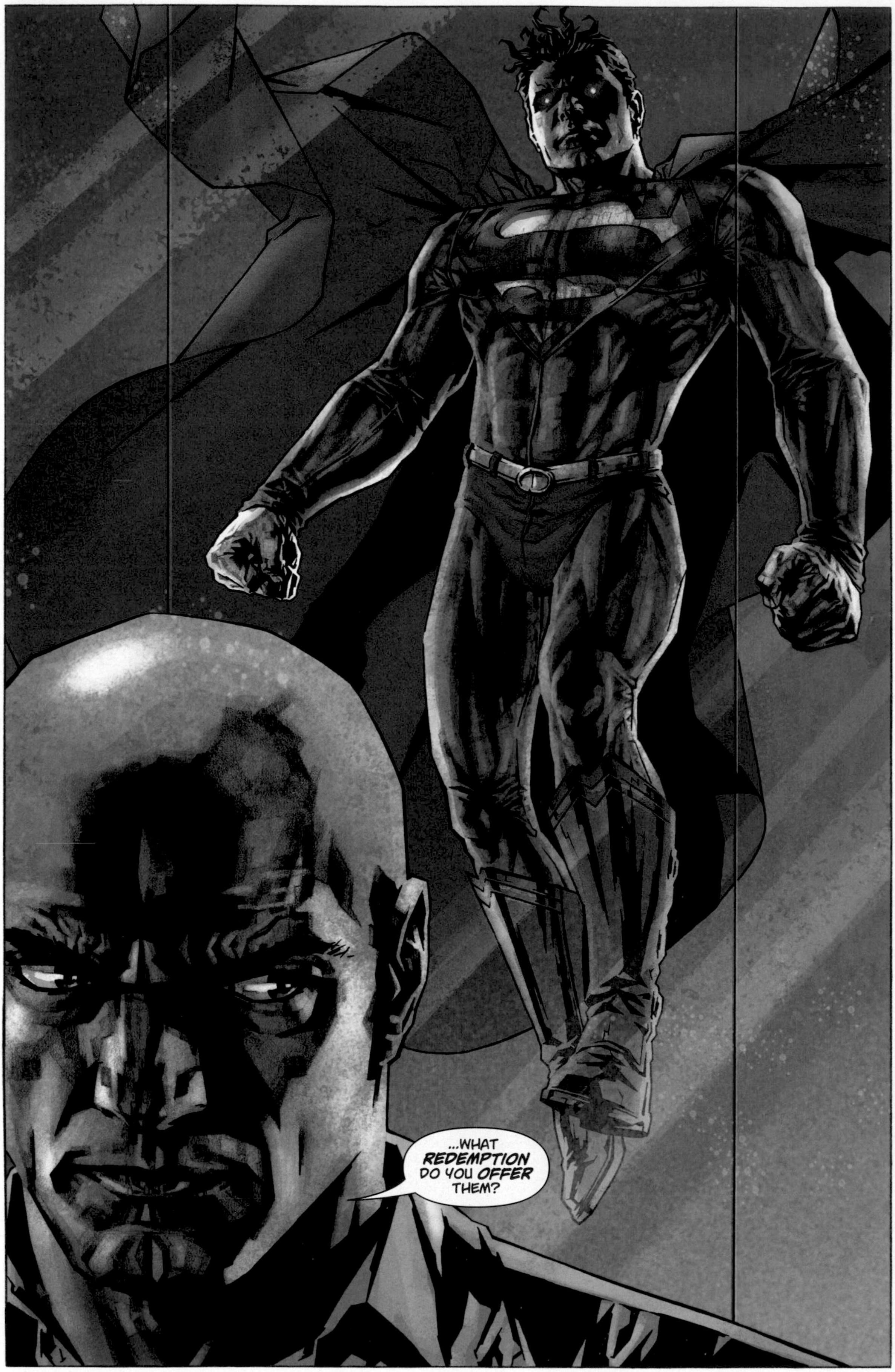
...WHAT REDEMPTION DO YOU OFFER THEM?

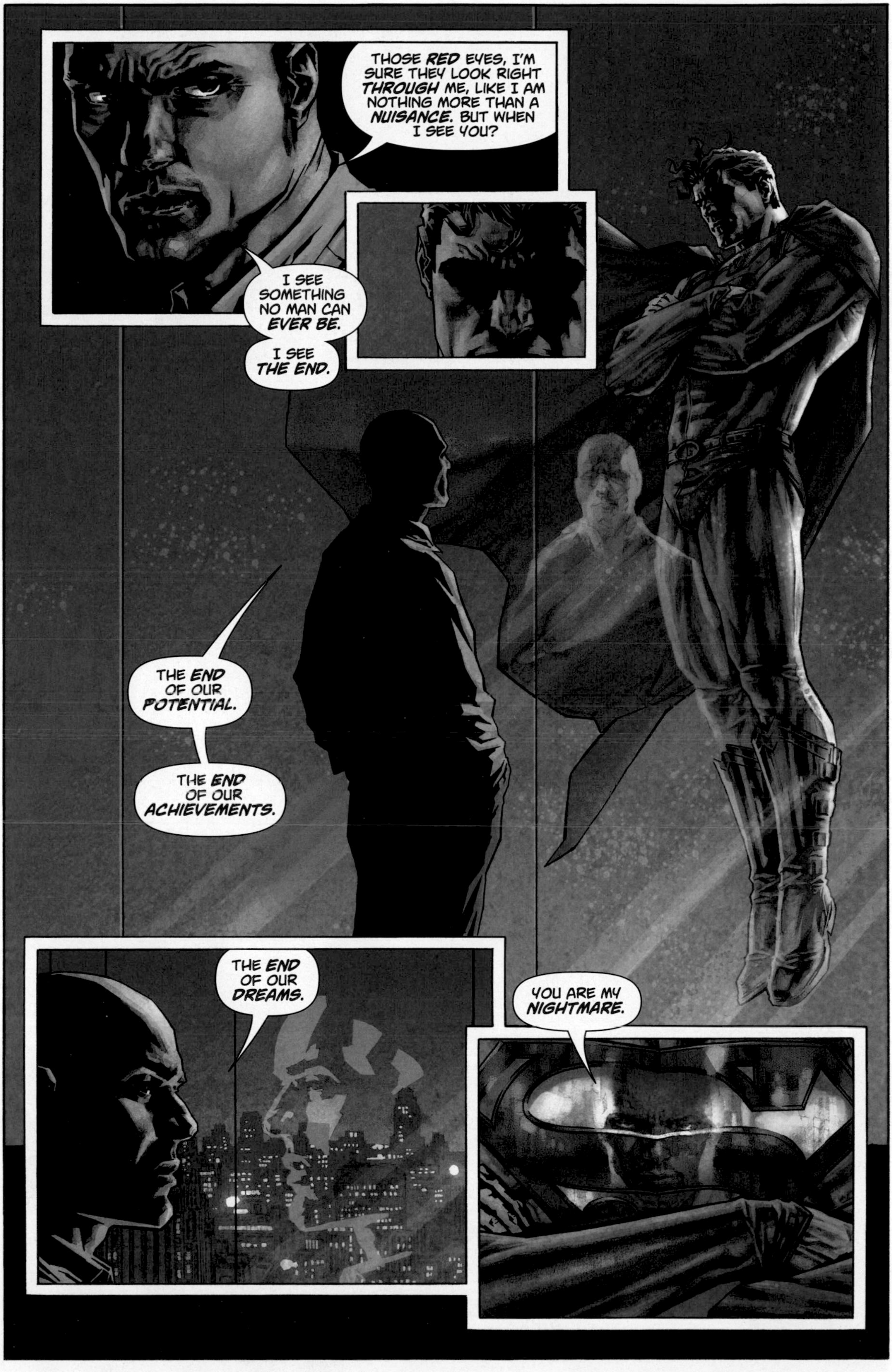
THOSE RED EYES, I'M SURE THEY LOOK RIGHT THROUGH ME, LIKE I AM NOTHING MORE THAN A NUISANCE. BUT WHEN I SEE YOU?
I SEE SOMETHING NO MAN CAN EVER BE.
I SEE THE END.
THE END OF OUR POTENTIAL.
THE END OF OUR ACHIEVEMENTS.
THE END OF OUR DREAMS.
YOU ARE MY NIGHTMARE.

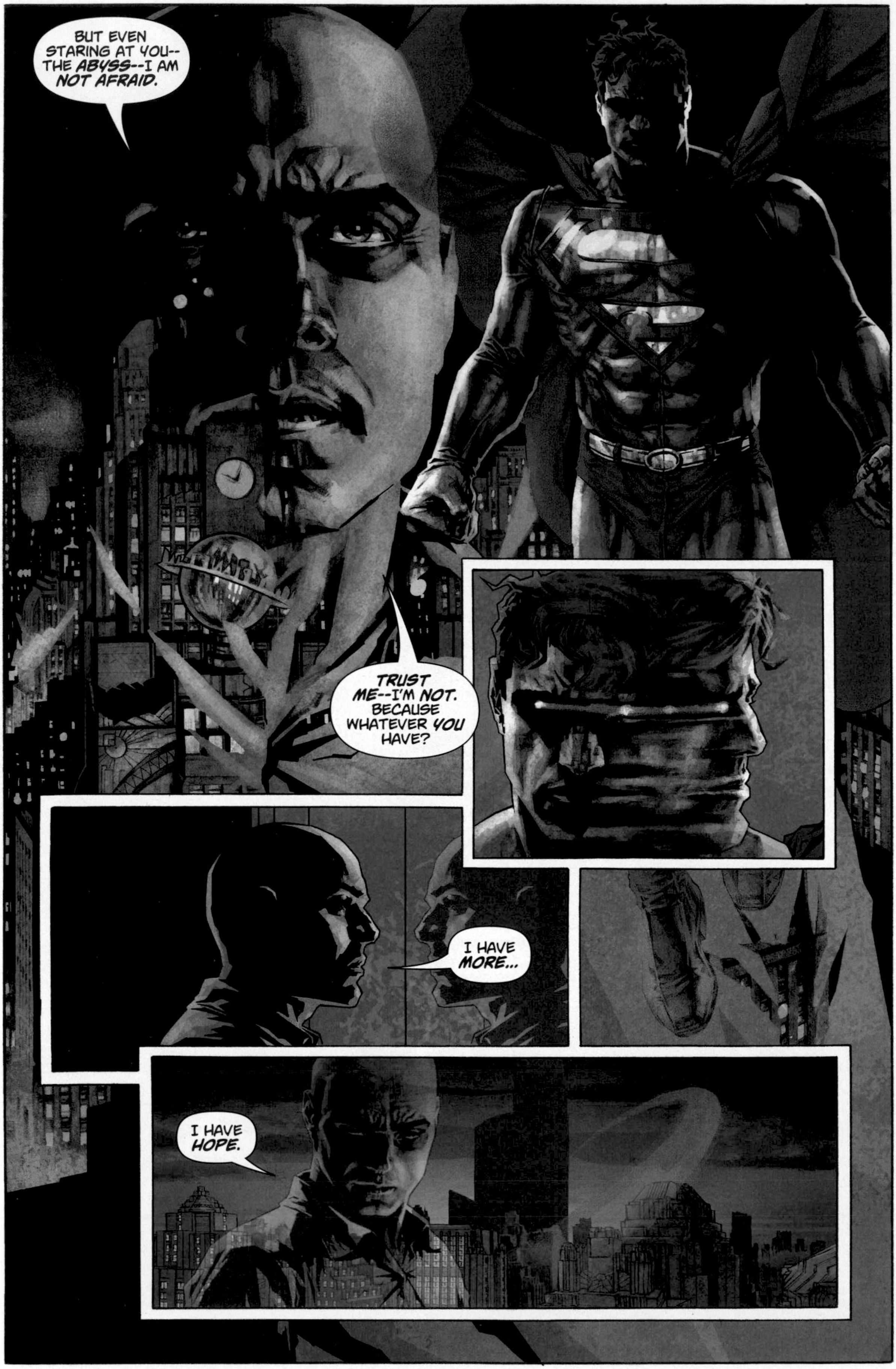
BUT EVEN STARING AT YOU--THE ABYSS--I AM NOT AFRAID.
TRUST ME--I'M NOT. BECAUSE WHATEVER YOU HAVE?
I HAVE MORE...
I HAVE HOPE.

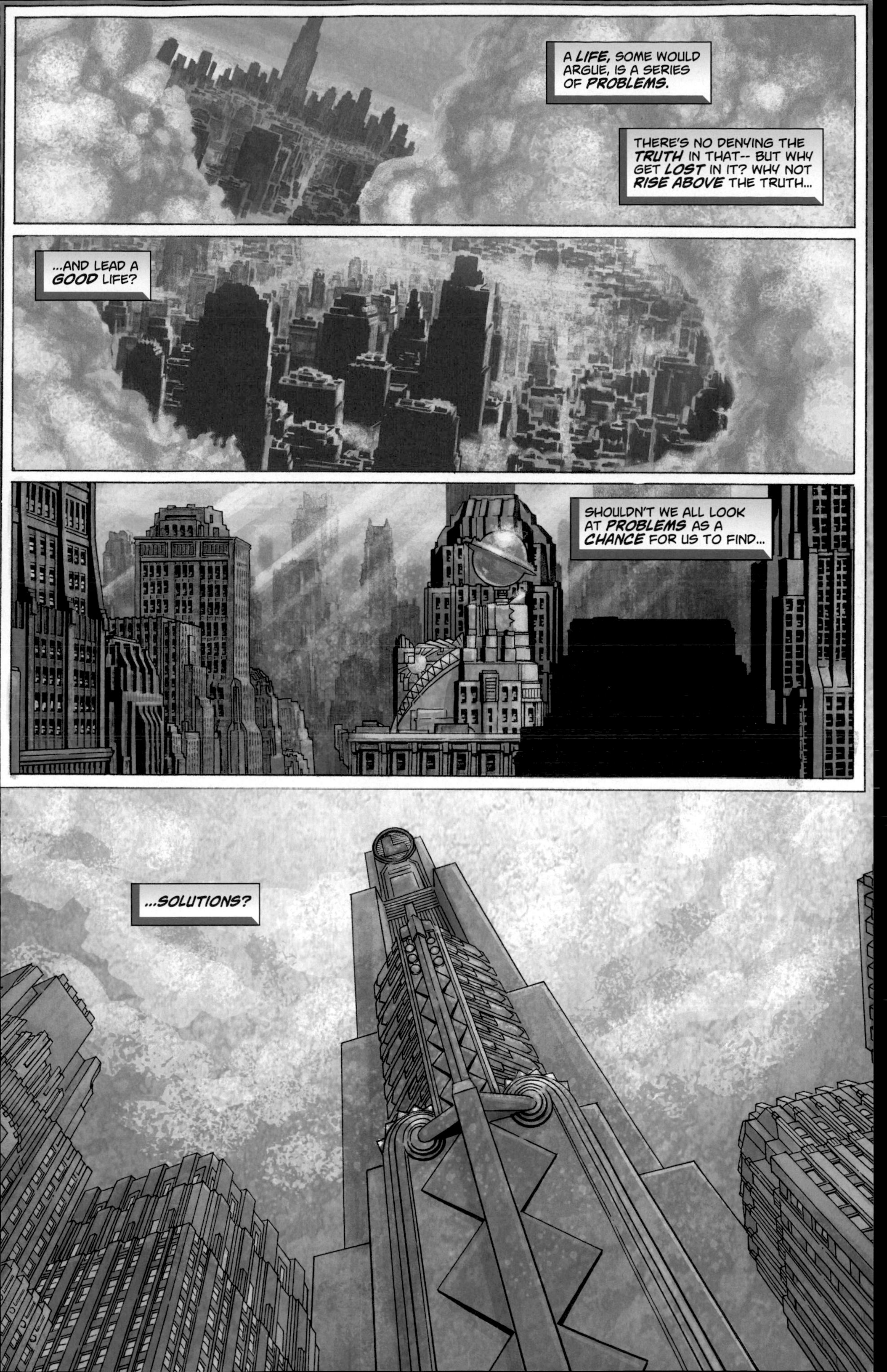
A LIFE, SOME WOULD ARGUE, IS A SERIES OF PROBLEMS.
THERE'S NO DENYING THE TRUTH IN THAT-- BUT WHY GET LOST IN IT? WHY NOT RISE ABOVE THE TRUTH...
...AND LEAD A GOOD LIFE?
SHOULDN'T WE ALL LOOK AT PROBLEMS AS A CHANCE FOR US TO FIND...
...SOLUTIONS?

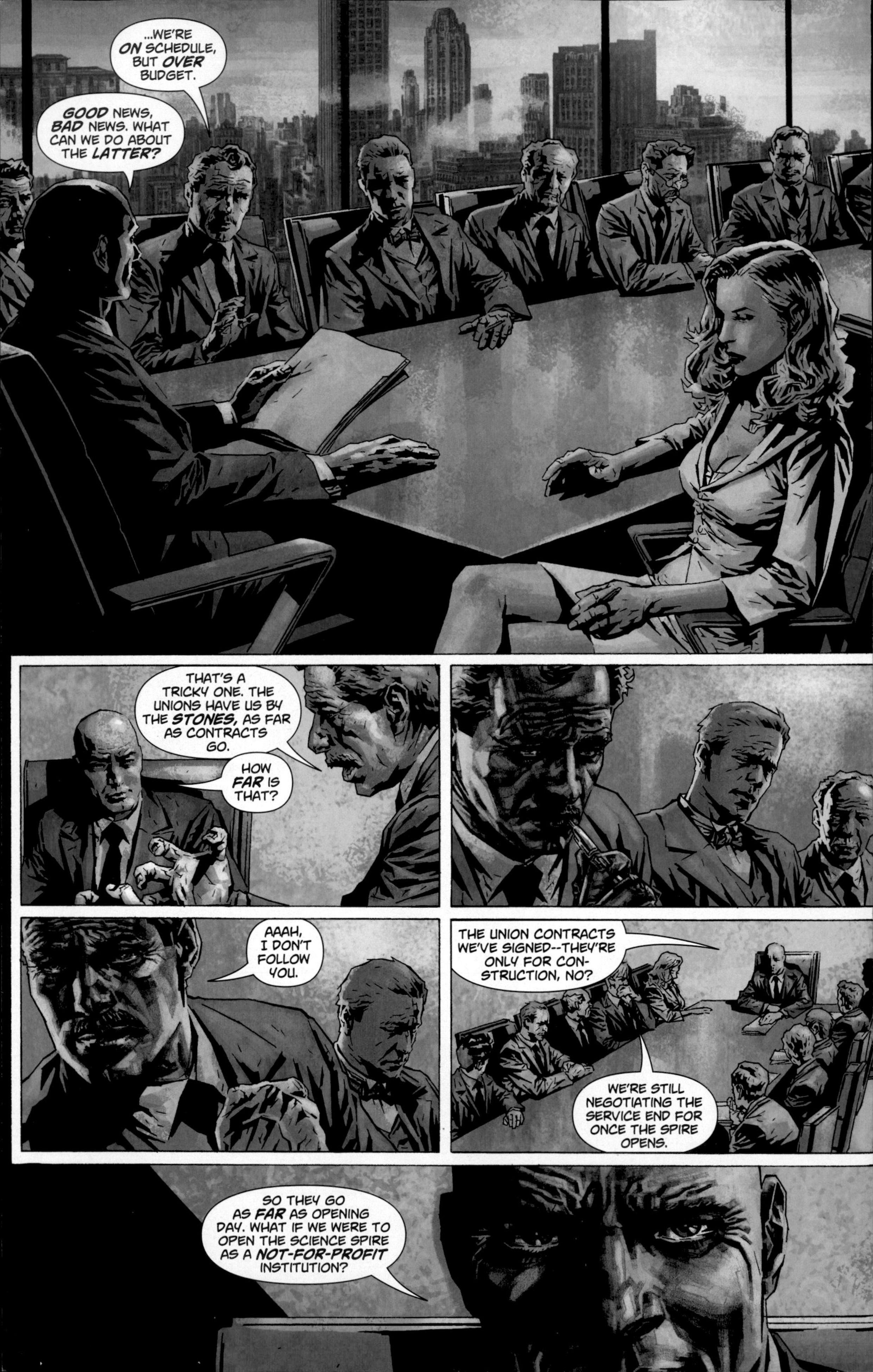

...WE'RE ON SCHEDULE, BUT OVER BUDGET.
GOOD NEWS, BAD NEWS. WHAT CAN WE DO ABOUT THE LATTER?
THAT'S A TRICKY ONE. THE UNIONS HAVE US BY THE STONES, AS FAR AS CONTRACTS GO.
HOW FAR IS THAT?
AAAH, I DON'T FOLLOW YOU.
THE UNION CONTRACTS WE'VE SIGNED--THEY'RE ONLY FOR CONSTRUCTION, NO?
WE'RE STILL NEGOTIATING THE SERVICE END FOR ONCE THE SPIRE OPENS.
SO THEY GO AS FAR AS OPENING DAY. WHAT IF WE WERE TO OPEN THE SCIENCE SPIRE AS A NOT-FOR-PROFIT INSTITUTION?

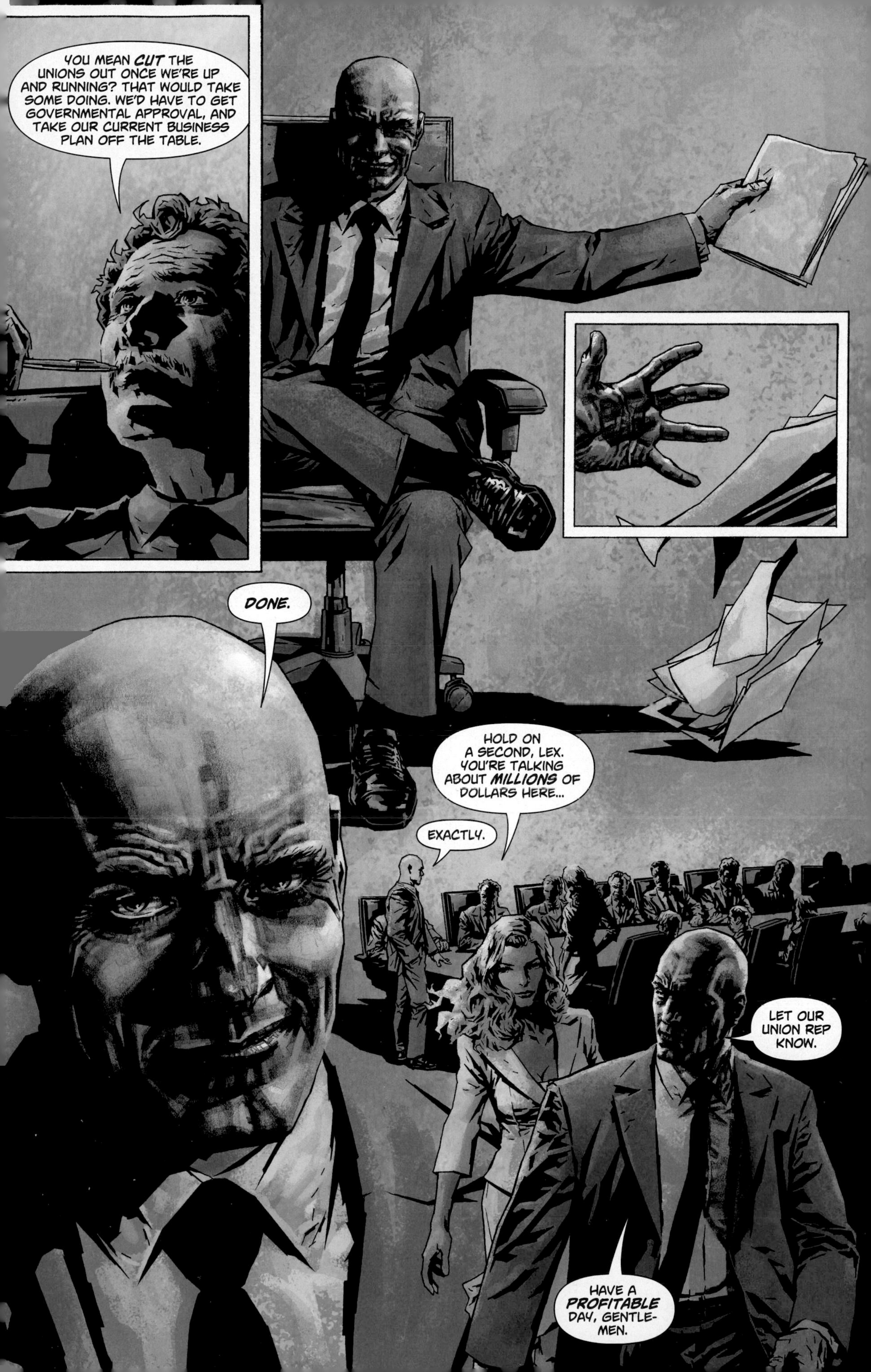
YOU MEAN CUT THE UNIONS OUT ONCE WE'RE UP AND RUNNING? THAT WOULD TAKE SOME DOING. WE'D HAVE TO GET GOVERNMENTAL APPROVAL, AND TAKE OUR CURRENT BUSINESS PLAN OFF THE TABLE.
DONE.
HOLD ON A SECOND, LEX. YOU'RE TALKING ABOUT MILLIONS OF DOLLARS HERE...
EXACTLY.
LET OUR UNION REP KNOW.
HAVE A PROFITABLE DAY, GENTLE- MEN.

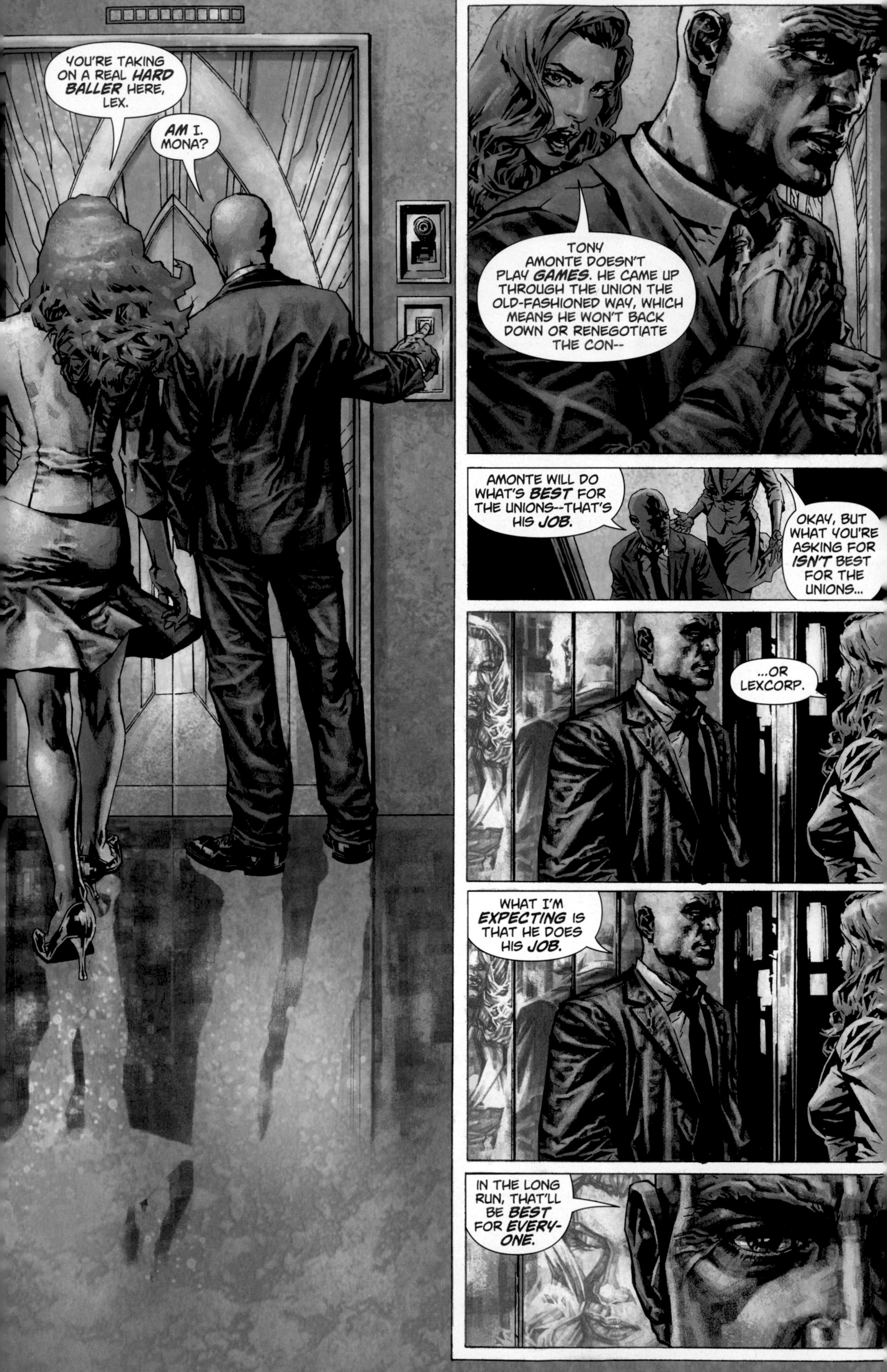
YOU'RE TAKING ON A REAL HARD BALLER HERE, LEX.
AM I. MONA?
TONY AMONTE DOESN'T PLAY GAMES. HE CAME UP THROUGH THE UNION THE OLD-FASHIONED WAY, WHICH MEANS HE WON'T BACK DOWN OR RENEGOTIATE THE CON--
AMONTE WILL DO WHAT'S BEST FOR THE UNIONS--THAT'S HIS JOB.
OKAY, BUT WHAT YOU'RE ASKING FOR ISN'T BEST FOR THE UNIONS...
...OR LEXCORP.
WHAT I'M EXPECTING IS THAT HE DOES HIS JOB.
IN THE LONG RUN, THAT'LL BE BEST FOR EVERY-ONE.

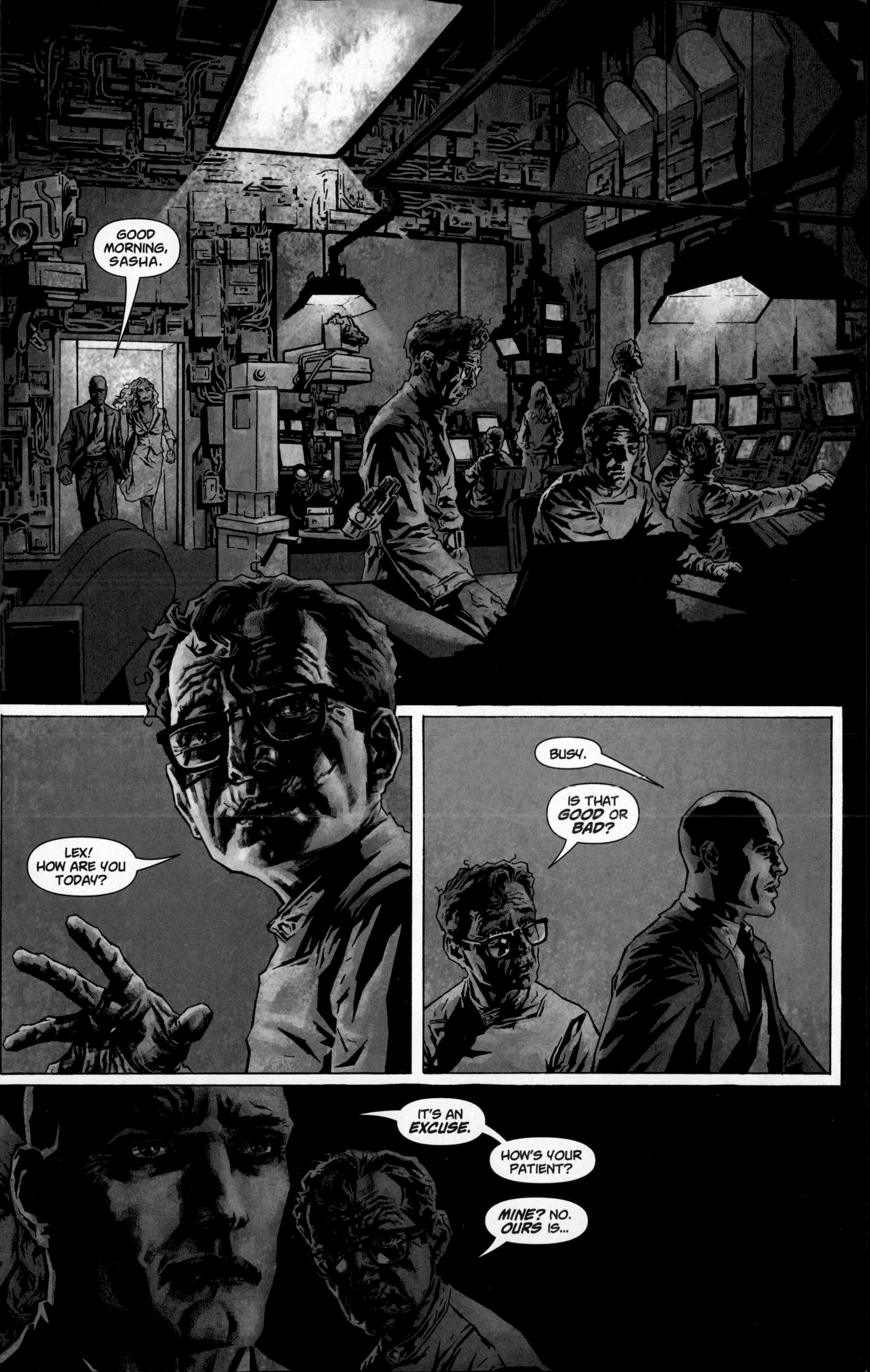
GOOD MORNING, SASHA.
LEX! HOW ARE YOU TODAY?
BUSY.
IS THAT GOOD OR BAD?
IT'S AN EXCUSE.
HOW'S YOUR PATIENT?
MINE? NO. OURS IS...

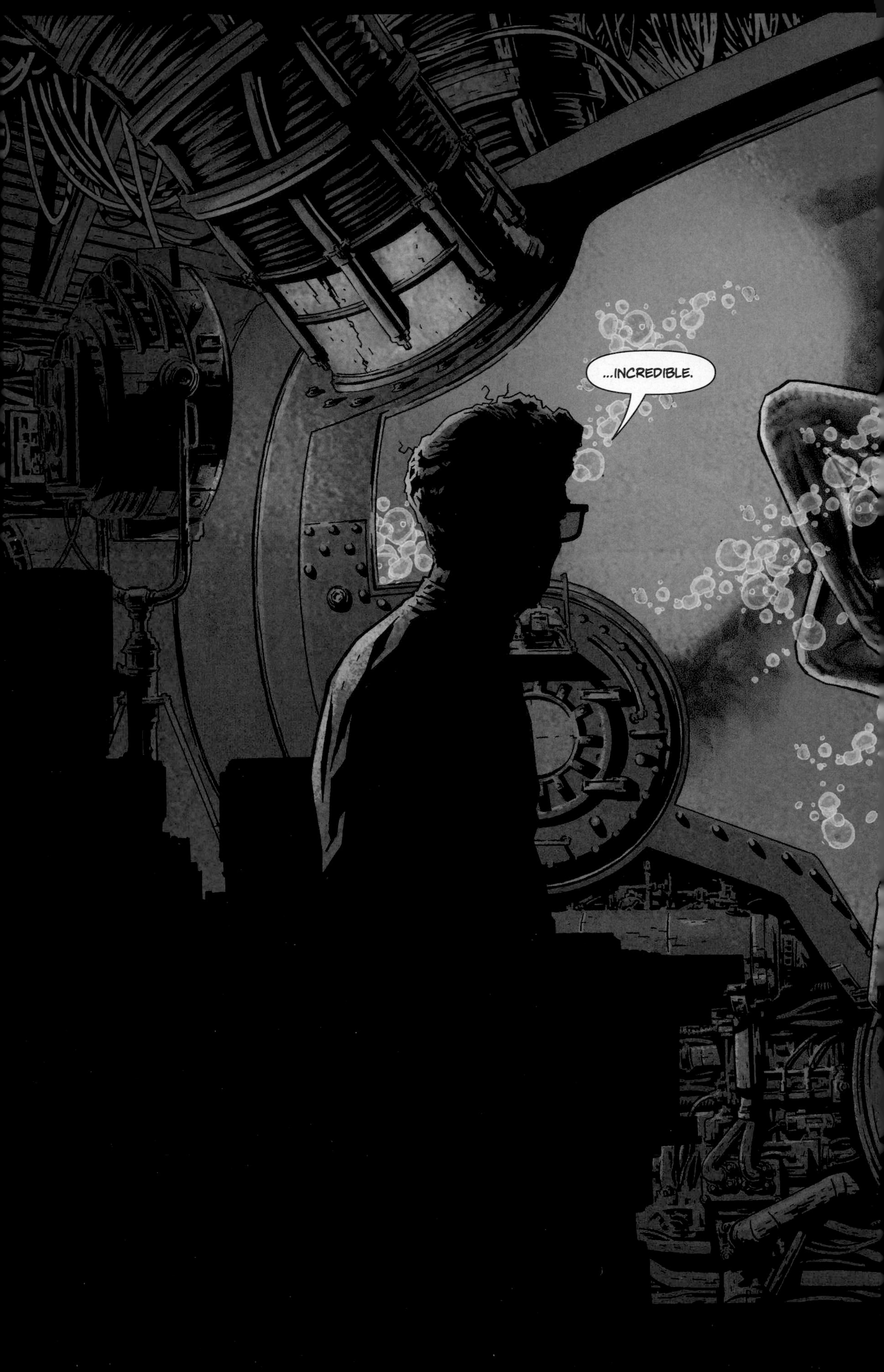
...INCREDIBLE.

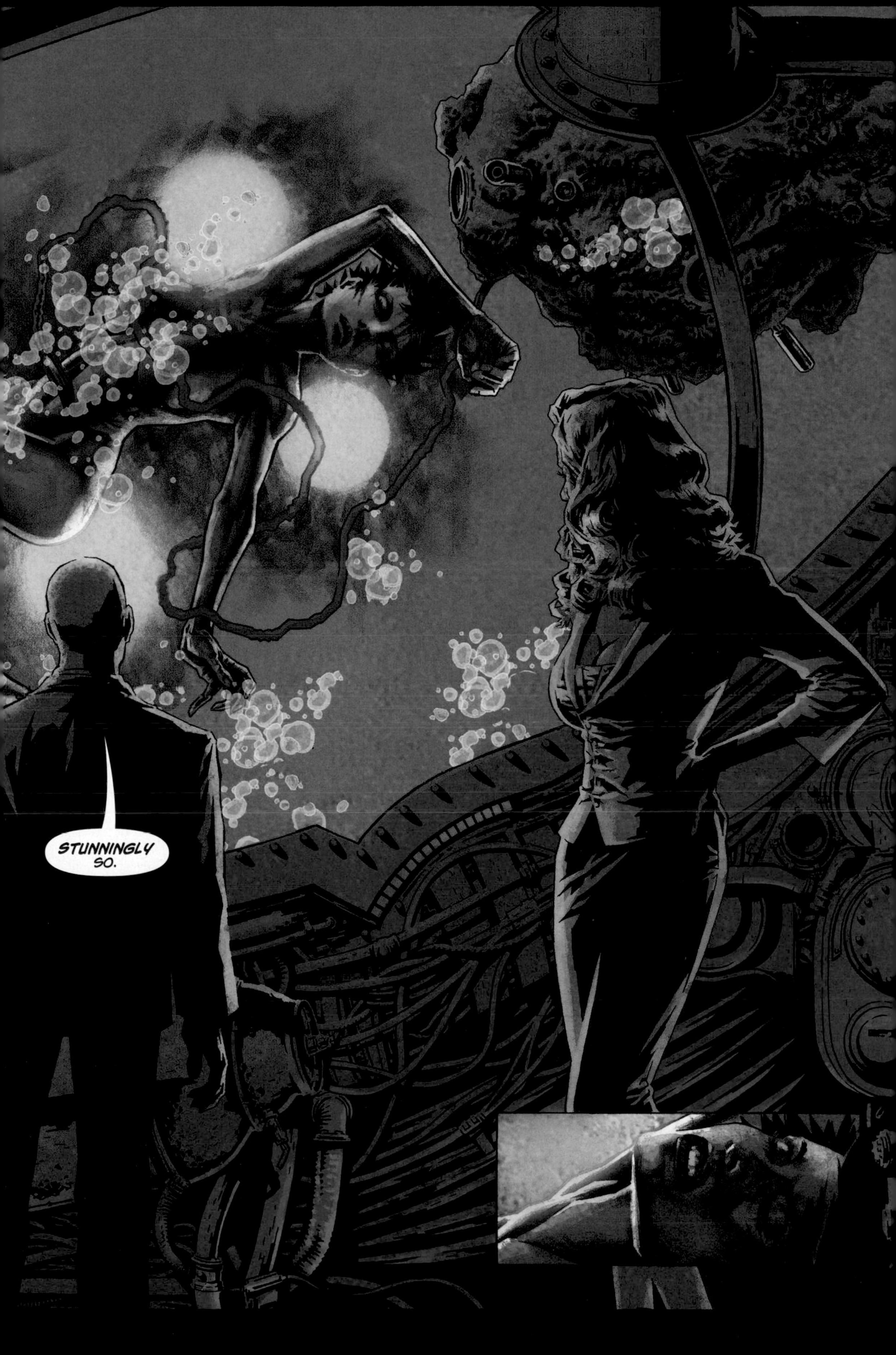
STUNNINGLY SO.

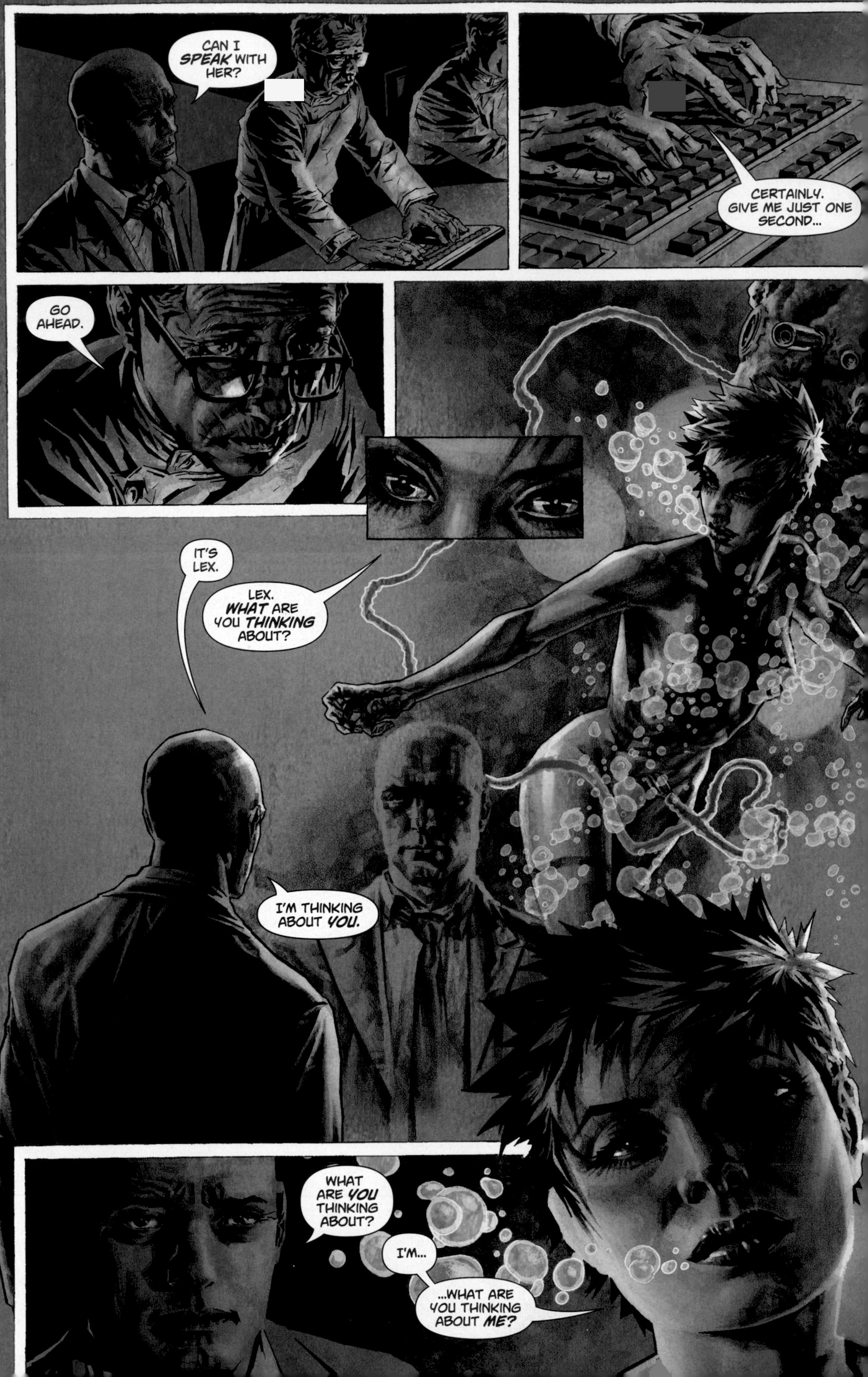
CAN I SPEAK WITH HER?
CERTAINLY. GIVE ME JUST ONE SECOND...
GO AHEAD.
IT'S LEX.
LEX. WHAT ARE YOU THINKING ABOUT?
I'M THINKING ABOUT YOU.
WHAT ARE YOU THINKING ABOUT?
I'M...
...WHAT ARE YOU THINKING ABOUT ME?

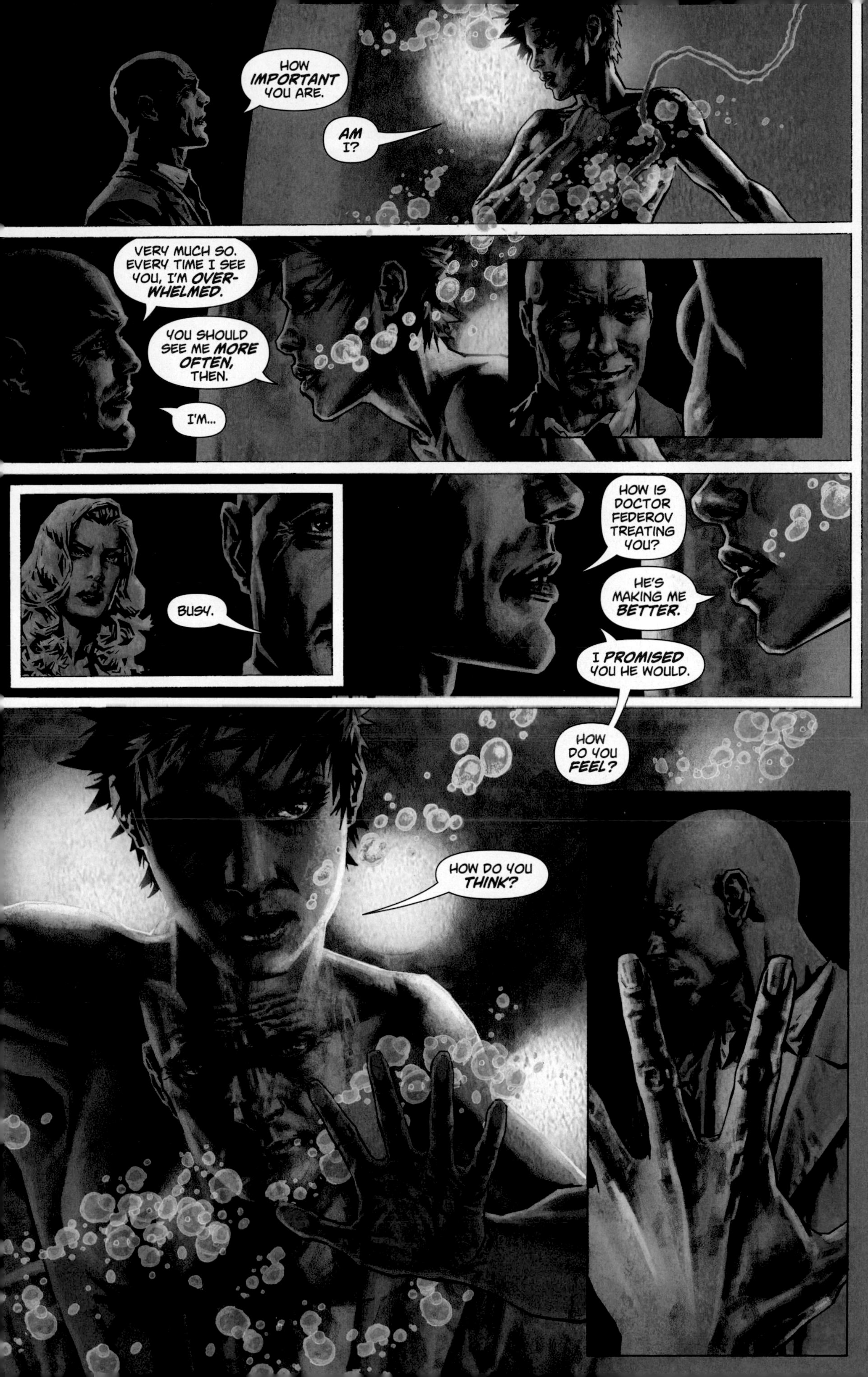
HOW IMPORTANT YOU ARE.
AM I?
VERY MUCH SO. EVERY TIME I SEE YOU, I'M OVER-WHELMED.
YOU SHOULD SEE ME MORE OFTEN, THEN.
I'M...
BUSY.
HOW IS DOCTOR FEDEROV TREATING YOU?
HE'S MAKING ME BETTER.
I PROMISED YOU HE WOULD.
HOW DO YOU FEEL?
HOW DO YOU THINK?

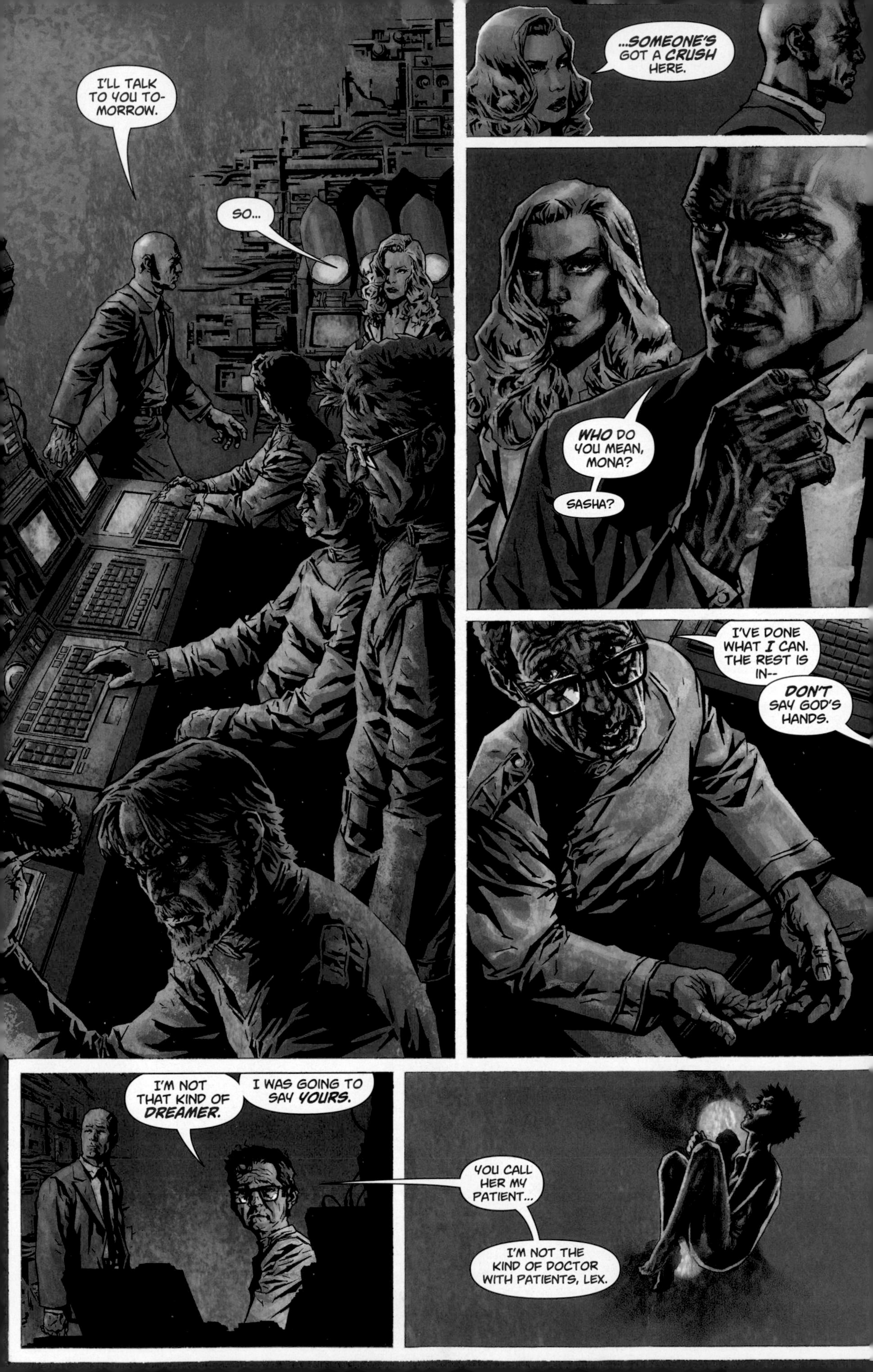
I'LL TALK TO YOU TO-MORROW.
SO...
...SOMEONE'S GOT A CRUSH HERE.
WHO DO YOU MEAN, MONA?
SASHA?
I'VE DONE WHAT I CAN. THE REST IS IN--
DON'T SAY GOD'S HANDS.
I'M NOT THAT KIND OF DREAMER.
I WAS GOING TO SAY YOURS.
YOU CALL HER MY PATIENT...
I'M NOT THE KIND OF DOCTOR WITH PATIENTS, LEX.

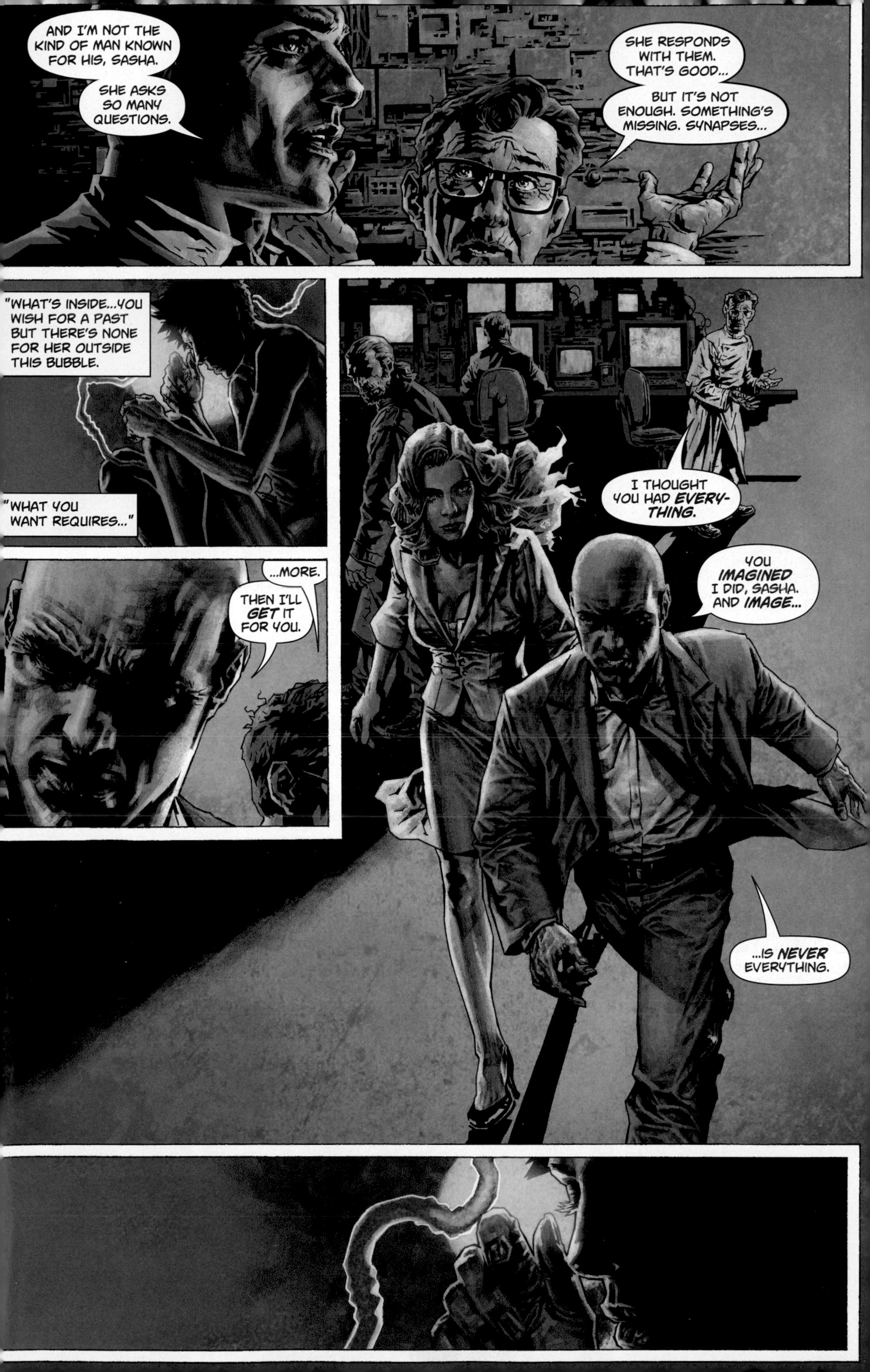
AND I'M NOT THE KIND OF MAN KNOWN FOR HIS, SASHA.
SHE ASKS SO MANY QUESTIONS.
SHE RESPONDS WITH THEM. THAT'S GOOD...
BUT IT'S NOT ENOUGH. SOMETHING'S MISSING. SYNAPSES...
"WHAT'S INSIDE...YOU WISH FOR A PAST BUT THERE'S NONE FOR HER OUTSIDE THIS BUBBLE.
"WHAT YOU WANT REQUIRES..."
...MORE.
THEN I'LL *GET* IT FOR YOU.
I THOUGHT YOU HAD *EVERYTHING.*
YOU *IMAGINED* I DID, SASHA. AND *IMAGE*...
...IS *NEVER* EVERYTHING.

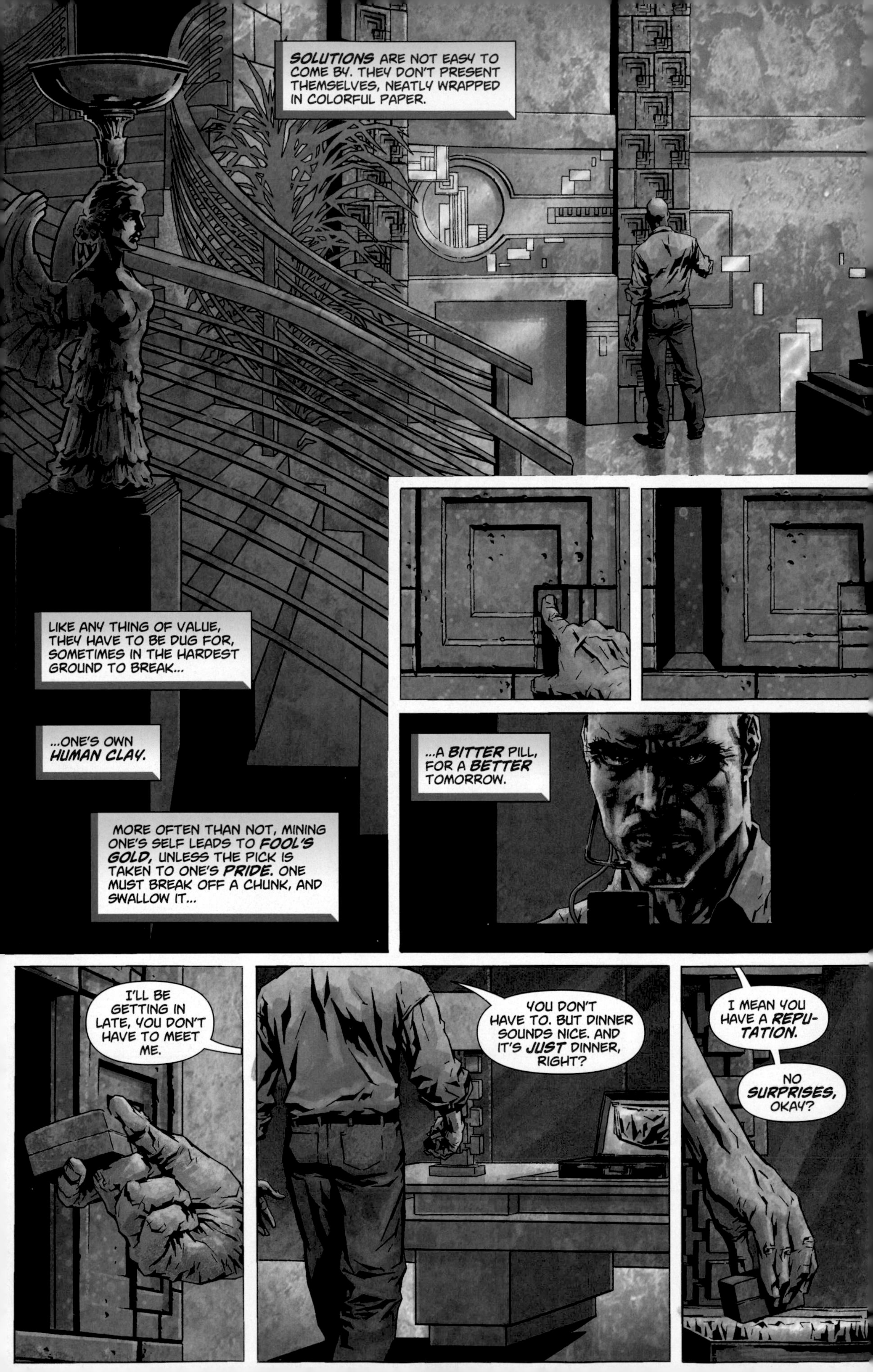
SOLUTIONS ARE NOT EASY TO COME BY. THEY DON'T PRESENT THEMSELVES, NEATLY WRAPPED IN COLORFUL PAPER.
LIKE ANY THING OF VALUE, THEY HAVE TO BE DUG FOR, SOMETIMES IN THE HARDEST GROUND TO BREAK...
...ONE'S OWN HUMAN CLAY.
MORE OFTEN THAN NOT, MINING ONE'S SELF LEADS TO FOOL'S GOLD, UNLESS THE PICK IS TAKEN TO ONE'S PRIDE. ONE MUST BREAK OFF A CHUNK, AND SWALLOW IT...
...A BITTER PILL, FOR A BETTER TOMORROW.
I'LL BE GETTING IN LATE, YOU DON'T HAVE TO MEET ME.
YOU DON'T HAVE TO. BUT DINNER SOUNDS NICE. AND IT'S JUST DINNER, RIGHT?
I MEAN YOU HAVE A REPU-TATION.
NO SURPRISES, OKAY?

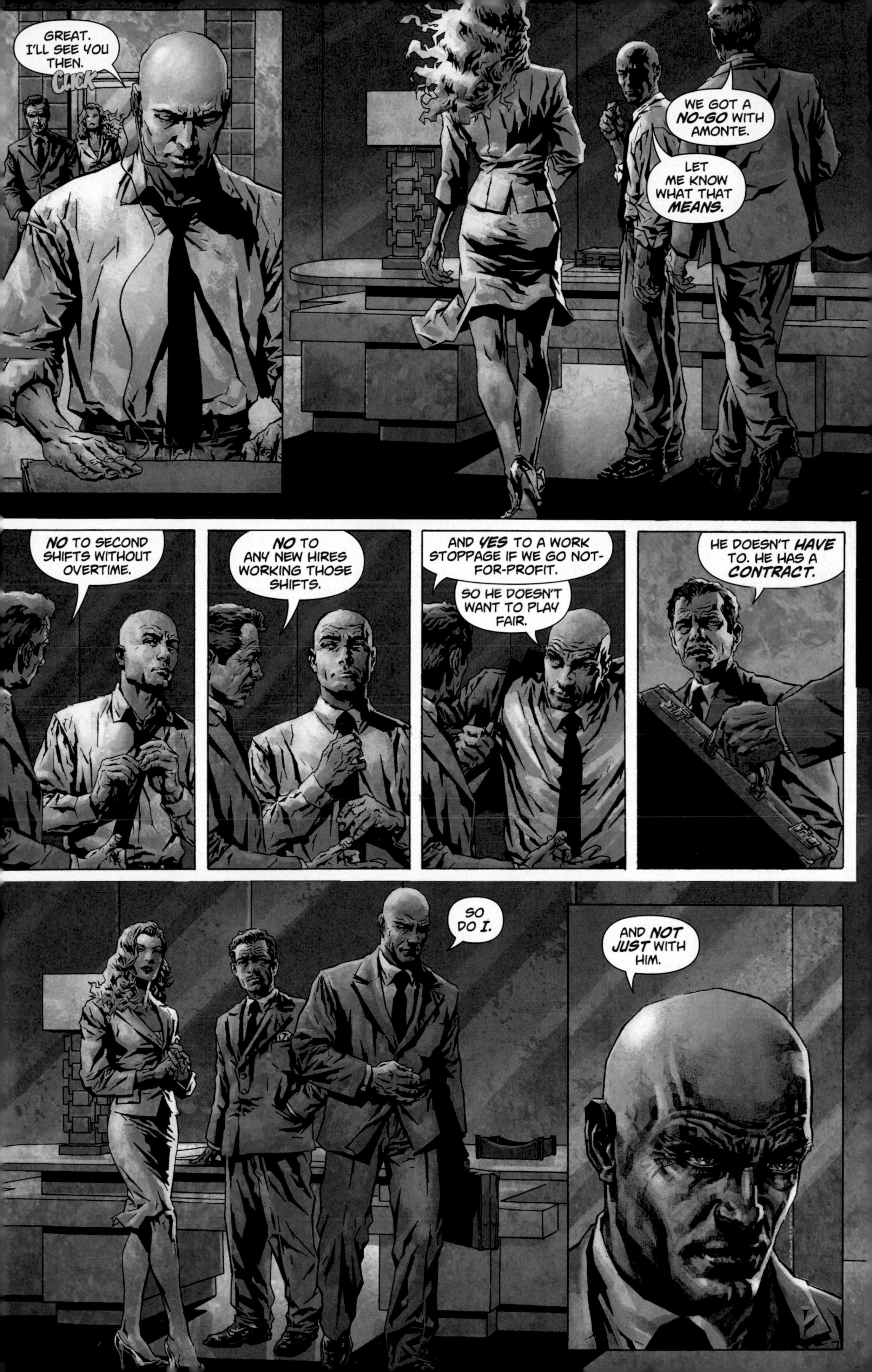
GREAT. I'LL SEE YOU THEN.
CLICK
WE GOT A NO-GO WITH AMONTE.
LET ME KNOW WHAT THAT MEANS.
NO TO SECOND SHIFTS WITHOUT OVERTIME.
NO TO ANY NEW HIRES WORKING THOSE SHIFTS.
AND YES TO A WORK STOPPAGE IF WE GO NOT-FOR-PROFIT.
SO HE DOESN'T WANT TO PLAY FAIR.
HE DOESN'T HAVE TO. HE HAS A CONTRACT.
SO DO I.
AND NOT JUST WITH HIM.

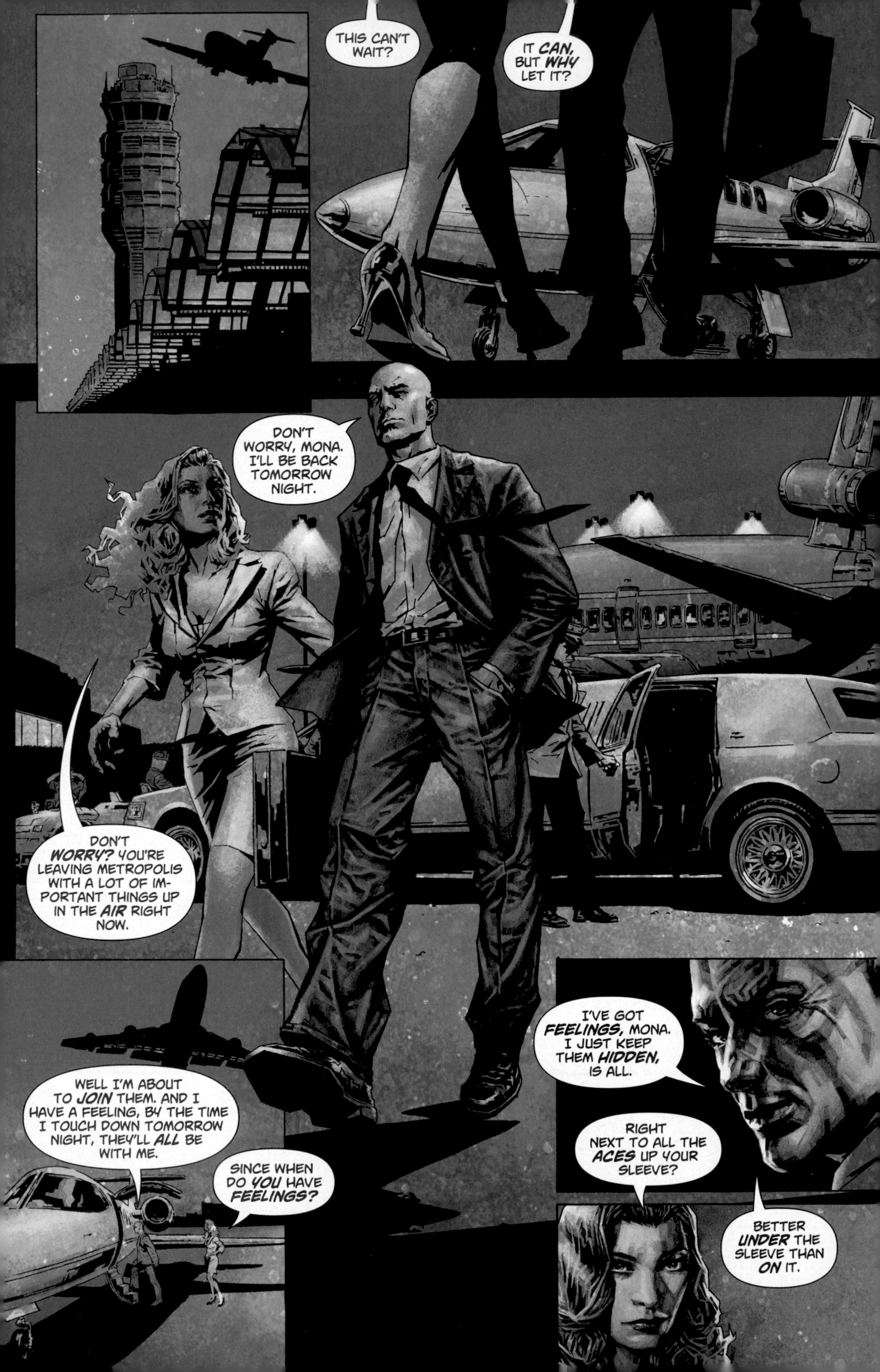
THIS CAN'T WAIT?
IT CAN, BUT WHY LET IT?
DON'T WORRY, MONA. I'LL BE BACK TOMORROW NIGHT.
DON'T WORRY? YOU'RE LEAVING METROPOLIS WITH A LOT OF IMPORTANT THINGS UP IN THE AIR RIGHT NOW.
WELL I'M ABOUT TO JOIN THEM. AND I HAVE A FEELING, BY THE TIME I TOUCH DOWN TOMORROW NIGHT, THEY'LL ALL BE WITH ME.
SINCE WHEN DO YOU HAVE FEELINGS?
I'VE GOT FEELINGS, MONA. I JUST KEEP THEM HIDDEN, IS ALL.
RIGHT NEXT TO ALL THE ACES UP YOUR SLEEVE?
BETTER UNDER THE SLEEVE THAN ON IT.

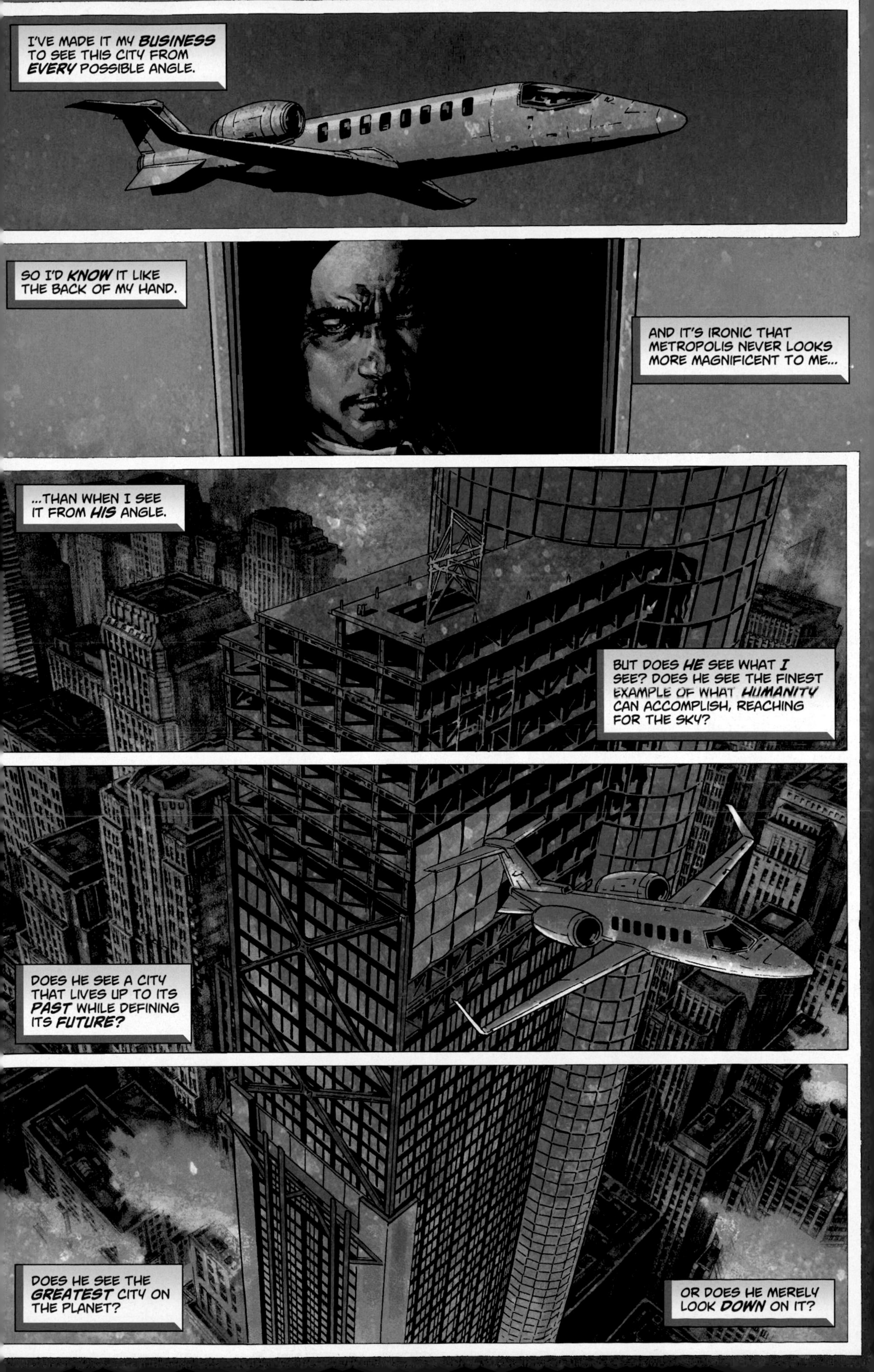
I'VE MADE IT MY BUSINESS TO SEE THIS CITY FROM EVERY POSSIBLE ANGLE.
SO I'D KNOW IT LIKE THE BACK OF MY HAND.
AND IT'S IRONIC THAT METROPOLIS NEVER LOOKS MORE MAGNIFICENT TO ME...
...THAN WHEN I SEE IT FROM HIS ANGLE.
BUT DOES HE SEE WHAT I SEE? DOES HE SEE THE FINEST EXAMPLE OF WHAT HUMANITY CAN ACCOMPLISH, REACHING FOR THE SKY?
DOES HE SEE A CITY THAT LIVES UP TO ITS PAST WHILE DEFINING ITS FUTURE?
DOES HE SEE THE GREATEST CITY ON THE PLANET?
OR DOES HE MERELY LOOK DOWN ON IT?

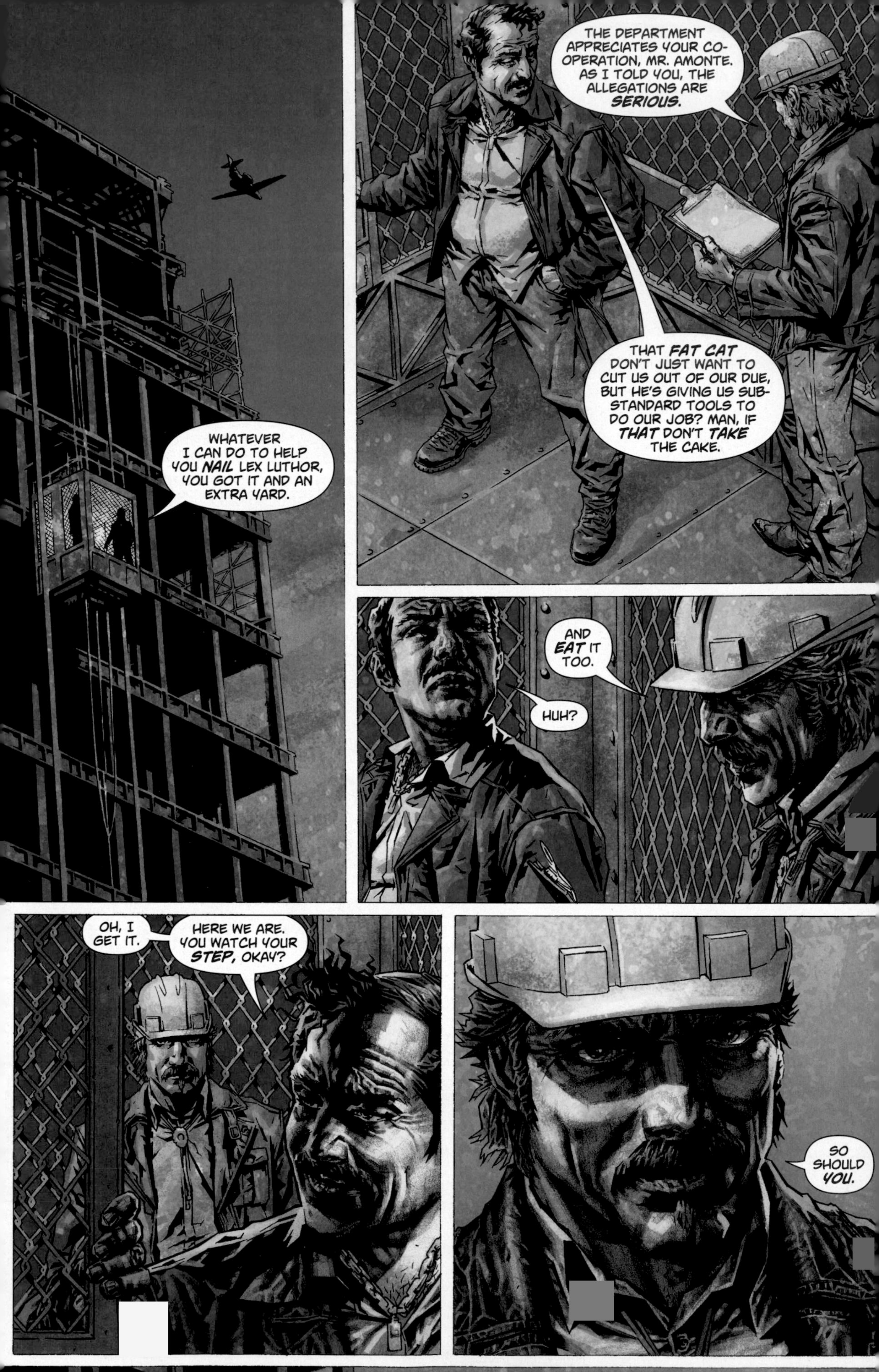
WHATEVER I CAN DO TO HELP YOU NAIL LEX LUTHOR, YOU GOT IT AND AN EXTRA YARD.
THE DEPARTMENT APPRECIATES YOUR CO-OPERATION, MR. AMONTE. AS I TOLD YOU, THE ALLEGATIONS ARE SERIOUS.
THAT FAT CAT DON'T JUST WANT TO CUT US OUT OF OUR DUE, BUT HE'S GIVING US SUB-STANDARD TOOLS TO DO OUR JOB? MAN, IF THAT DON'T TAKE THE CAKE.
AND EAT IT TOO.
HUH?
OH, I GET IT.
HERE WE ARE. YOU WATCH YOUR STEP, OKAY?
SO SHOULD YOU.

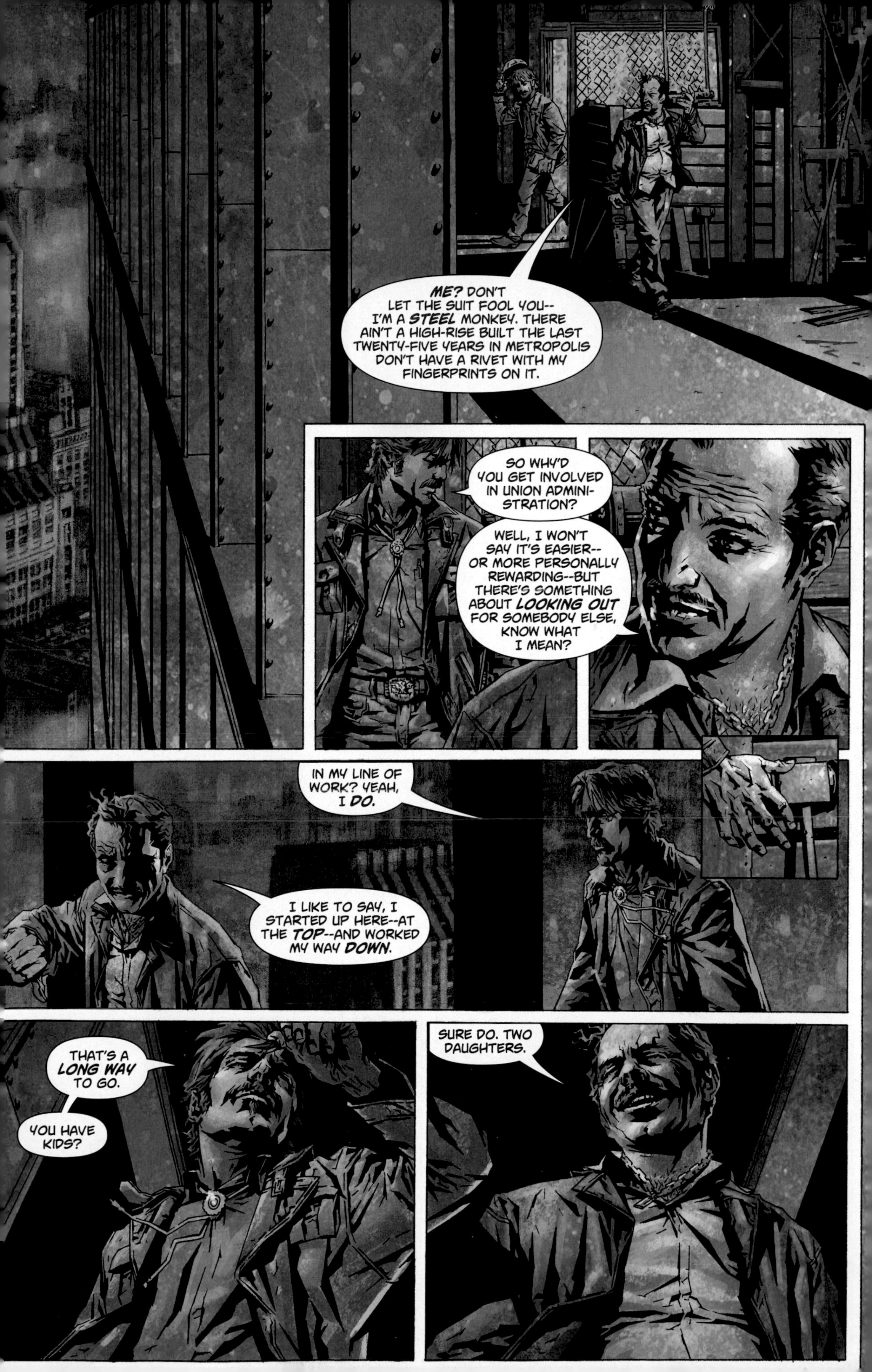
ME? DON'T LET THE SUIT FOOL YOU-- I'M A STEEL MONKEY. THERE AIN'T A HIGH-RISE BUILT THE LAST TWENTY-FIVE YEARS IN METROPOLIS DON'T HAVE A RIVET WITH MY FINGERPRINTS ON IT.
SO WHY'D YOU GET INVOLVED IN UNION ADMINI-STRATION?
WELL, I WON'T SAY IT'S EASIER-- OR MORE PERSONALLY REWARDING--BUT THERE'S SOMETHING ABOUT LOOKING OUT FOR SOMEBODY ELSE, KNOW WHAT I MEAN?
IN MY LINE OF WORK? YEAH, I DO.
I LIKE TO SAY, I STARTED UP HERE--AT THE TOP--AND WORKED MY WAY DOWN.
THAT'S A LONG WAY TO GO.
YOU HAVE KIDS?
SURE DO. TWO DAUGHTERS.

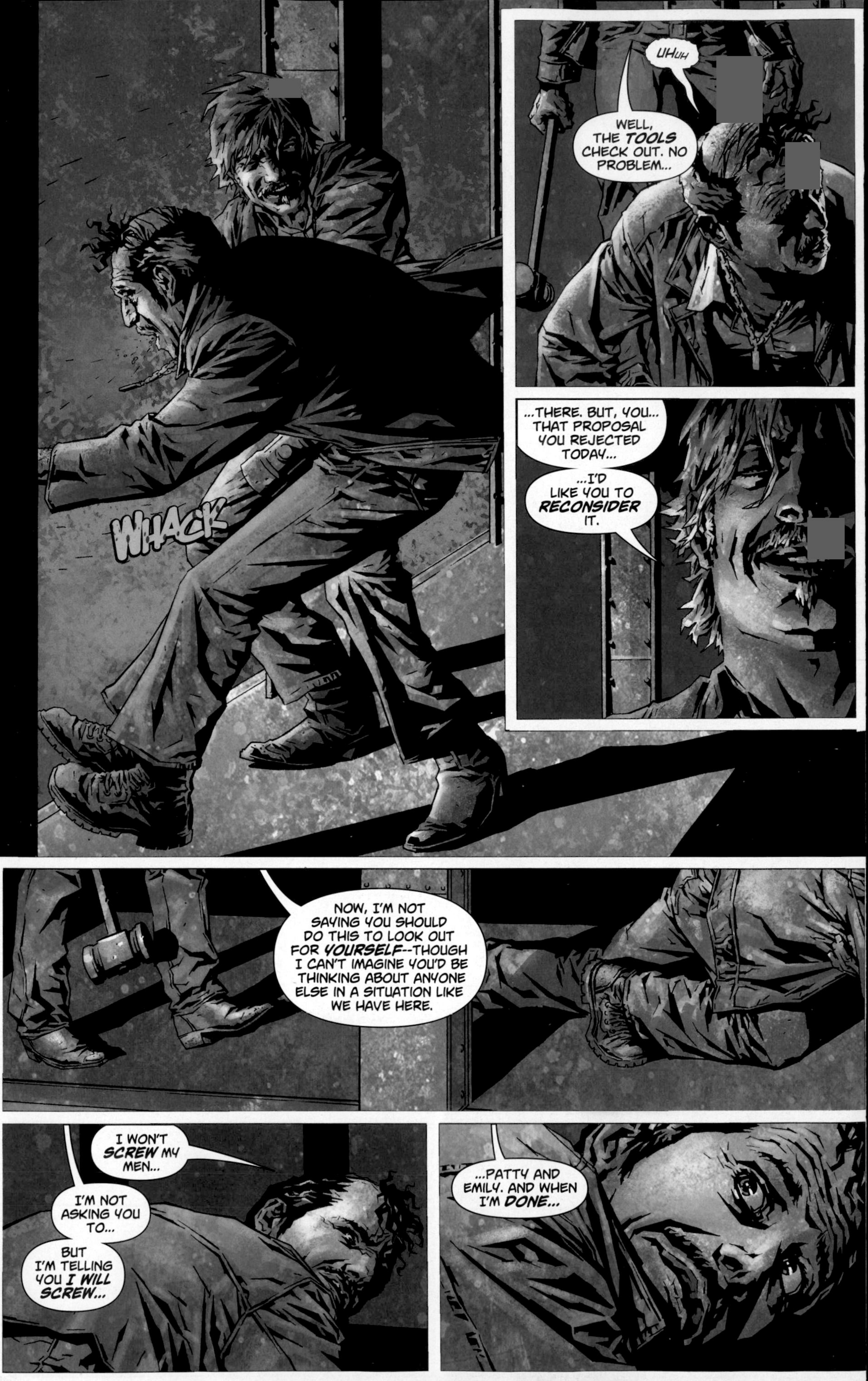

WHACK
UHUH
WELL, THE TOOLS CHECK OUT. NO PROBLEM...
...THERE. BUT, YOU... THAT PROPOSAL YOU REJECTED TODAY...
...I'D LIKE YOU TO RECONSIDER IT.
NOW, I'M NOT SAYING YOU SHOULD DO THIS TO LOOK OUT FOR YOURSELF--THOUGH I CAN'T IMAGINE YOU'D BE THINKING ABOUT ANYONE ELSE IN A SITUATION LIKE WE HAVE HERE.
I WON'T SCREW MY MEN...
I'M NOT ASKING YOU TO...
BUT I'M TELLING YOU I WILL SCREW...
...PATTY AND EMILY. AND WHEN I'M DONE...

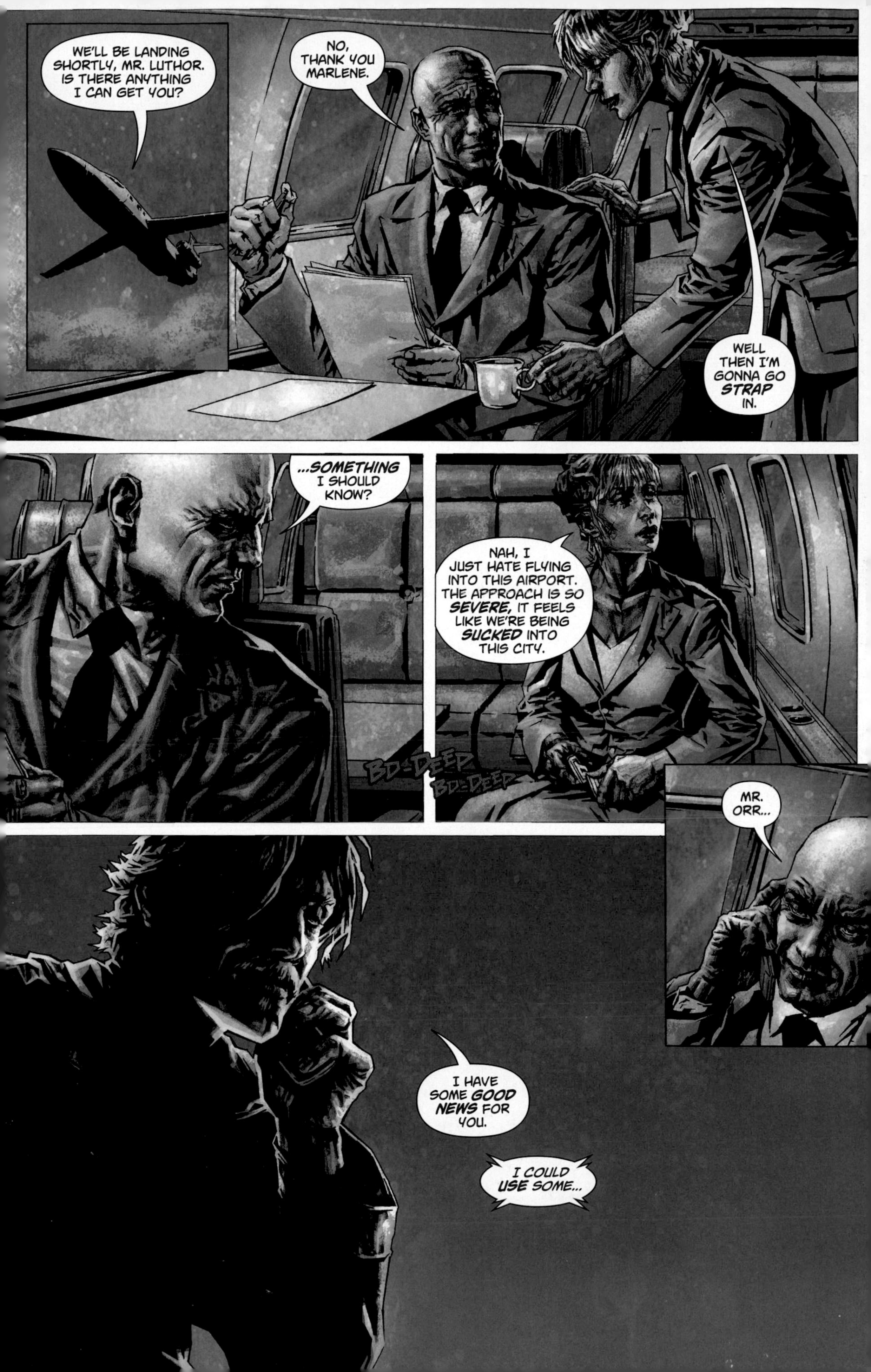
WE'LL BE LANDING SHORTLY, MR. LUTHOR. IS THERE ANYTHING I CAN GET YOU?
NO, THANK YOU MARLENE.
WELL THEN I'M GONNA GO STRAP IN.
...SOMETHING I SHOULD KNOW?
NAH, I JUST HATE FLYING INTO THIS AIRPORT. THE APPROACH IS SO SEVERE, IT FEELS LIKE WE'RE BEING SUCKED INTO THIS CITY.
BD-DEEP
BD-DEEP
MR. ORR...
I HAVE SOME GOOD NEWS FOR YOU.
I COULD USE SOME...

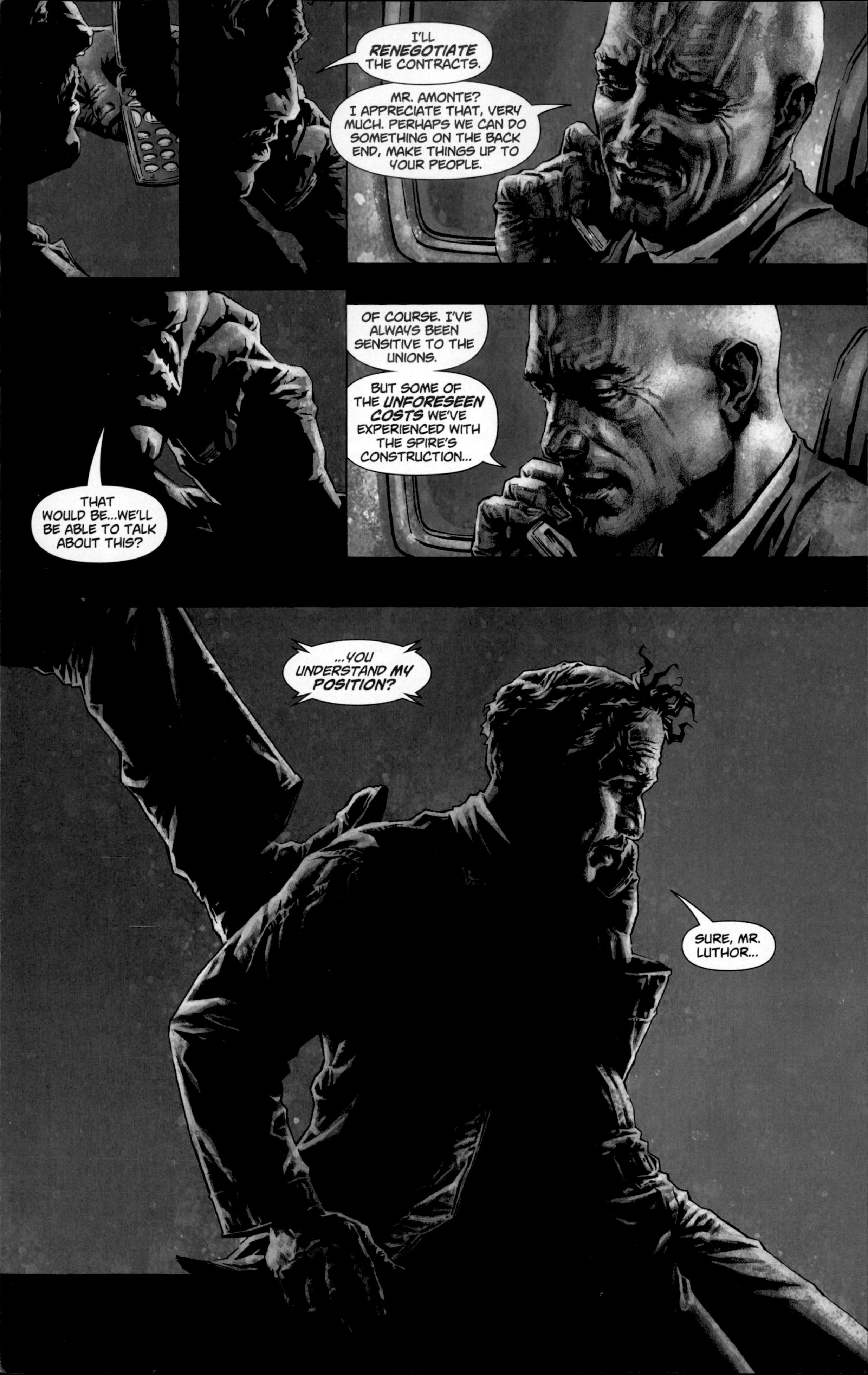
I'LL RENEGOTIATE THE CONTRACTS.
MR. AMONTE? I APPRECIATE THAT, VERY MUCH. PERHAPS WE CAN DO SOMETHING ON THE BACK END, MAKE THINGS UP TO YOUR PEOPLE.
OF COURSE. I'VE ALWAYS BEEN SENSITIVE TO THE UNIONS.
BUT SOME OF THE UNFORESEEN COSTS WE'VE EXPERIENCED WITH THE SPIRE'S CONSTRUCTION...
THAT WOULD BE...WE'LL BE ABLE TO TALK ABOUT THIS?
...YOU UNDERSTAND MY POSITION?
SURE, MR. LUTHOR...

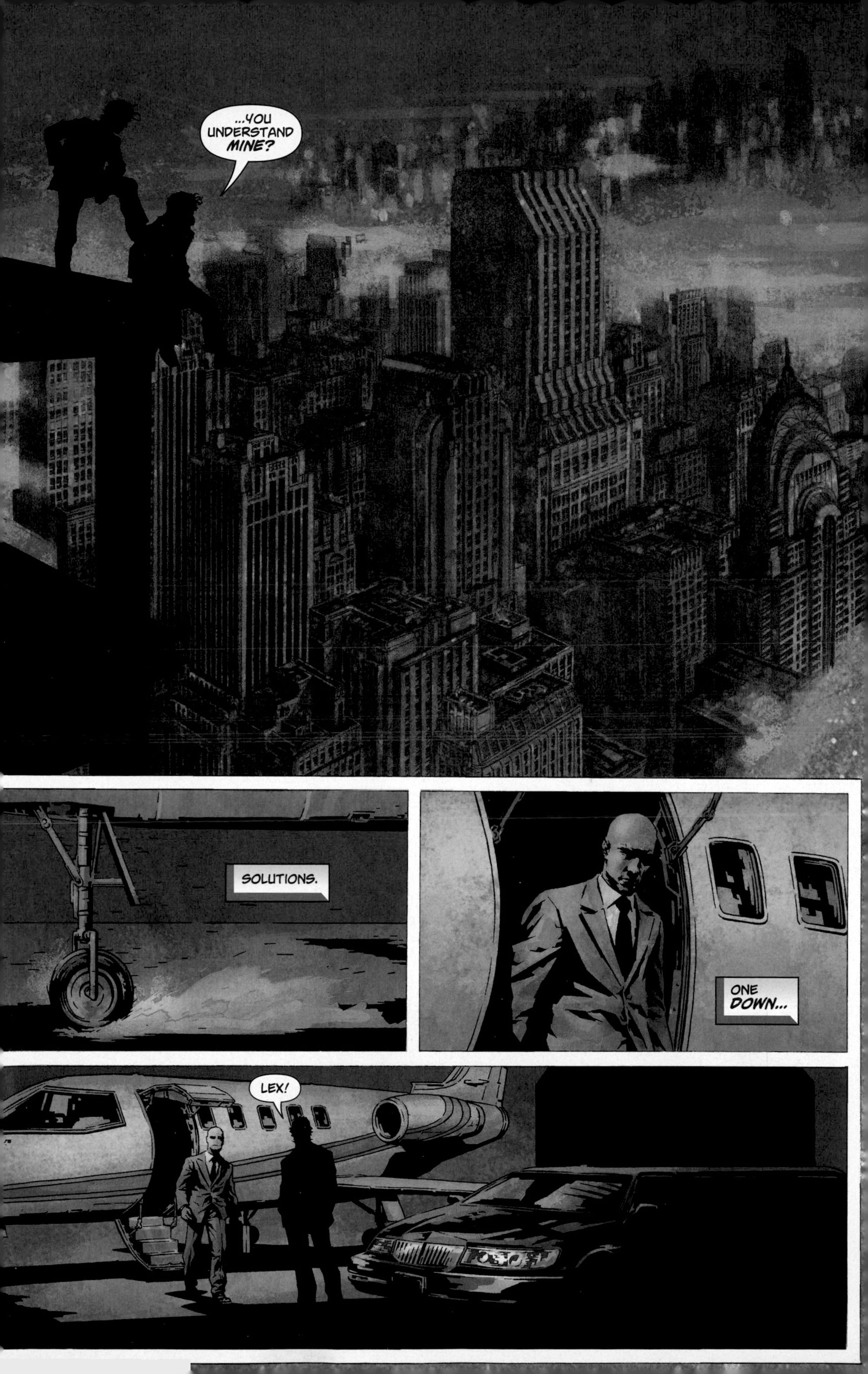
...YOU UNDERSTAND MINE?
SOLUTIONS.
ONE DOWN...
LEX!

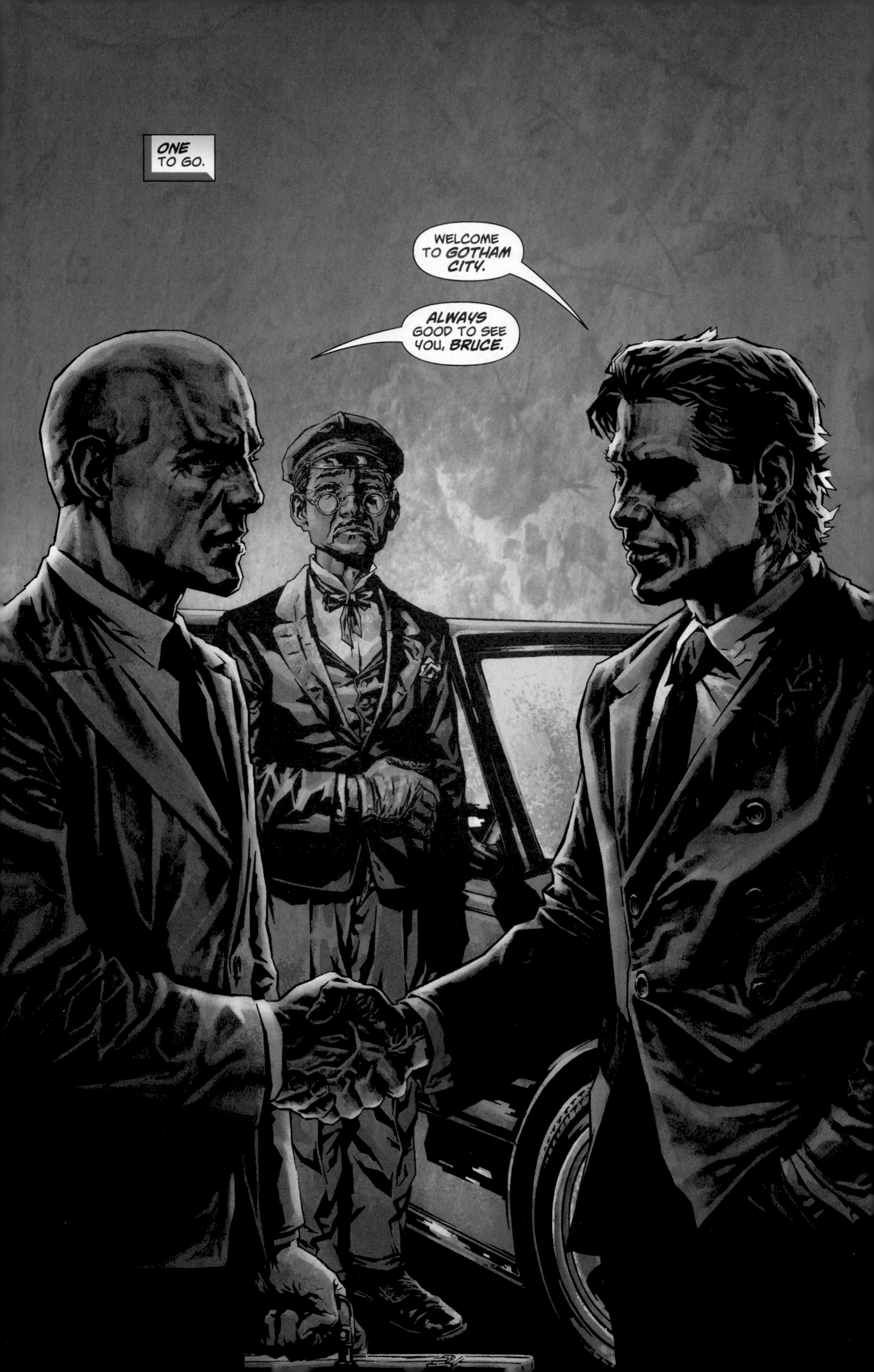
ONE TO GO.
WELCOME TO GOTHAM CITY.
ALWAYS GOOD TO SEE YOU, BRUCE.

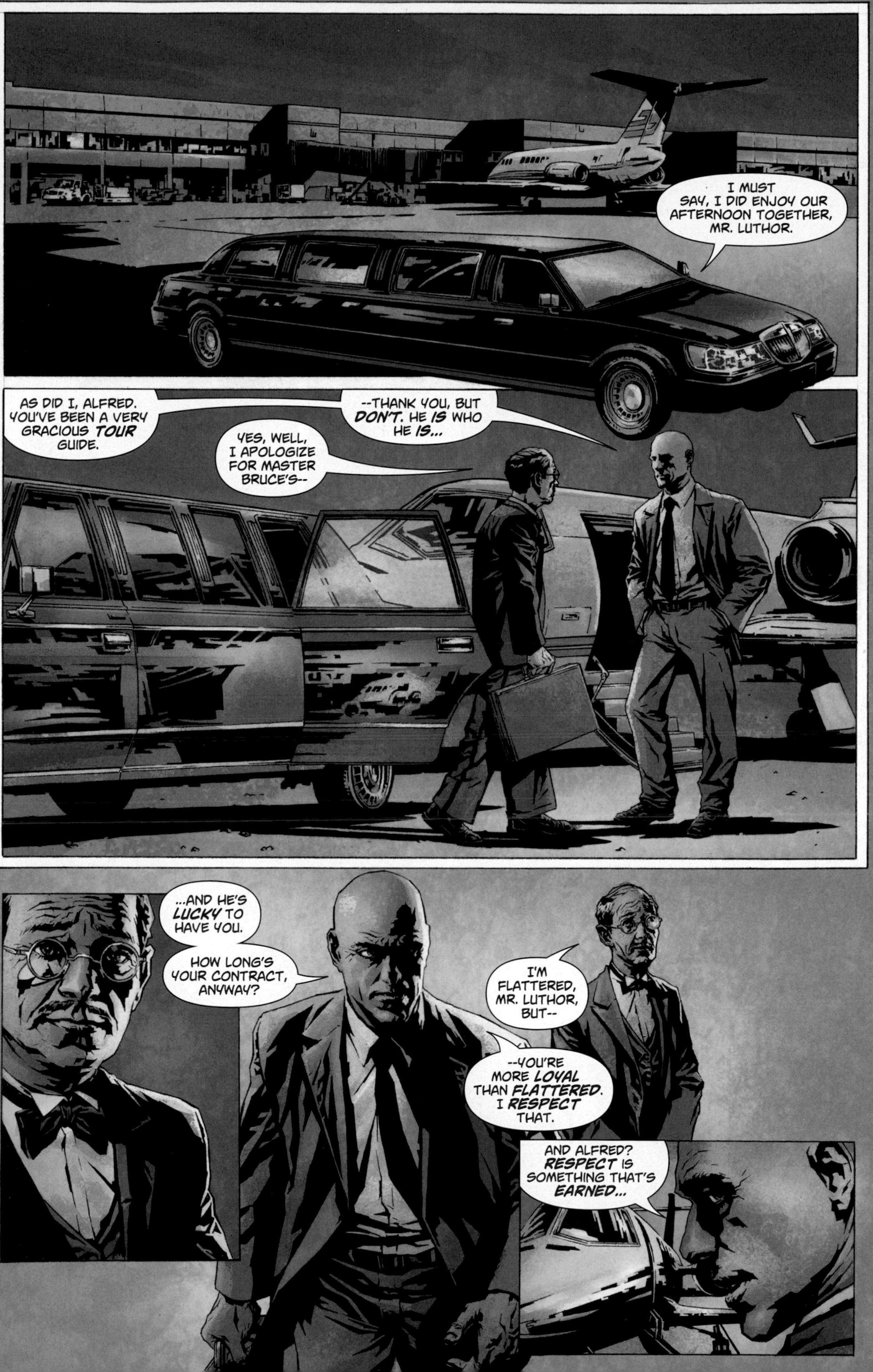
I MUST SAY, I DID ENJOY OUR AFTERNOON TOGETHER, MR. LUTHOR.
AS DID I, ALFRED. YOU'VE BEEN A VERY GRACIOUS TOUR GUIDE.
YES, WELL, I APOLOGIZE FOR MASTER BRUCE'S--
--THANK YOU, BUT DON'T. HE IS WHO HE IS...
...AND HE'S LUCKY TO HAVE YOU.
HOW LONG'S YOUR CONTRACT, ANYWAY?
I'M FLATTERED, MR. LUTHOR, BUT--
--YOU'RE MORE LOYAL THAN FLATTERED. I RESPECT THAT.
AND ALFRED? RESPECT IS SOMETHING THAT'S EARNED...

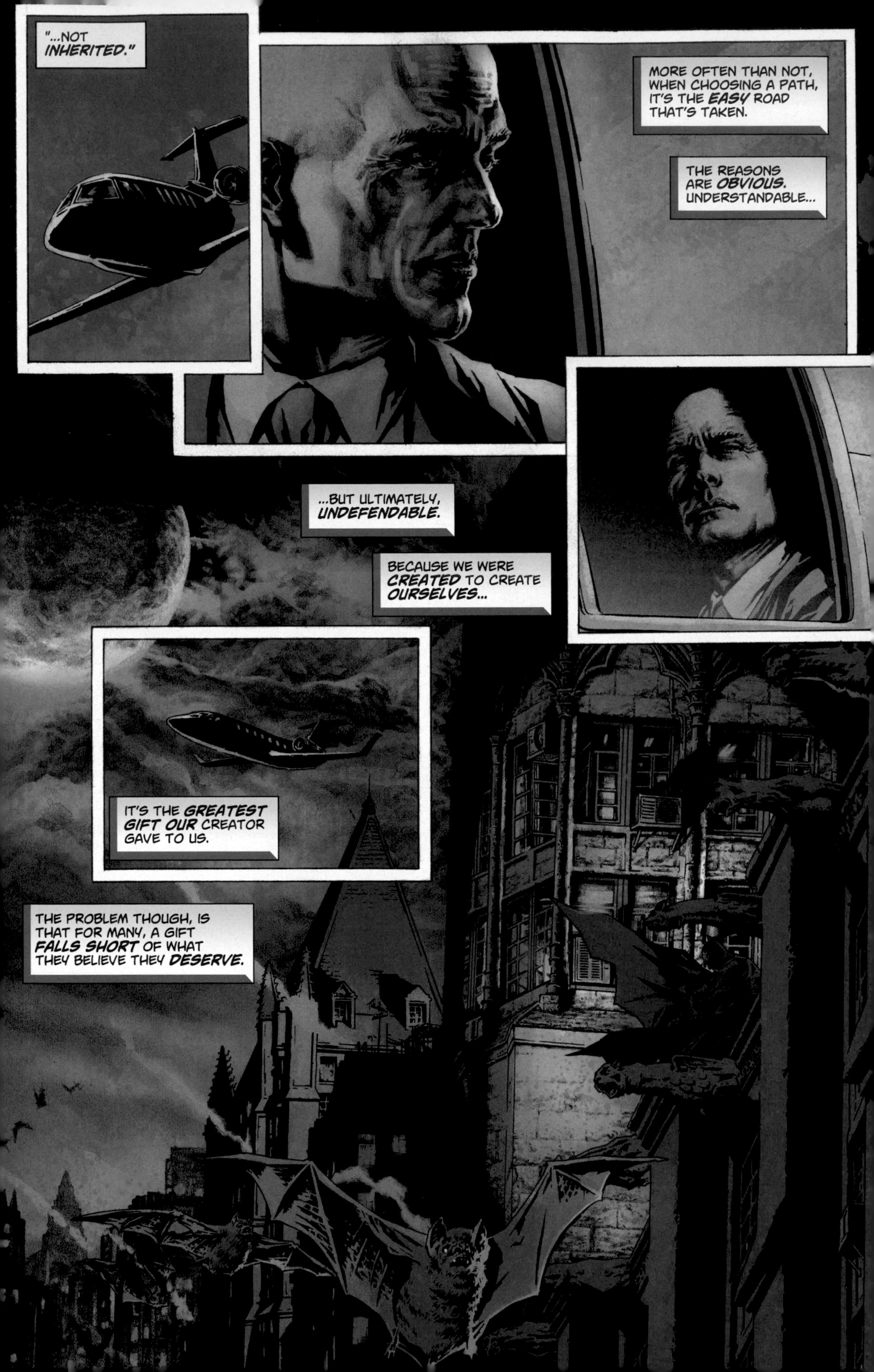
"...NOT *INHERITED.*"
MORE OFTEN THAN NOT, WHEN CHOOSING A PATH, IT'S THE *EASY* ROAD THAT'S TAKEN.
THE REASONS ARE *OBVIOUS.* UNDERSTANDABLE...
...BUT ULTIMATELY, *UNDEFENDABLE.*
BECAUSE WE WERE *CREATED* TO CREATE *OURSELVES...*
IT'S THE *GREATEST GIFT OUR* CREATOR GAVE TO US.
THE PROBLEM THOUGH, IS THAT FOR MANY, A GIFT *FALLS SHORT* OF WHAT THEY BELIEVE THEY *DESERVE.*

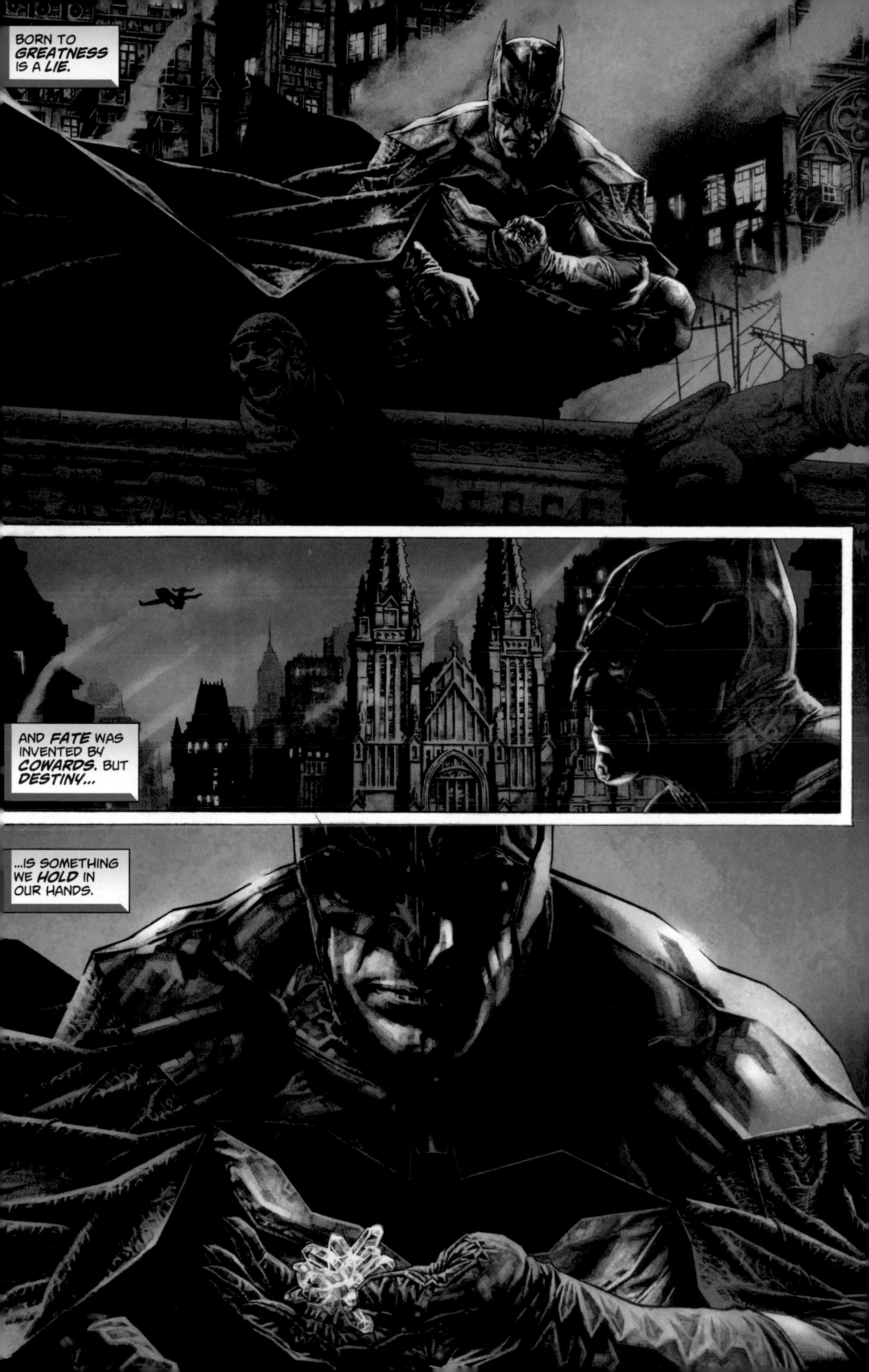
BORN TO GREATNESS IS A LIE.
AND FATE WAS INVENTED BY COWARDS. BUT DESTINY...
...IS SOMETHING WE HOLD IN OUR HANDS.

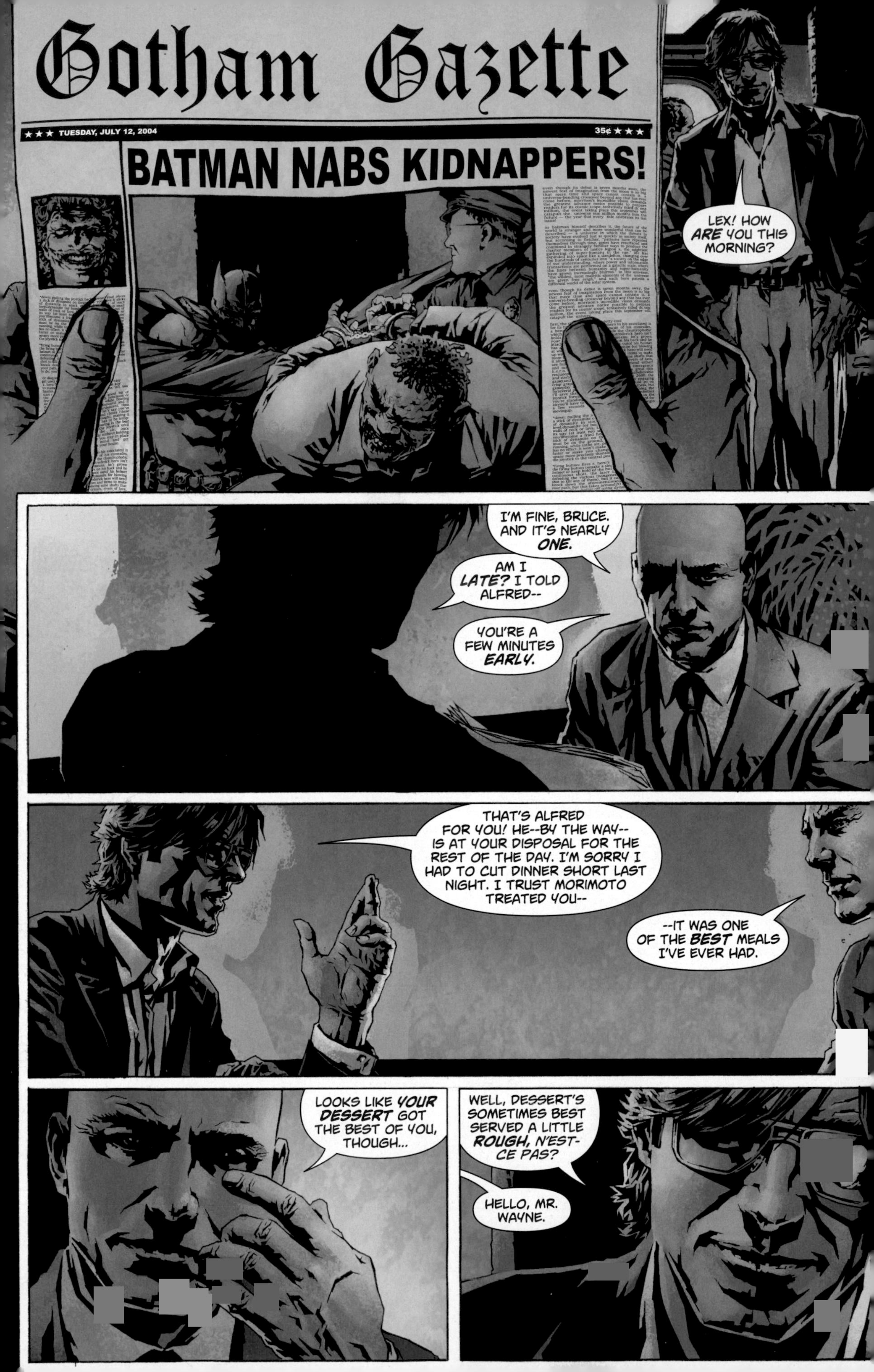
Gotham Gazette
TUESDAY, JULY 12, 2004
35¢
BATMAN NABS KIDNAPPERS!
LEX! HOW *ARE* YOU THIS MORNING?
I'M FINE, BRUCE. AND IT'S NEARLY *ONE*.
AM I *LATE?* I TOLD ALFRED--
YOU'RE A FEW MINUTES *EARLY*.
THAT'S ALFRED FOR YOU! HE--BY THE WAY--IS AT YOUR DISPOSAL FOR THE REST OF THE DAY. I'M SORRY I HAD TO CUT DINNER SHORT LAST NIGHT. I TRUST MORIMOTO TREATED YOU--
--IT WAS ONE OF THE *BEST* MEALS I'VE EVER HAD.
LOOKS LIKE *YOUR DESSERT* GOT THE BEST OF YOU, THOUGH...
WELL, DESSERT'S SOMETIMES BEST SERVED A LITTLE *ROUGH, N'EST-CE PAS?*
HELLO, MR. WAYNE.

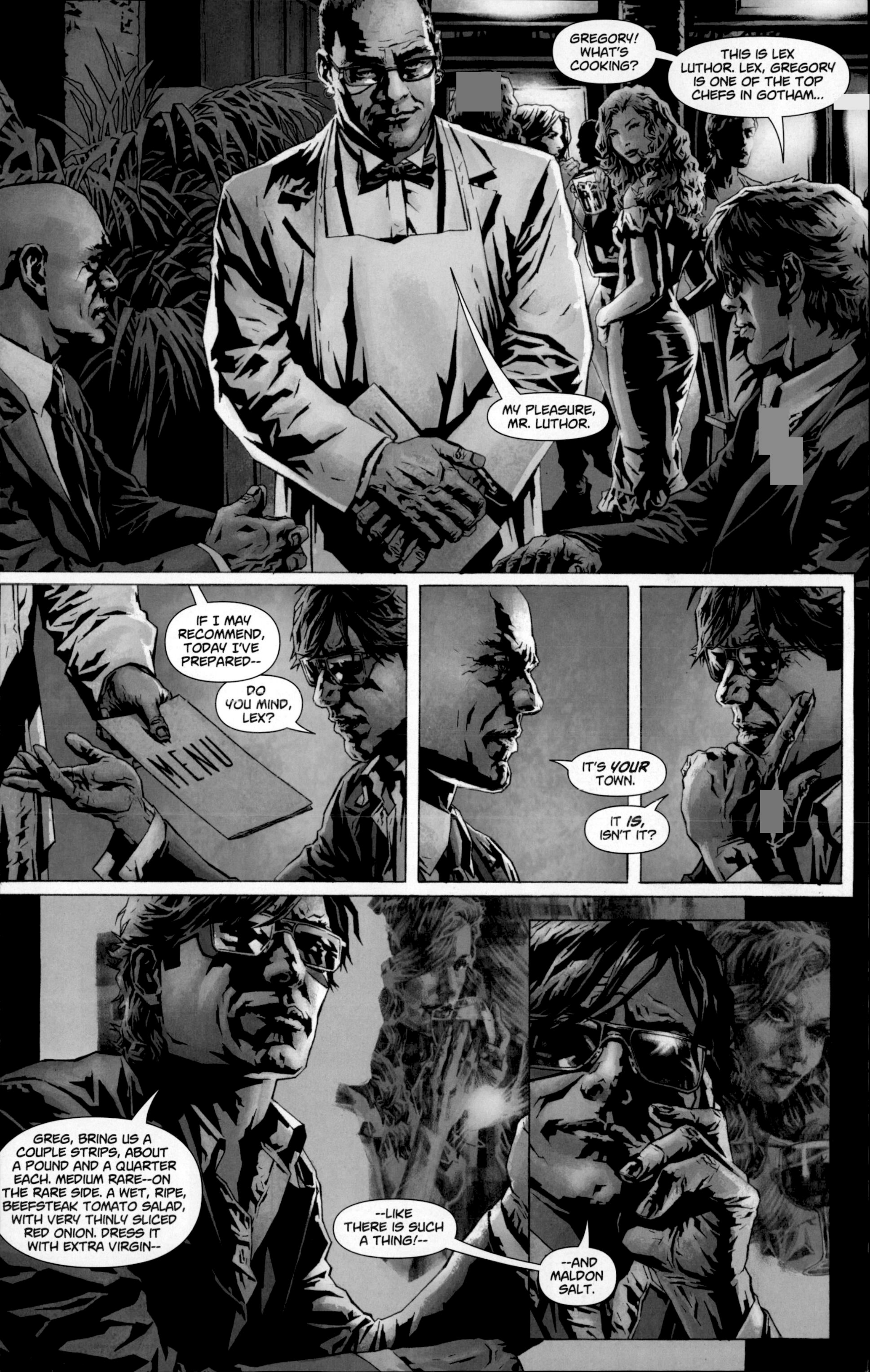
GREGORY! WHAT'S COOKING?
THIS IS LEX LUTHOR. LEX, GREGORY IS ONE OF THE TOP CHEFS IN GOTHAM...
MY PLEASURE, MR. LUTHOR.
IF I MAY RECOMMEND, TODAY I'VE PREPARED--
DO YOU MIND, LEX?
MENU
IT'S *YOUR* TOWN.
IT *IS*, ISN'T IT?
GREG, BRING US A COUPLE STRIPS, ABOUT A POUND AND A QUARTER EACH. MEDIUM RARE--ON THE RARE SIDE. A WET, RIPE, BEEFSTEAK TOMATO SALAD, WITH VERY THINLY SLICED RED ONION. DRESS IT WITH EXTRA VIRGIN--
--LIKE THERE IS SUCH A THING!--
--AND MALDON SALT.

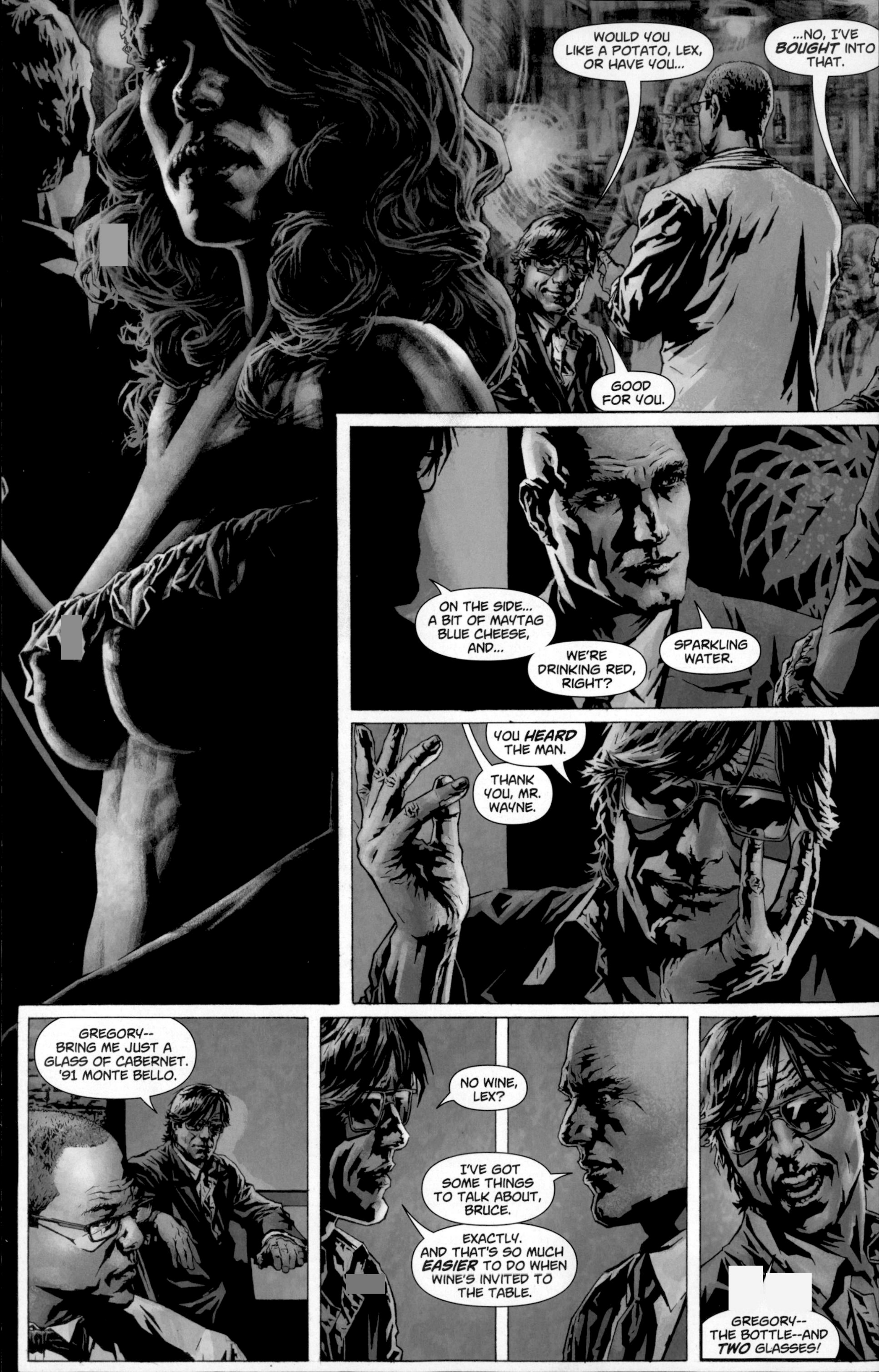
WOULD YOU LIKE A POTATO, LEX, OR HAVE YOU...
...NO, I'VE **BOUGHT** INTO THAT.
GOOD FOR YOU.
ON THE SIDE... A BIT OF MAYTAG BLUE CHEESE, AND...
WE'RE DRINKING RED, RIGHT?
SPARKLING WATER.
YOU **HEARD** THE MAN.
THANK YOU, MR. WAYNE.
GREGORY-- BRING ME JUST A GLASS OF CABERNET. '91 MONTE BELLO.
NO WINE, LEX?
I'VE GOT SOME THINGS TO TALK ABOUT, BRUCE.
EXACTLY. AND THAT'S SO MUCH ***EASIER*** TO DO WHEN WINE'S INVITED TO THE TABLE.
GREGORY-- THE BOTTLE--AND ***TWO*** GLASSES!

I *WANT* TO *LIKE* BRUCE WAYNE...

AND IT'S NOT JUST BECAUSE HE MAY GO OUT OF HIS WAY TO TRY TO MAKE CERTAIN THAT I *DON'T*...

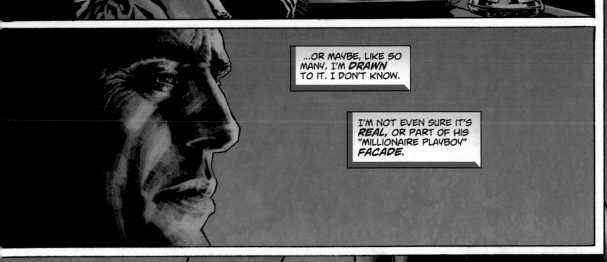

OR THAT HE *RELISHES* A PART OF LIFE I'M... *UNCOMFORTABLE* WITH.

HE CONVEYS...*ANIMAL MAGNETISM.* MAYBE I'M JEALOUS OF THAT...

...OR MAYBE, LIKE SO MANY, I'M *DRAWN* TO IT. I DON'T KNOW.

I'M NOT EVEN SURE IT'S *REAL,* OR PART OF HIS "MILLIONAIRE PLAYBOY" *FACADE.*

BUT ONE THING'S CLEAR ABOUT BRUCE. BEYOND THE MASK HE WEARS...

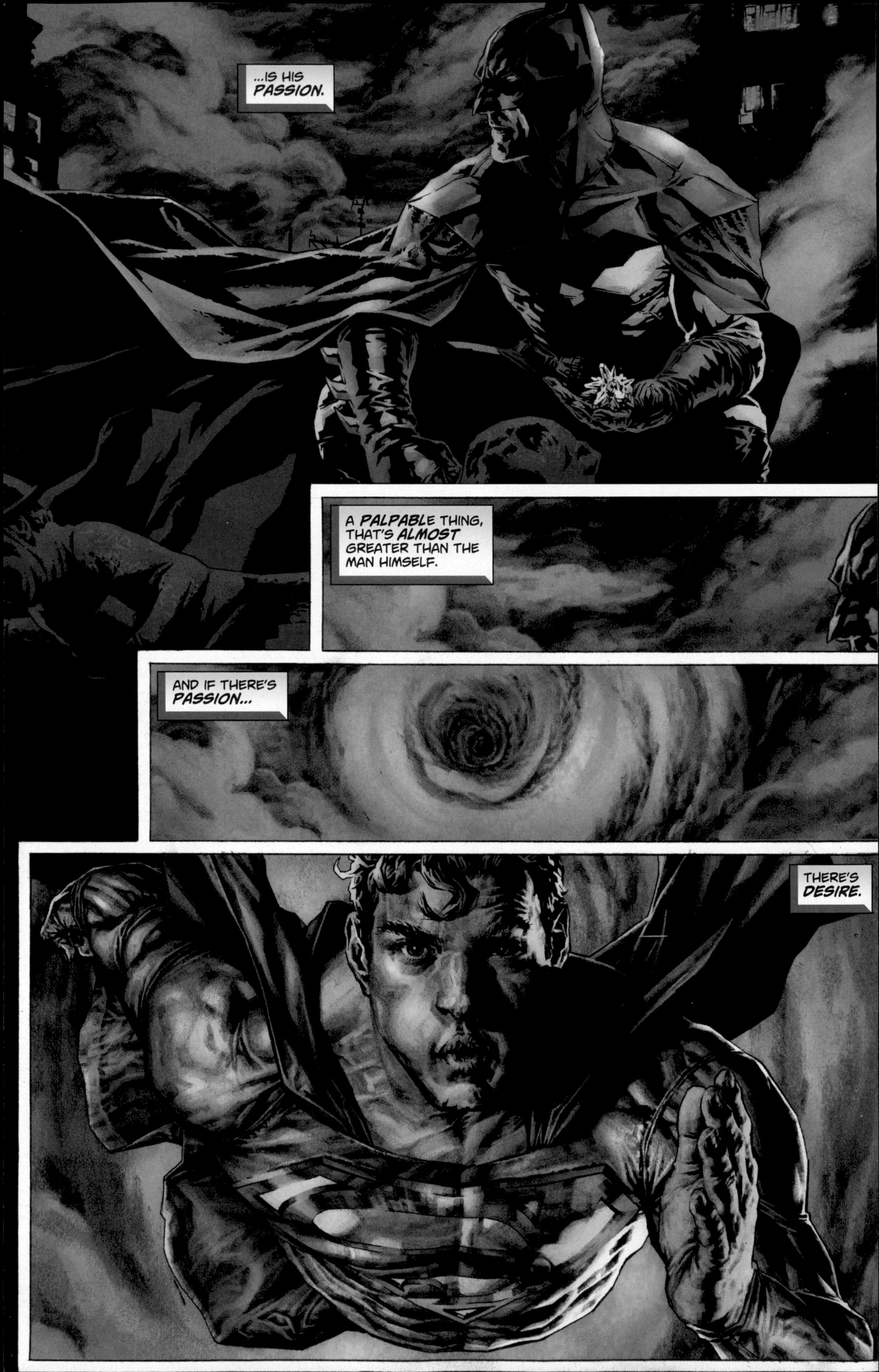

...IS HIS PASSION.
A PALPABLE THING, THAT'S ALMOST GREATER THAN THE MAN HIMSELF.
AND IF THERE'S PASSION...
THERE'S DESIRE.

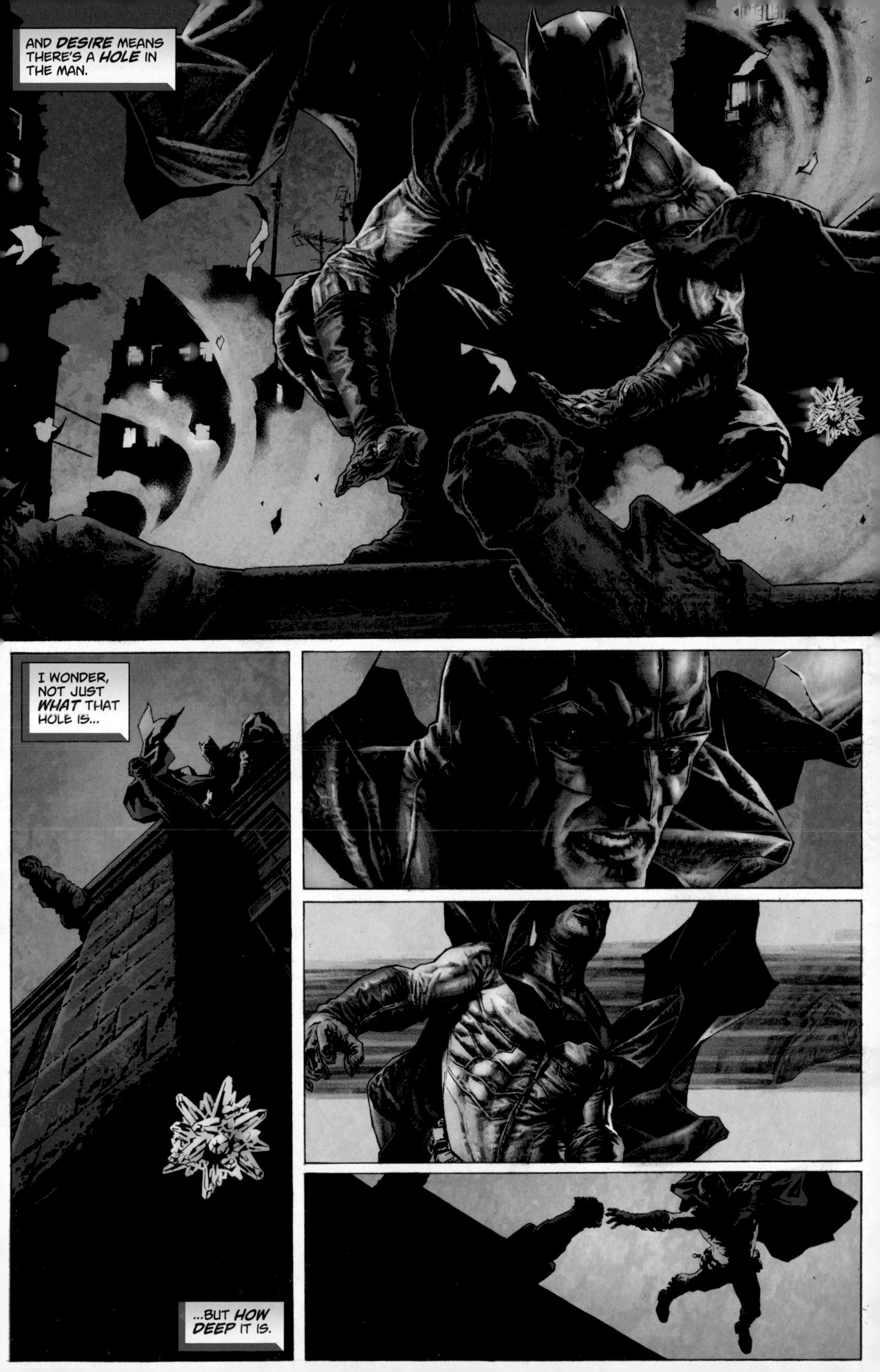
AND DESIRE MEANS THERE'S A HOLE IN THE MAN.
I WONDER, NOT JUST WHAT THAT HOLE IS...
...BUT HOW DEEP IT IS.

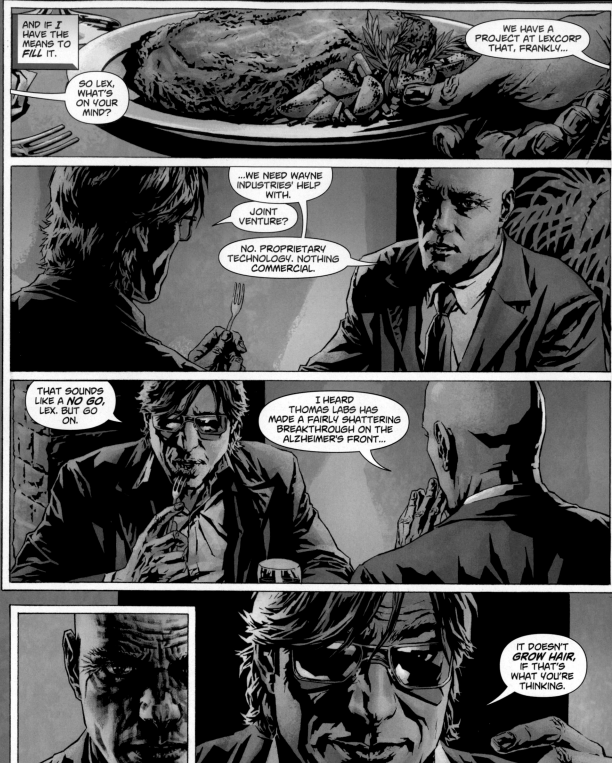

AND IF *I* HAVE THE MEANS TO *FILL* IT.

SO LEX, WHAT'S ON YOUR MIND?

WE HAVE A PROJECT AT LEXCORP THAT, FRANKLY...

...WE NEED WAYNE INDUSTRIES' HELP WITH.

JOINT VENTURE?

NO. PROPRIETARY TECHNOLOGY. NOTHING COMMERCIAL.

THAT SOUNDS LIKE A *NO GO*, LEX. BUT GO ON.

I HEARD THOMAS LABS HAS MADE A FAIRLY SHATTERING BREAKTHROUGH ON THE ALZHEIMER'S FRONT...

IT DOESN'T *GROW HAIR*, IF THAT'S WHAT YOU'RE THINKING.

...I THINK IT COULD BE BENEFICIAL ON ANOTHER.

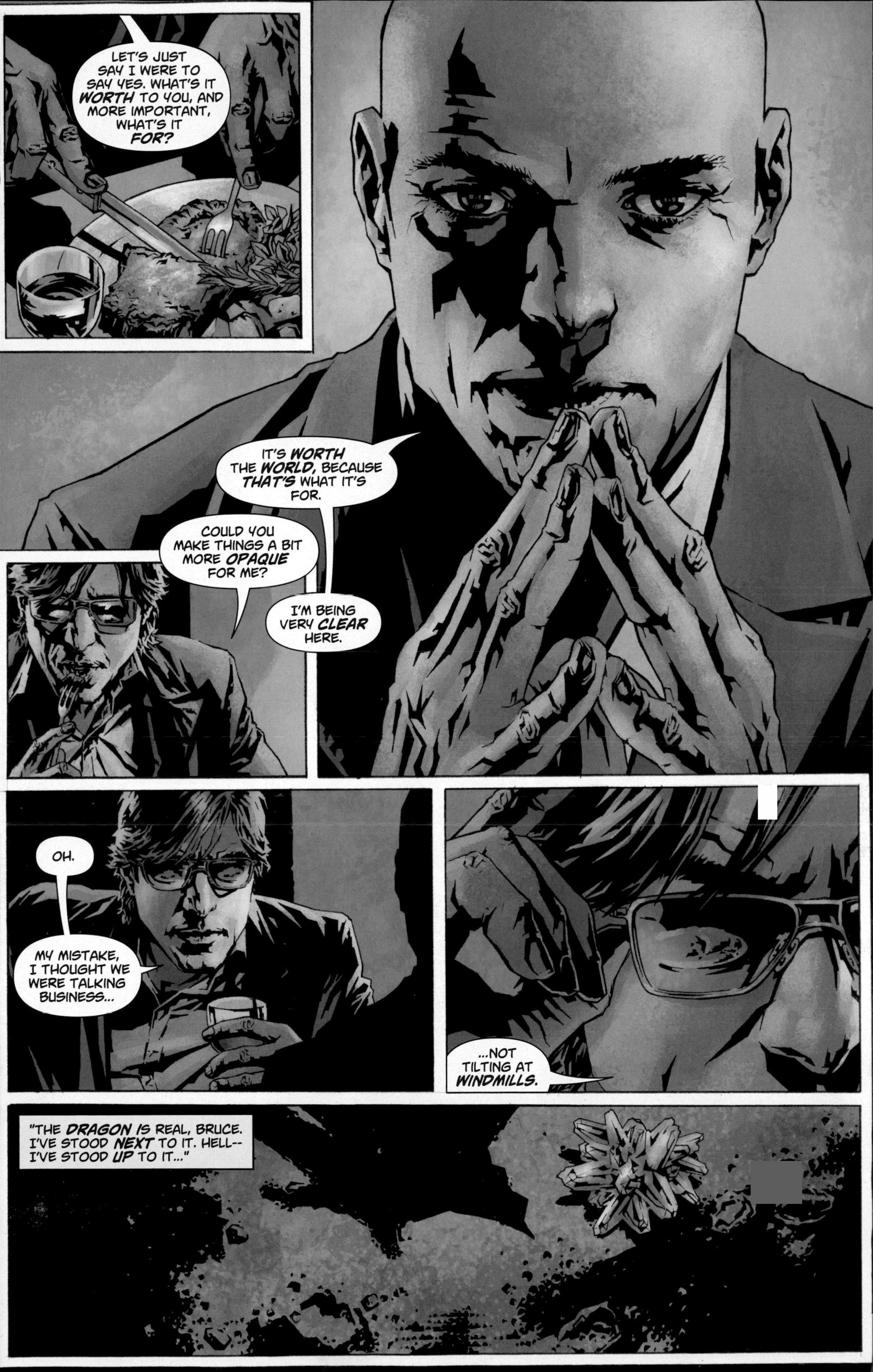

LET'S JUST SAY I WERE TO SAY YES. WHAT'S IT WORTH TO YOU, AND MORE IMPORTANT, WHAT'S IT FOR?
IT'S WORTH THE WORLD, BECAUSE THAT'S WHAT IT'S FOR.
COULD YOU MAKE THINGS A BIT MORE OPAQUE FOR ME?
I'M BEING VERY CLEAR HERE.
OH.
MY MISTAKE, I THOUGHT WE WERE TALKING BUSINESS...
...NOT TILTING AT WINDMILLS.
"THE DRAGON IS REAL, BRUCE. I'VE STOOD NEXT TO IT. HELL-- I'VE STOOD UP TO IT..."

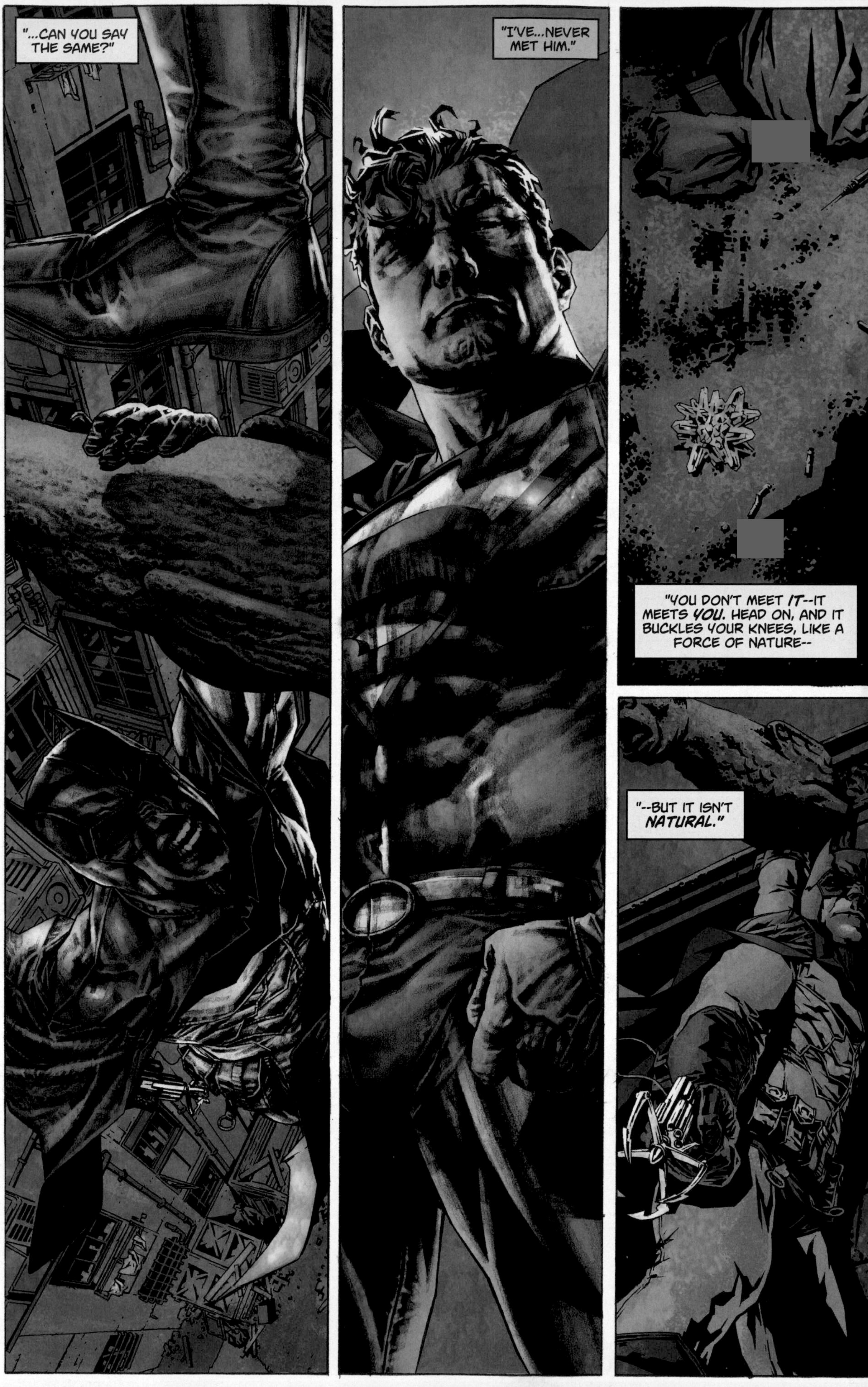
"...CAN YOU SAY THE SAME?"
"I'VE...NEVER MET HIM."
"YOU DON'T MEET *IT*--IT MEETS ***YOU***. HEAD ON, AND IT BUCKLES YOUR KNEES, LIKE A FORCE OF NATURE--
"--BUT IT ISN'T ***NATURAL.***"

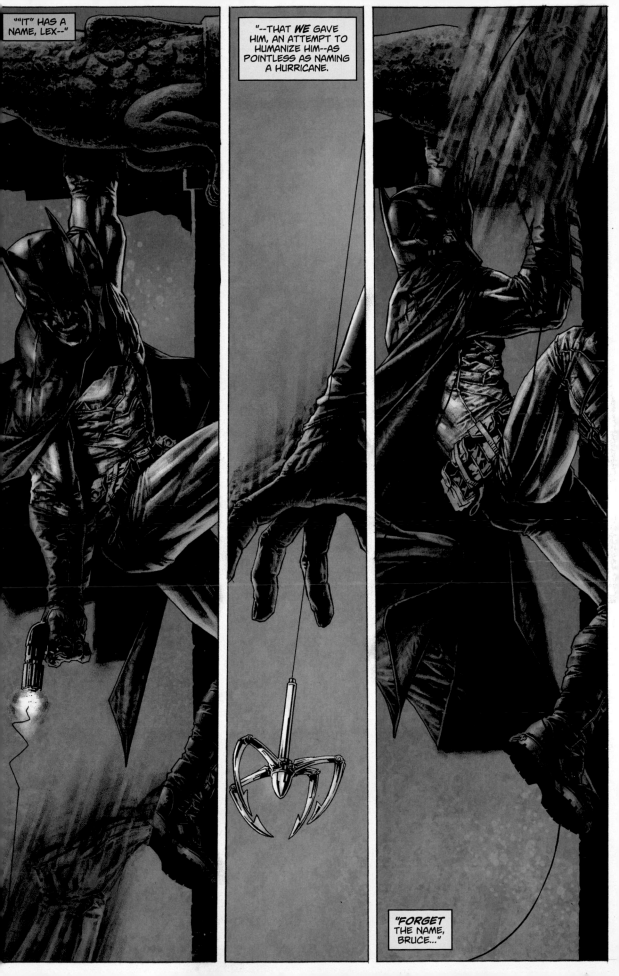

"'IT' HAS A NAME, LEX--"

"--THAT *WE* GAVE HIM, AN ATTEMPT TO HUMANIZE HIM--AS POINTLESS AS NAMING A HURRICANE.

"*FORGET* THE NAME, BRUCE..."

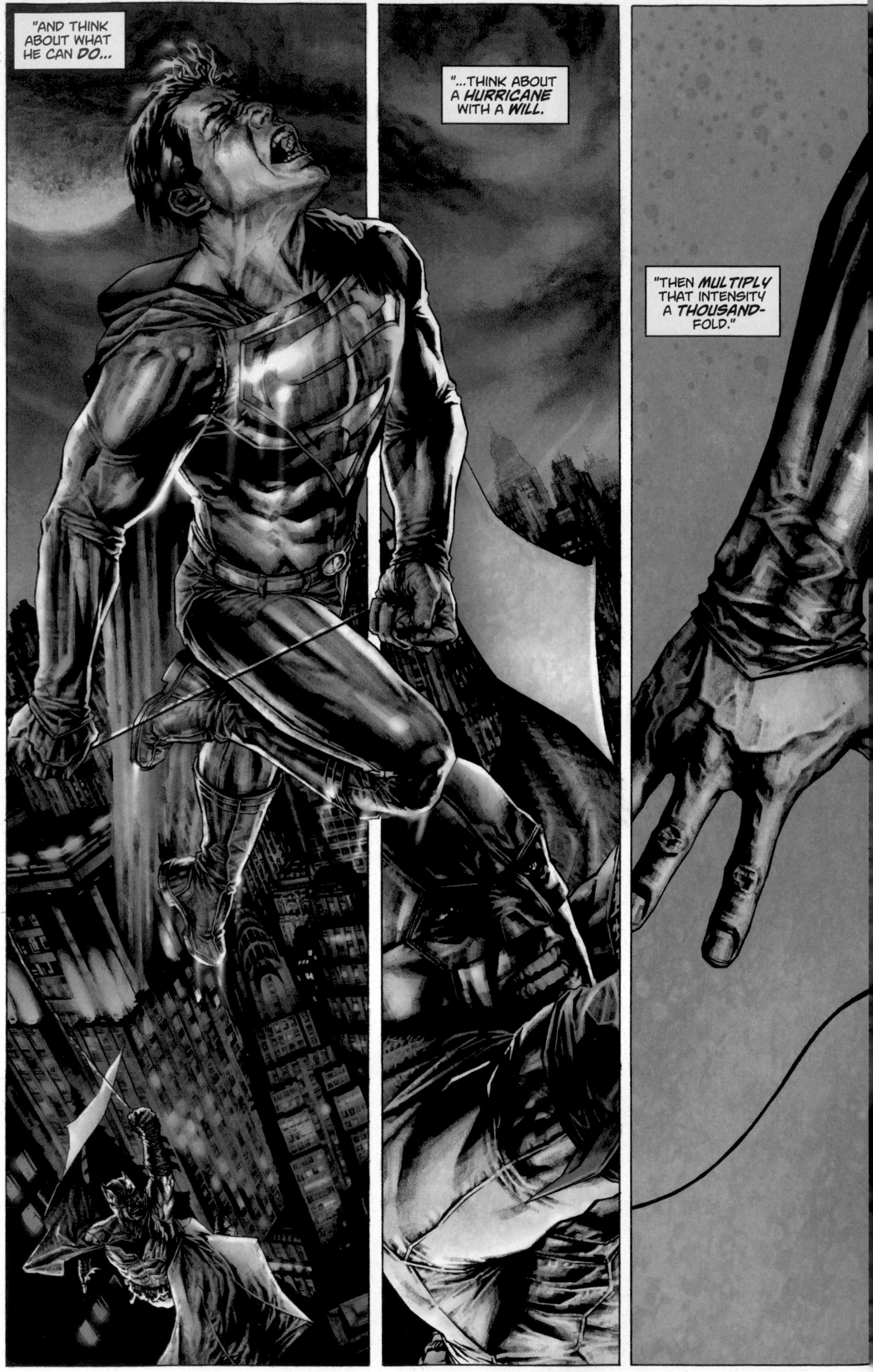
"AND THINK ABOUT WHAT HE CAN *DO*...
"...THINK ABOUT A *HURRICANE* WITH A *WILL*.
"THEN *MULTIPLY* THAT INTENSITY A *THOUSAND*-FOLD."

THAT'S SOME STORM.

GOOD THING HE'S ON **OUR** SIDE.

WHAT IF HE **CHANGES** HIS MIND?

WHAT IF...TONIGHT--HE LOOKS DOWN AT US AND **DECIDES** WE'RE **NOT CAPABLE** TO MANIFEST OUR OWN DESTINY?

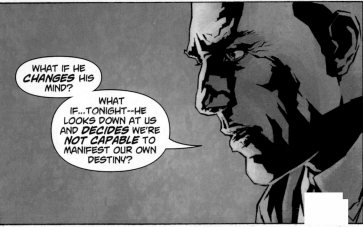

WHAT IF TOMORROW HE WAKES UP BELIEVING HE KNOWS WHAT'S **BEST** FOR US?

THAT IT'S NOT ENOUGH TO **PROTECT** THE WORLD...

...WHEN HE CAN **RULE** IT? THE ONLY **SAFEGUARD** WE HAVE AGAINST THAT HAPPENING...

...IS HIS **WORD.**

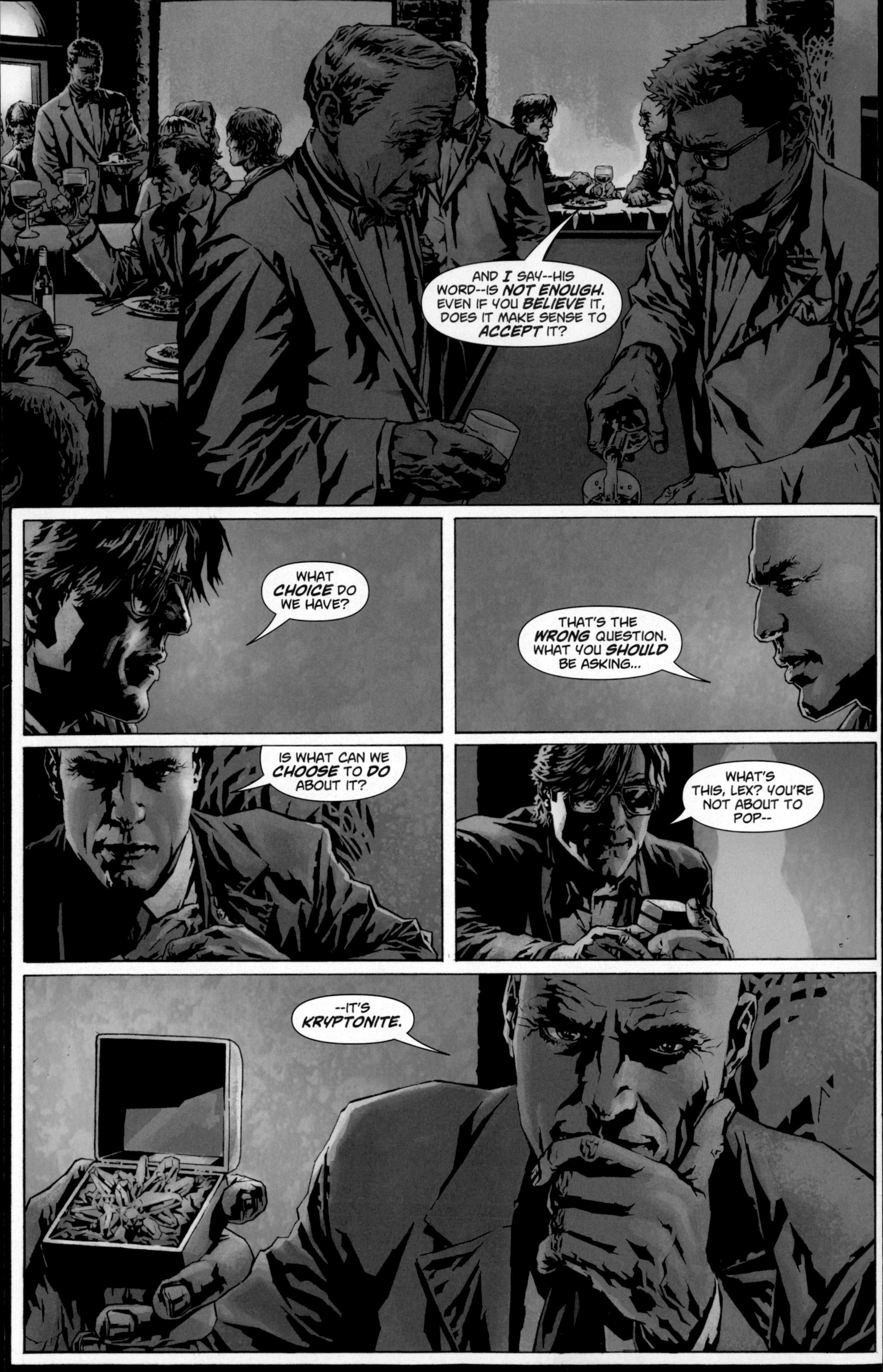
AND I SAY--HIS WORD--IS NOT ENOUGH. EVEN IF YOU BELIEVE IT, DOES IT MAKE SENSE TO ACCEPT IT?
WHAT CHOICE DO WE HAVE?
THAT'S THE WRONG QUESTION. WHAT YOU SHOULD BE ASKING...
IS WHAT CAN WE CHOOSE TO DO ABOUT IT?
WHAT'S THIS, LEX? YOU'RE NOT ABOUT TO POP--
--IT'S KRYPTONITE.

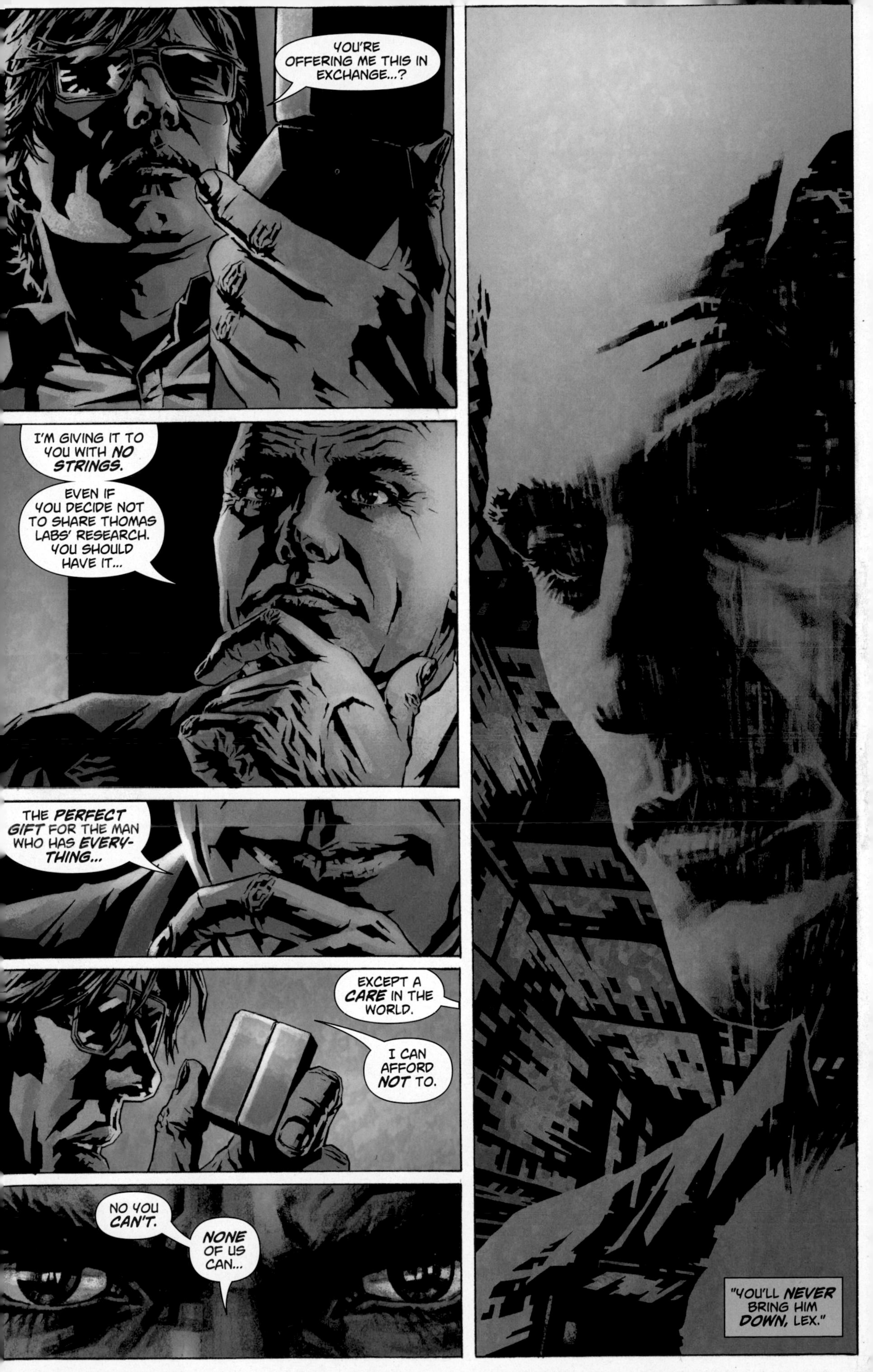
YOU'RE OFFERING ME THIS IN EXCHANGE...?
I'M GIVING IT TO YOU WITH NO STRINGS.
EVEN IF YOU DECIDE NOT TO SHARE THOMAS LABS' RESEARCH. YOU SHOULD HAVE IT...
THE PERFECT GIFT FOR THE MAN WHO HAS EVERY-THING...
EXCEPT A CARE IN THE WORLD.
I CAN AFFORD NOT TO.
NO YOU CAN'T.
NONE OF US CAN...
"YOU'LL NEVER BRING HIM DOWN, LEX."

I'M NOT INTERESTED IN BRINGING *HIM DOWN...*

...BUT *OBSESSED* WITH BRINGING *US UP.*

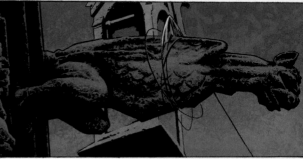

ALL OF US--*EVERYONE*-- DESERVES A CHANCE AT *GREATNESS.*

ALL THAT TAKES IS THE *BELIEF* THAT IT *EXISTS.*

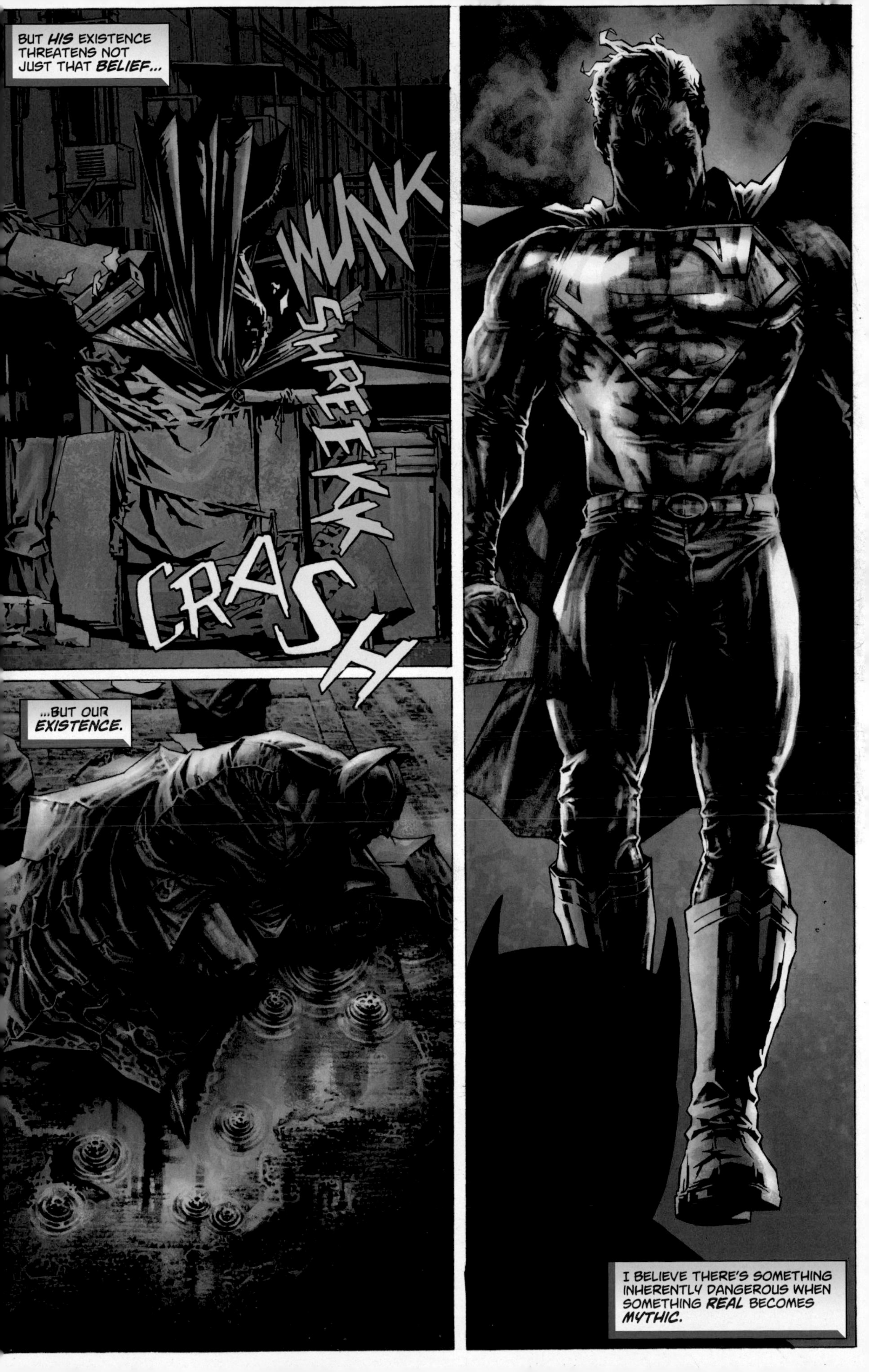
BUT HIS EXISTENCE THREATENS NOT JUST THAT BELIEF...
WUNK
SHREEKK
CRASH
...BUT OUR EXISTENCE.
I BELIEVE THERE'S SOMETHING INHERENTLY DANGEROUS WHEN SOMETHING REAL BECOMES MYTHIC.

I BELIEVE WHEN THAT HAPPENS, WE LOSE THE PART OF OURSELVES THAT *YEARNS* TO BE *GREAT*.

BECAUSE WHEN FACED WITH A *MYTH?*

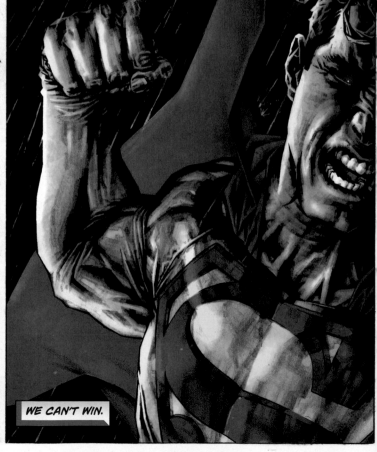

WE CAN'T WIN.

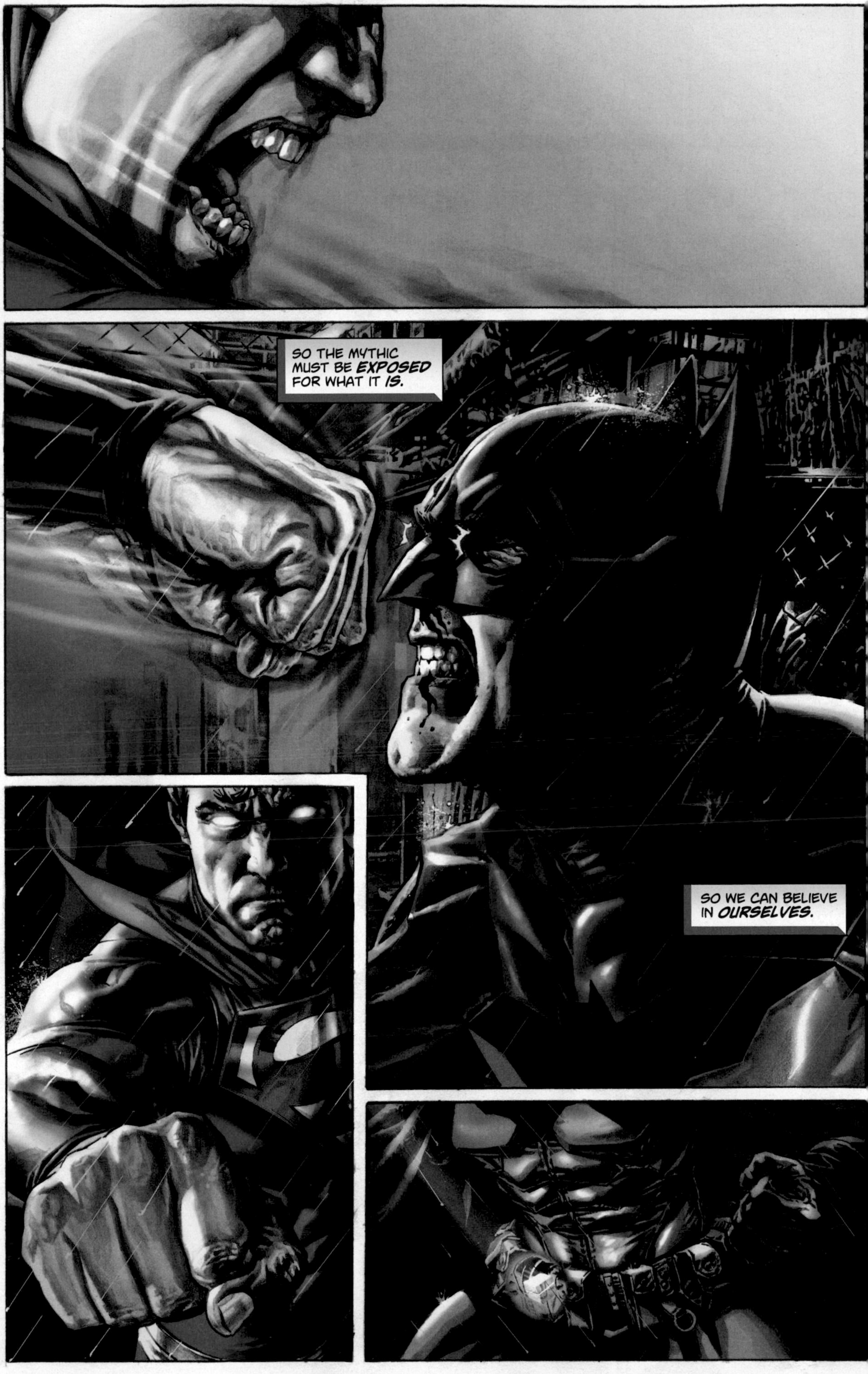
SO THE MYTHIC MUST BE EXPOSED FOR WHAT IT IS.
SO WE CAN BELIEVE IN OURSELVES.

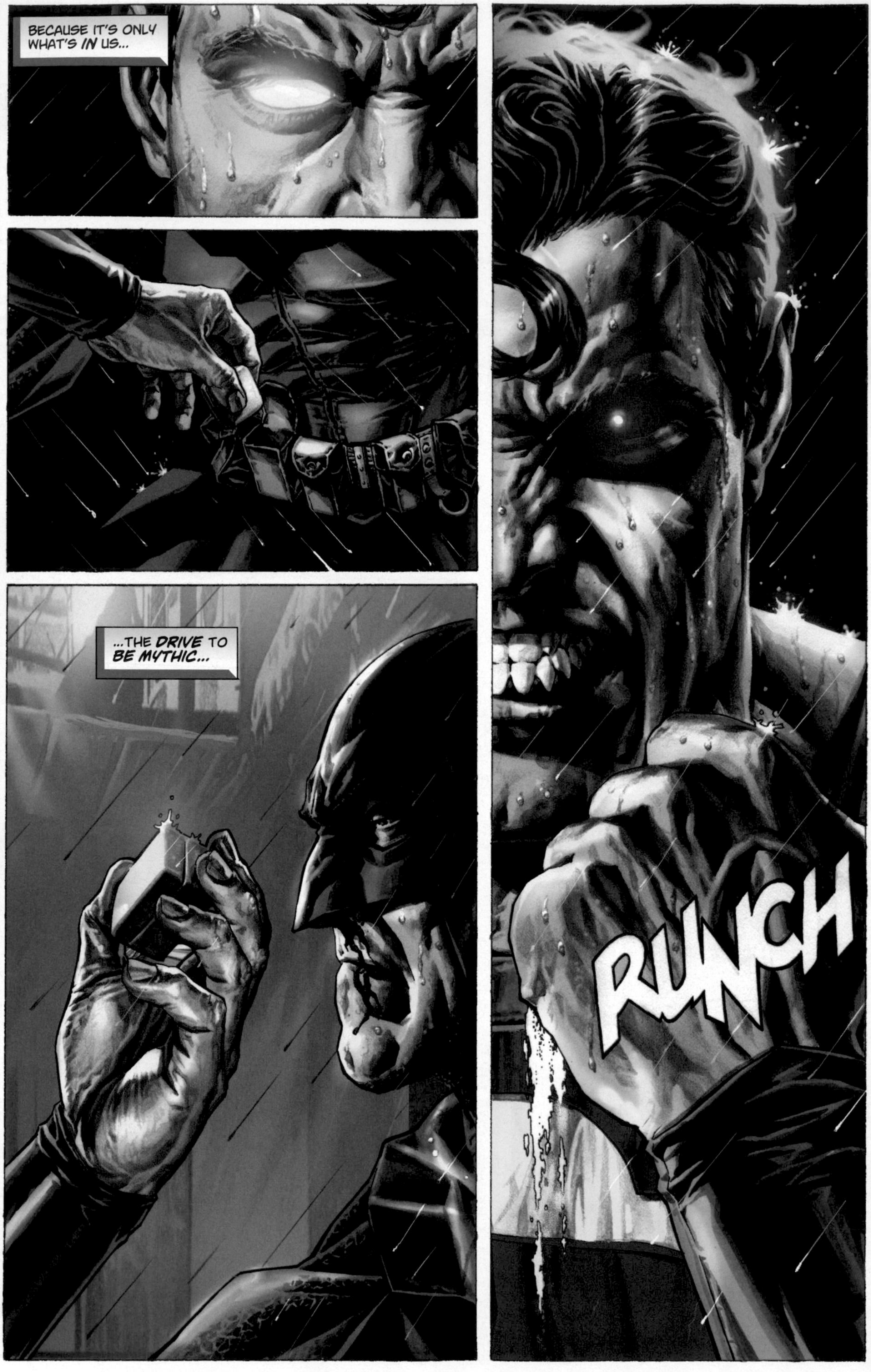
BECAUSE IT'S ONLY WHAT'S IN US...
...THE DRIVE TO BE MYTHIC...
RUNCH

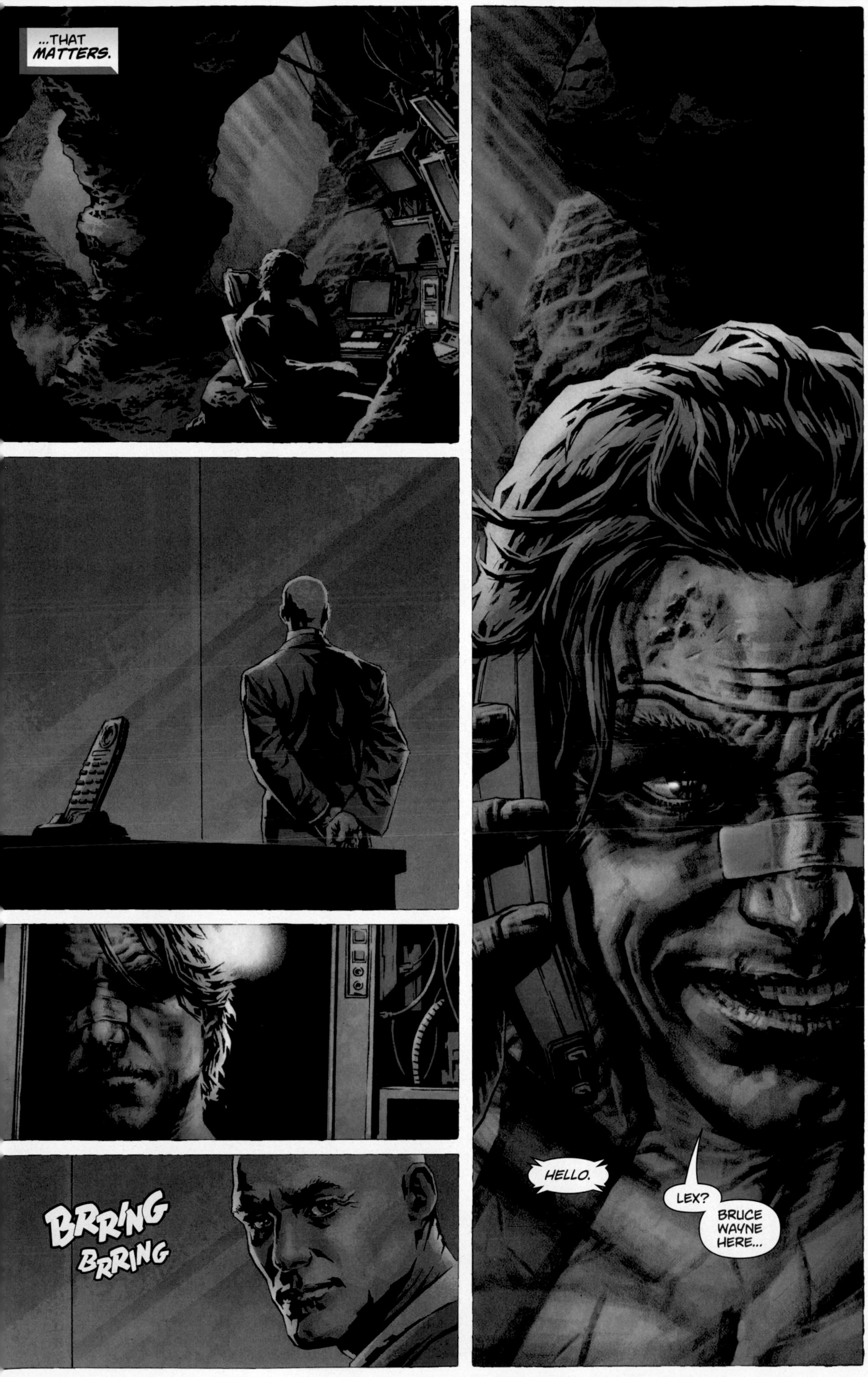
...THAT MATTERS.
BRRING
BRRING
HELLO.
LEX?
BRUCE WAYNE HERE...

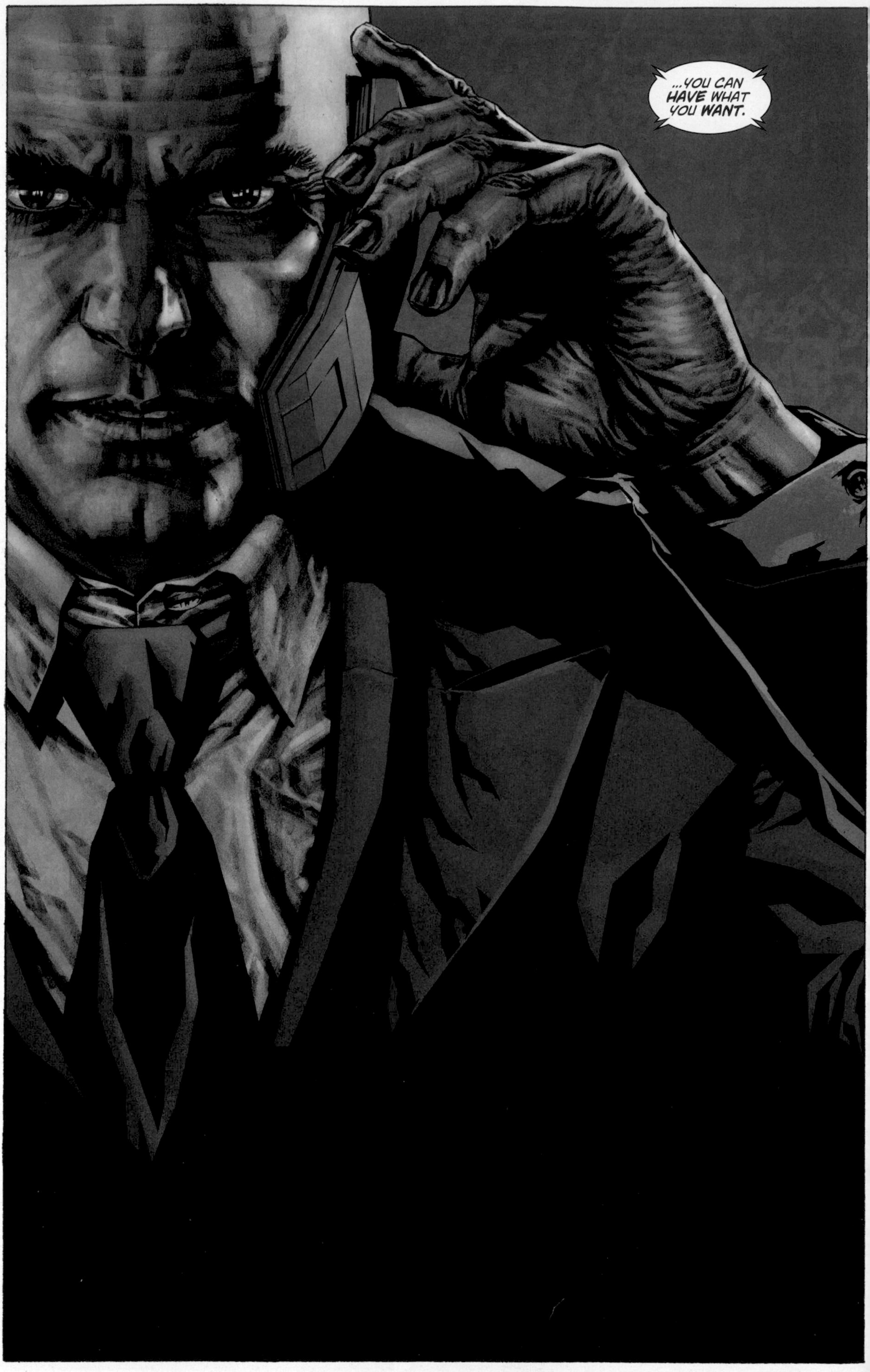
...YOU CAN HAVE WHAT YOU WANT.

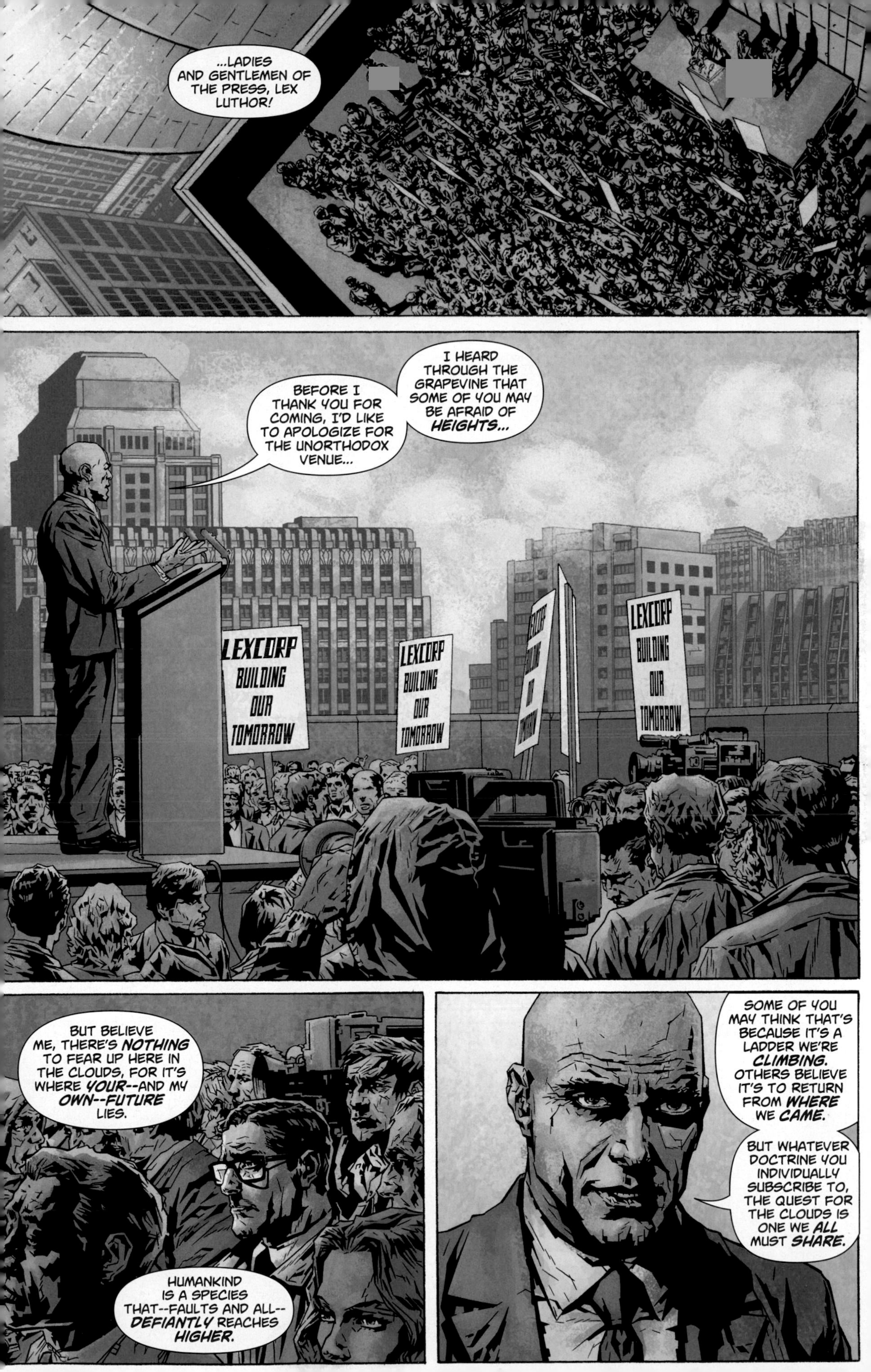
...LADIES AND GENTLEMEN OF THE PRESS, LEX LUTHOR!
BEFORE I THANK YOU FOR COMING, I'D LIKE TO APOLOGIZE FOR THE UNORTHODOX VENUE...
I HEARD THROUGH THE GRAPEVINE THAT SOME OF YOU MAY BE AFRAID OF HEIGHTS...
LEXCORP BUILDING OUR TOMORROW
LEXCORP BUILDING OUR TOMORROW
LEXCORP BUILDING OUR TOMORROW
BUT BELIEVE ME, THERE'S NOTHING TO FEAR UP HERE IN THE CLOUDS, FOR IT'S WHERE YOUR--AND MY OWN--FUTURE LIES.
HUMANKIND IS A SPECIES THAT--FAULTS AND ALL--DEFIANTLY REACHES HIGHER.
SOME OF YOU MAY THINK THAT'S BECAUSE IT'S A LADDER WE'RE CLIMBING. OTHERS BELIEVE IT'S TO RETURN FROM WHERE WE CAME.
BUT WHATEVER DOCTRINE YOU INDIVIDUALLY SUBSCRIBE TO, THE QUEST FOR THE CLOUDS IS ONE WE ALL MUST SHARE.

ALL OF US. EVERY MAN, WOMAN, AND CHILD--WE MUST STRIVE TO MAKE TODAY BETTER THAN YESTERDAY...

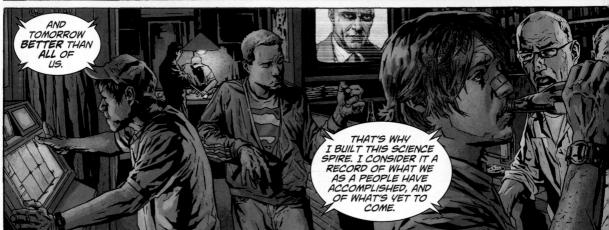

AND TOMORROW BETTER THAN ALL OF US.

THAT'S WHY I BUILT THIS SCIENCE SPIRE. I CONSIDER IT A RECORD OF WHAT WE AS A PEOPLE HAVE ACCOMPLISHED, AND OF WHAT'S YET TO COME.

EVERY FLOOR IS DEDICATED TO OUR GREATEST ACHIEVEMENTS. FROM PICKING UP A BONE, TO...

WHO KNOWS? BECAUSE WE ARE NOT DONE. AND THIS BUILDING WON'T BE EITHER. THE TOP FLOORS WILL BE LEFT AS YOU SEE THEM NOW...

...WAITING, FOR YOU, TO FINISH THEM.

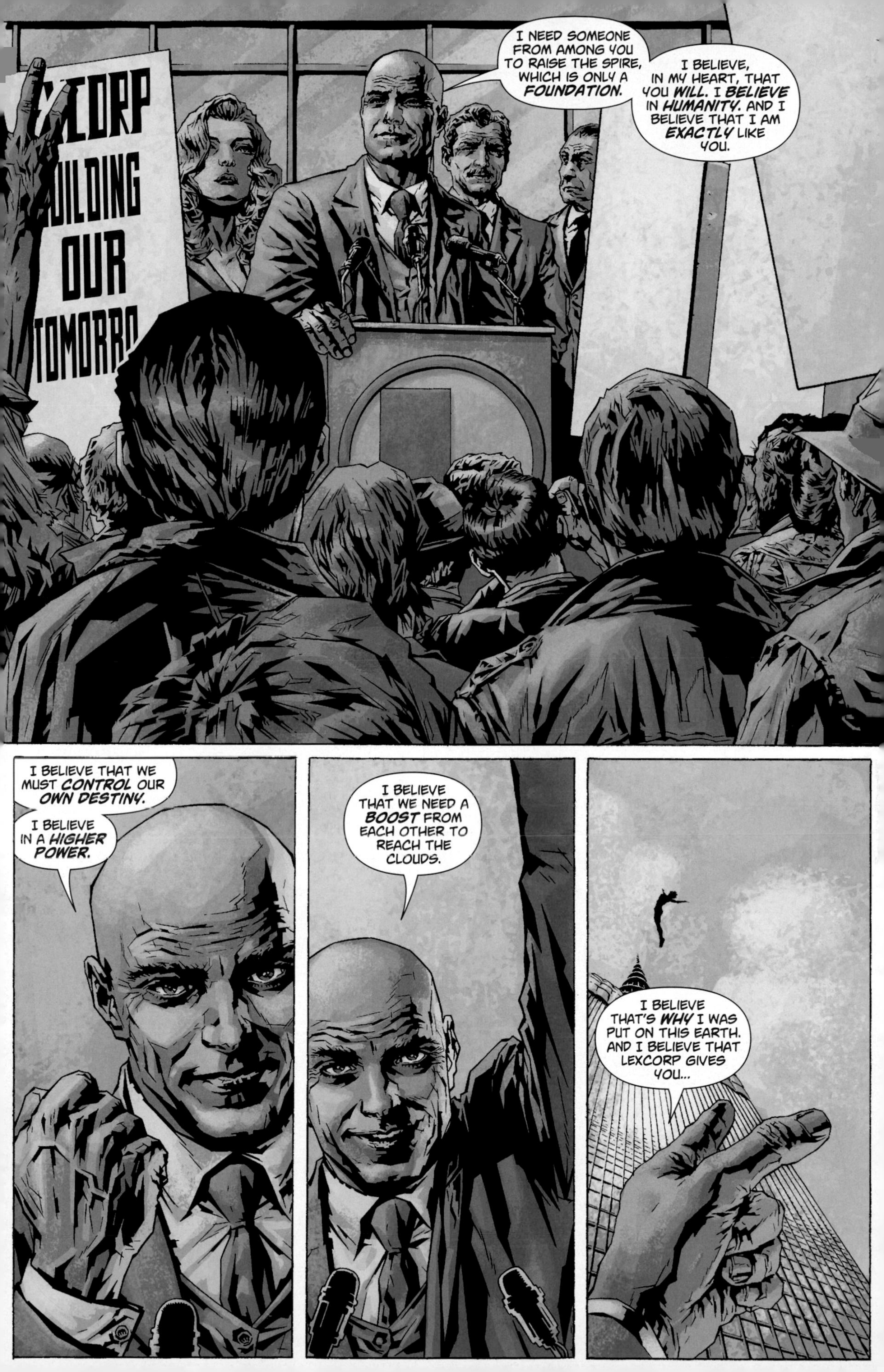

CORP BUILDING OUR TOMORRO
I NEED SOMEONE FROM AMONG YOU TO RAISE THE SPIRE, WHICH IS ONLY A FOUNDATION.
I BELIEVE, IN MY HEART, THAT YOU WILL. I BELIEVE IN HUMANITY. AND I BELIEVE THAT I AM EXACTLY LIKE YOU.
I BELIEVE THAT WE MUST CONTROL OUR OWN DESTINY.
I BELIEVE IN A HIGHER POWER.
I BELIEVE THAT WE NEED A BOOST FROM EACH OTHER TO REACH THE CLOUDS.
I BELIEVE THAT'S WHY I WAS PUT ON THIS EARTH. AND I BELIEVE THAT LEXCORP GIVES YOU...

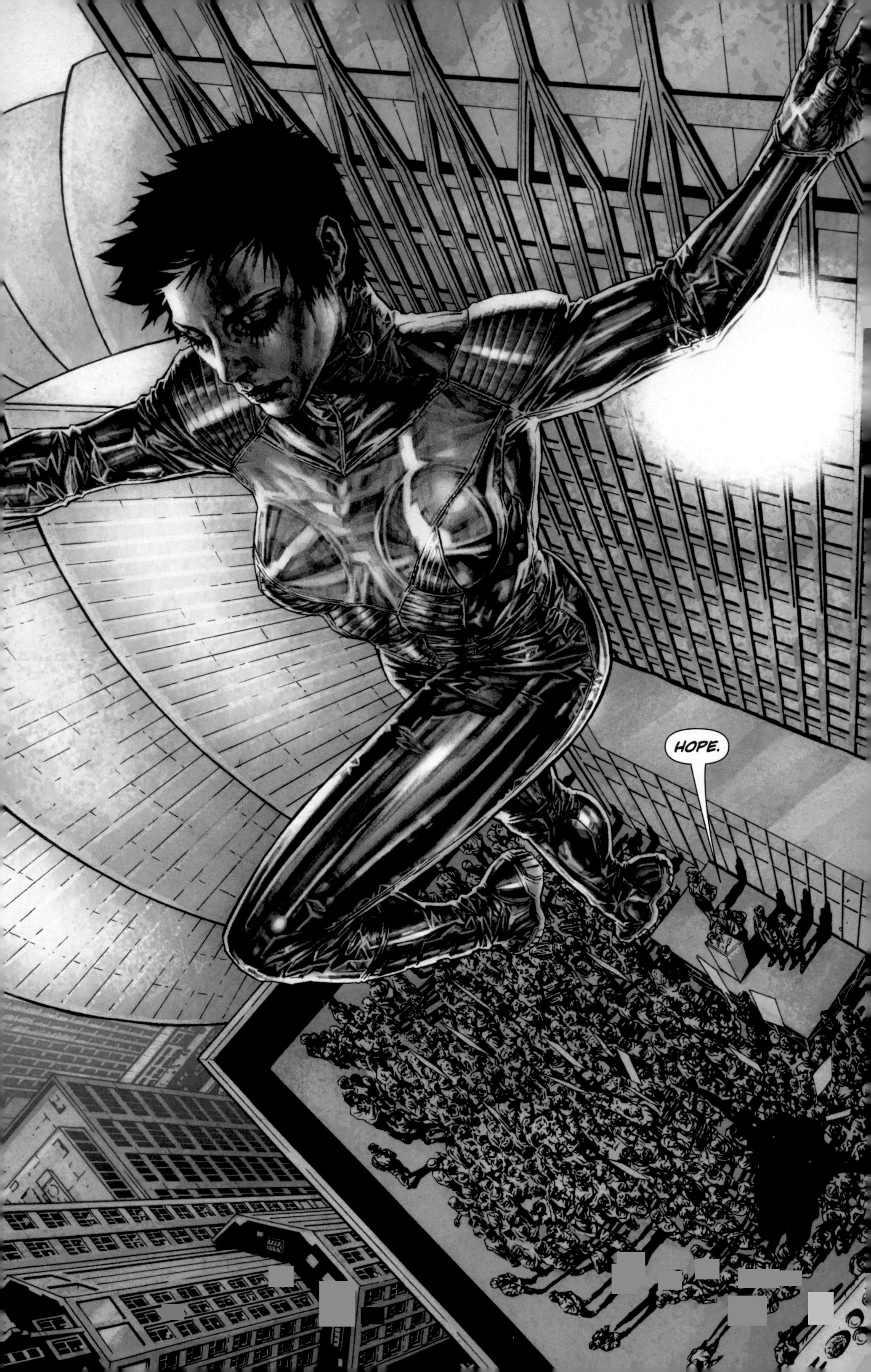
HOPE.

HOPE

IT'S BEEN NEARLY A MONTH SINCE HER DEBUT, BUT IN THAT SHORT SPAN SHE'S CAPTURED NOT JUST THE *IMAGINATION*, BUT THE *HEART* OF METROPOLIS.

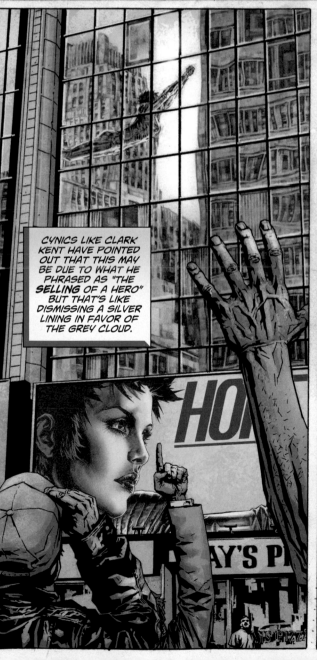

CYNICS LIKE CLARK KENT HAVE POINTED OUT THAT THIS MAY BE DUE TO WHAT HE PHRASED AS "THE *SELLING OF A HERO*" BUT THAT'S LIKE DISMISSING A SILVER LINING IN FAVOR OF THE GREY CLOUD.

MAYBE I SHOULD BUY THE DAILY PLANET AND *FIRE* HIM. CERTAINLY THERE ARE OTHERS IN MY POSITION THAT *CONTROL* THE MEDIA.

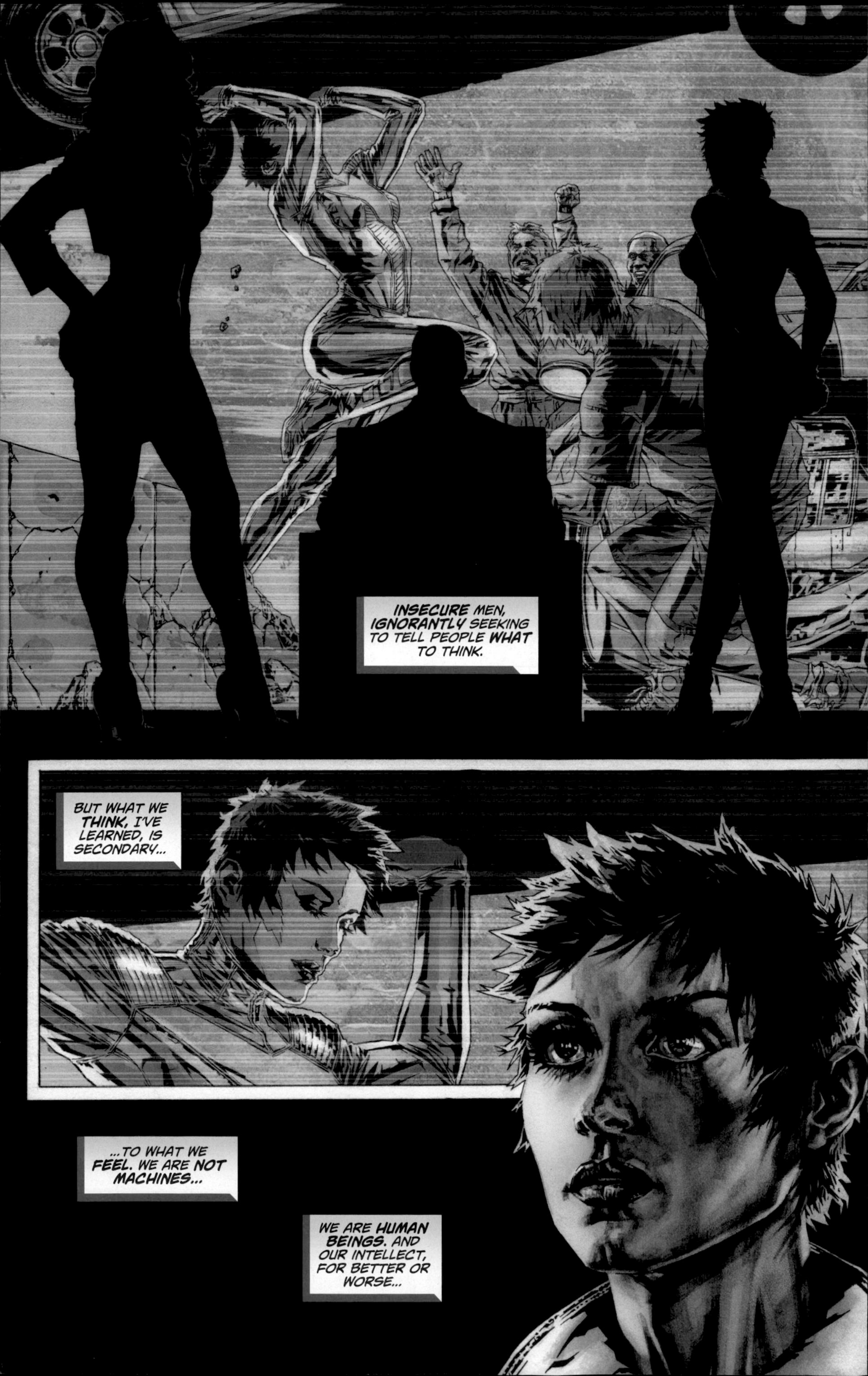
INSECURE MEN, IGNORANTLY SEEKING TO TELL PEOPLE WHAT TO THINK.
BUT WHAT WE THINK, I'VE LEARNED, IS SECONDARY...
...TO WHAT WE FEEL. WE ARE NOT MACHINES...
WE ARE HUMAN BEINGS. AND OUR INTELLECT, FOR BETTER OR WORSE...

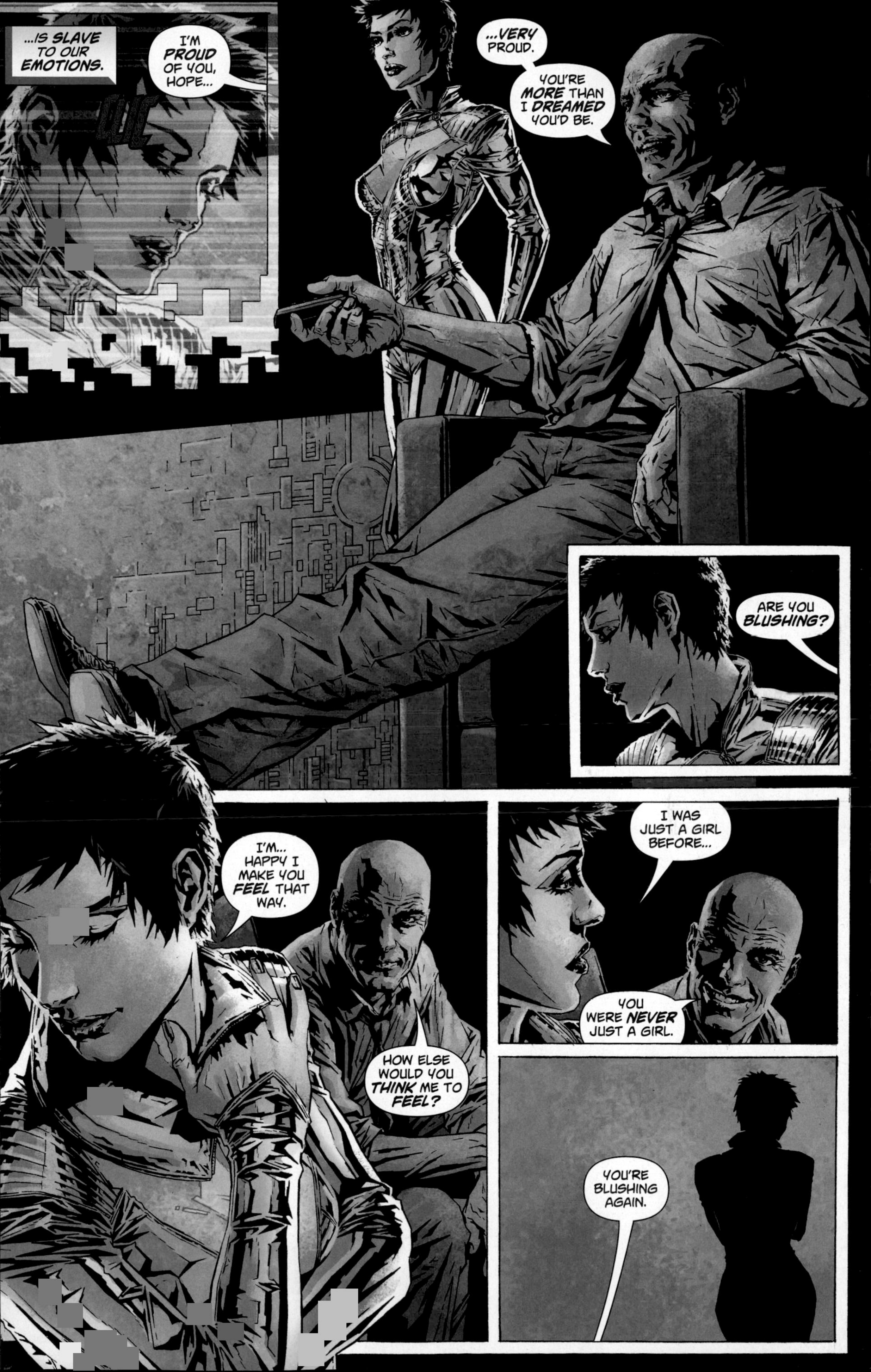
...IS SLAVE TO OUR EMOTIONS.
I'M PROUD OF YOU, HOPE...
...VERY PROUD.
YOU'RE MORE THAN I DREAMED YOU'D BE.
ARE YOU BLUSHING?
I'M... HAPPY I MAKE YOU FEEL THAT WAY.
HOW ELSE WOULD YOU THINK ME TO FEEL?
I WAS JUST A GIRL BEFORE...
YOU WERE NEVER JUST A GIRL.
YOU'RE BLUSHING AGAIN.

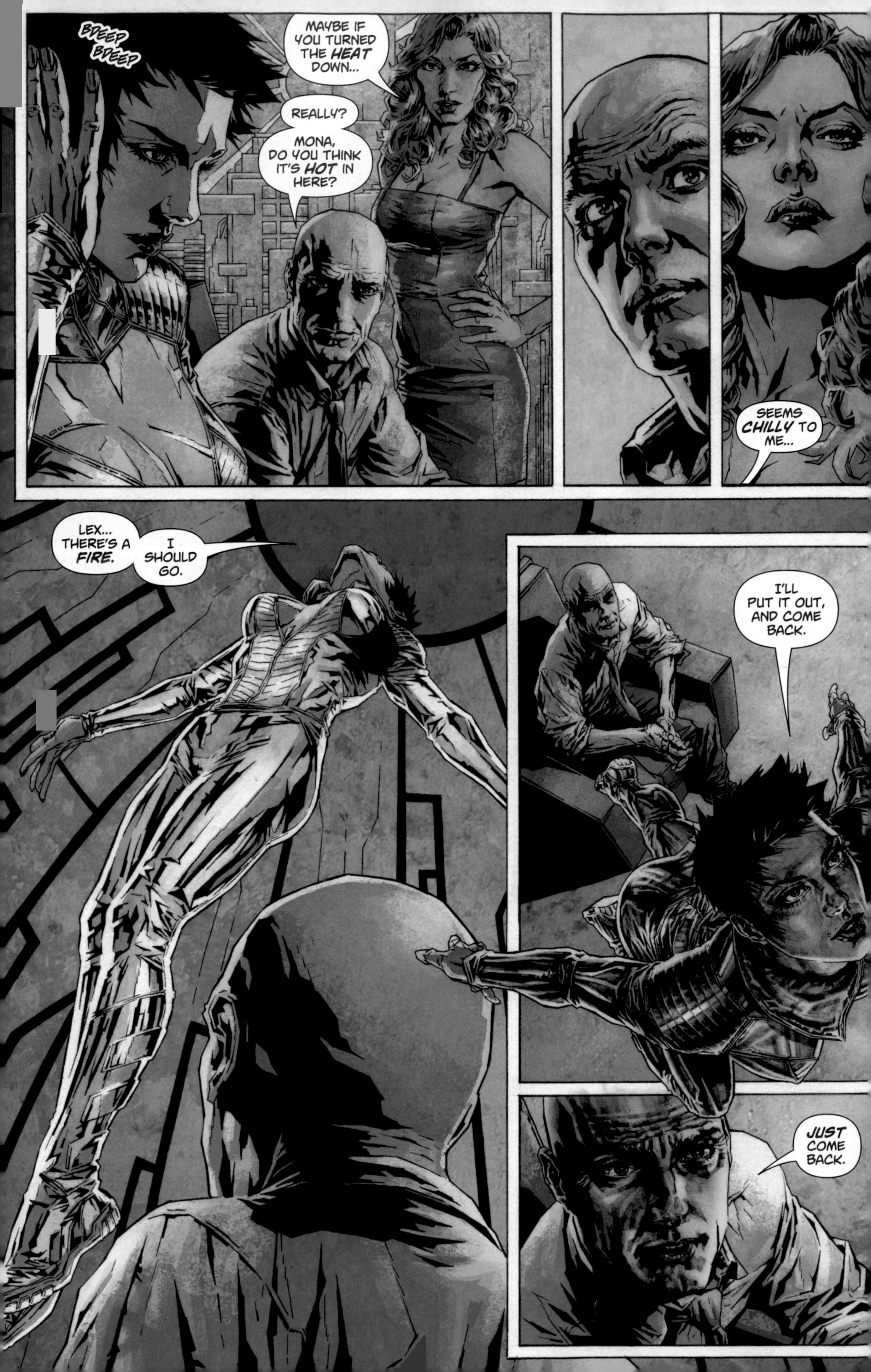
BDEEP BDEEP
MAYBE IF YOU TURNED THE HEAT DOWN...
REALLY?
MONA, DO YOU THINK IT'S HOT IN HERE?
SEEMS CHILLY TO ME...
LEX... THERE'S A FIRE.
I SHOULD GO.
I'LL PUT IT OUT, AND COME BACK.
JUST COME BACK.

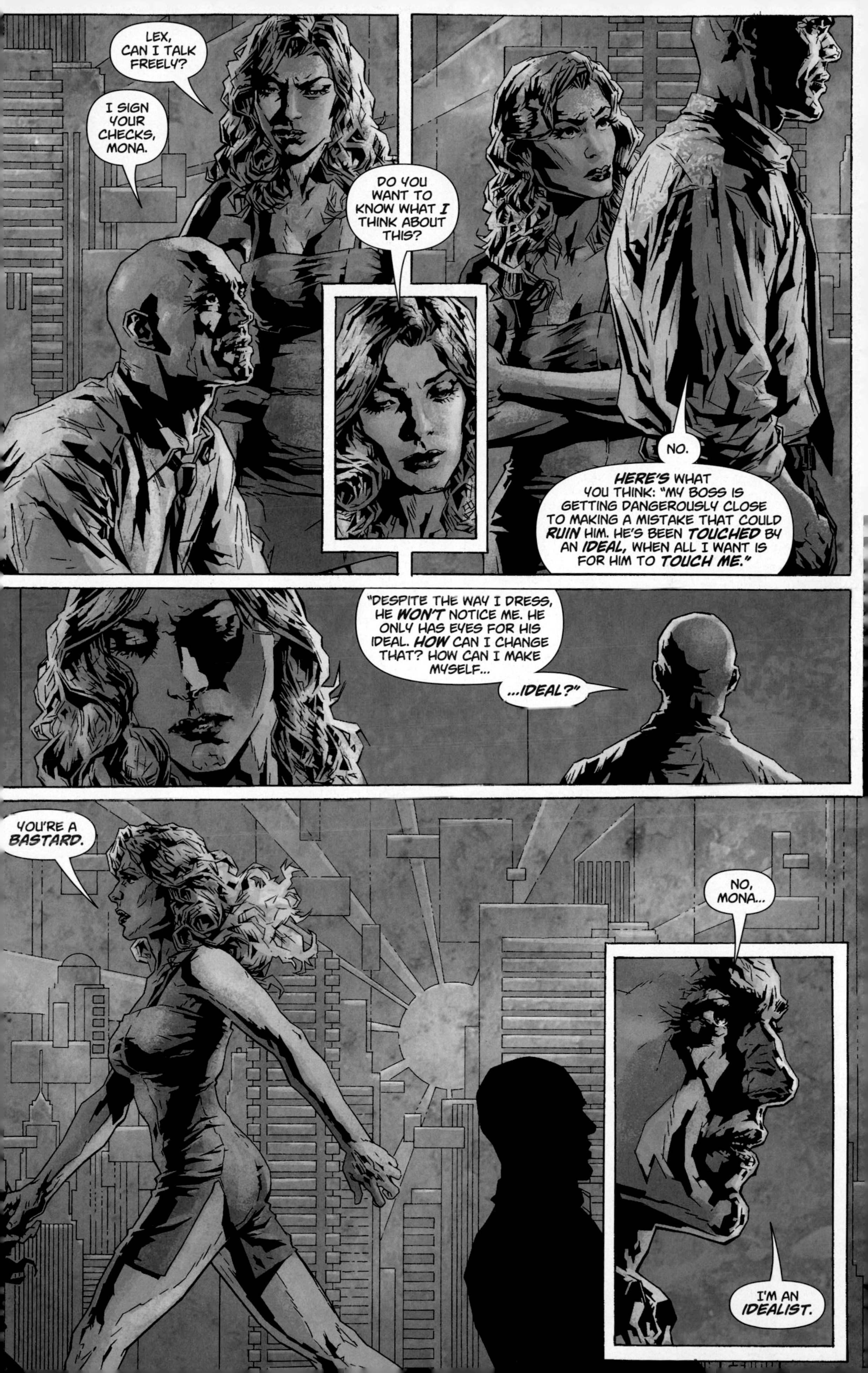
LEX, CAN I TALK FREELY?
I SIGN YOUR CHECKS, MONA.
DO YOU WANT TO KNOW WHAT *I* THINK ABOUT THIS?
NO.
HERE'S WHAT YOU THINK: "MY BOSS IS GETTING DANGEROUSLY CLOSE TO MAKING A MISTAKE THAT COULD ***RUIN*** HIM. HE'S BEEN ***TOUCHED*** BY AN ***IDEAL,*** WHEN ALL I WANT IS FOR HIM TO ***TOUCH ME.***"
"DESPITE THE WAY I DRESS, HE ***WON'T*** NOTICE ME. HE ONLY HAS EYES FOR HIS IDEAL. ***HOW*** CAN I CHANGE THAT? HOW CAN I MAKE MYSELF...
...IDEAL?"
YOU'RE A ***BASTARD.***
NO, MONA...
I'M AN ***IDEALIST.***

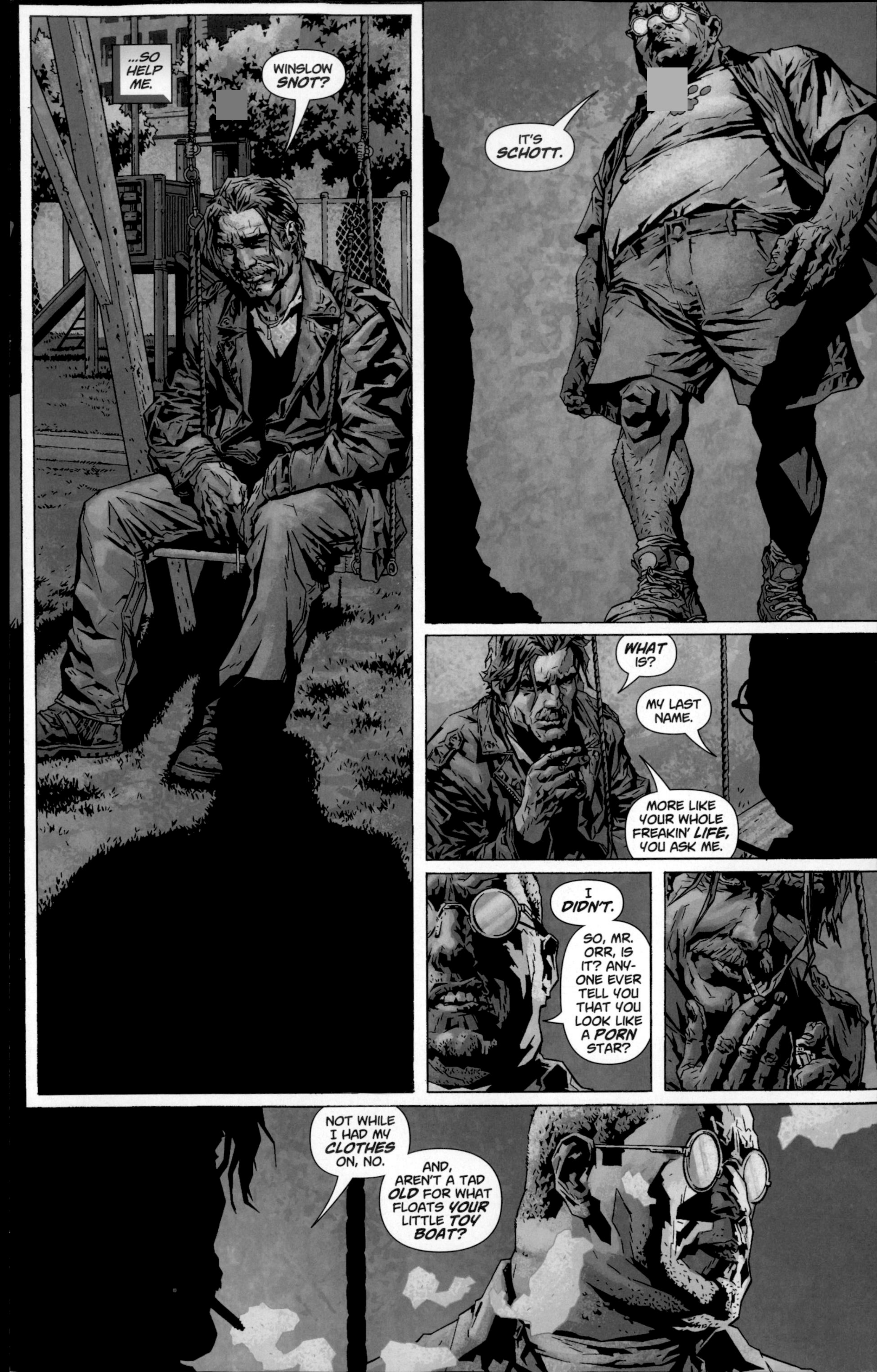
...SO HELP ME.
WINSLOW SNOT?
IT'S SCHOTT.
WHAT IS?
MY LAST NAME.
MORE LIKE YOUR WHOLE FREAKIN' LIFE, YOU ASK ME.
I DIDN'T.
SO, MR. ORR, IS IT? ANY-ONE EVER TELL YOU THAT YOU LOOK LIKE A PORN STAR?
NOT WHILE I HAD MY CLOTHES ON, NO.
AND, AREN'T A TAD OLD FOR WHAT FLOATS YOUR LITTLE TOY BOAT?

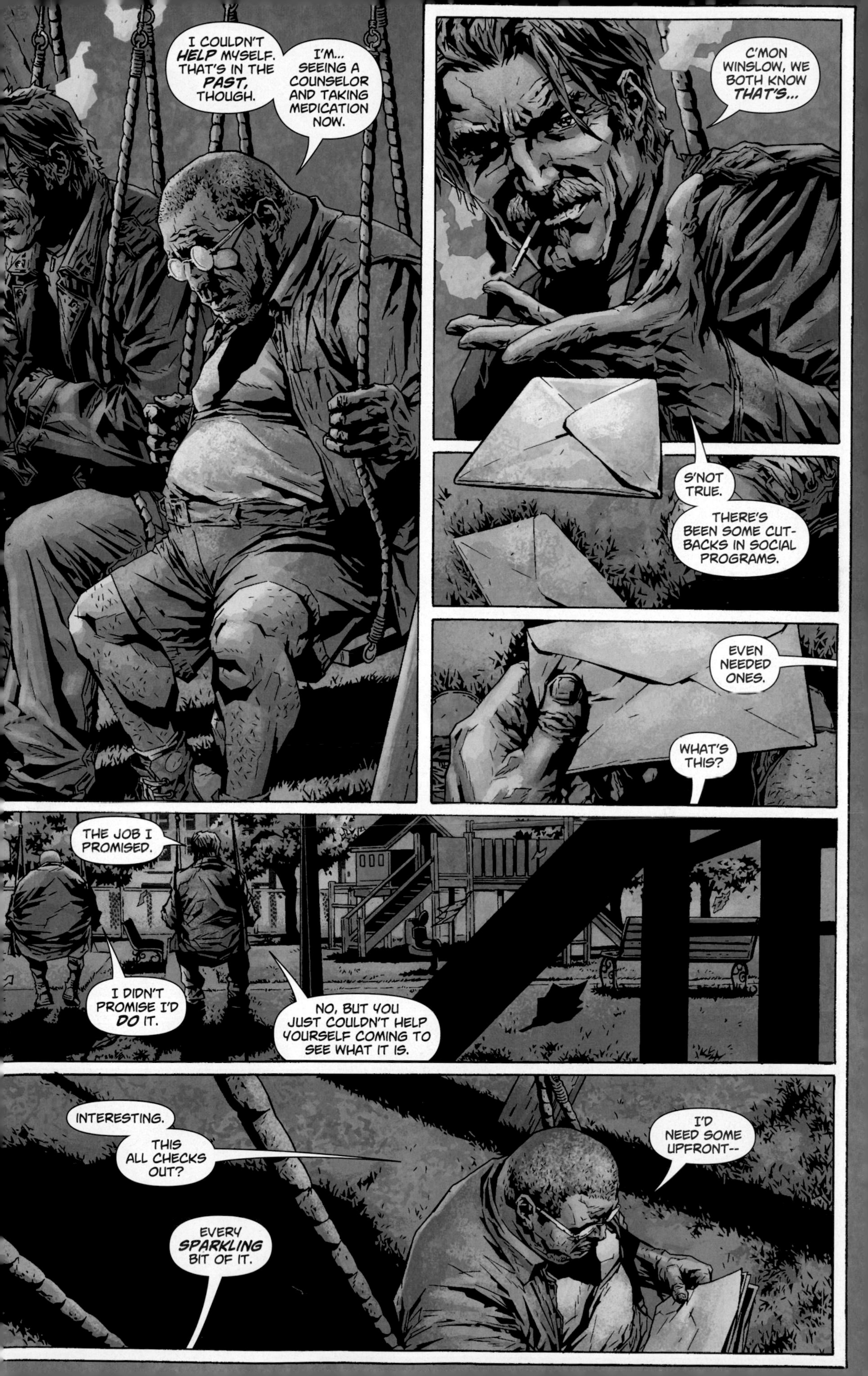
I COULDN'T HELP MYSELF. THAT'S IN THE PAST, THOUGH.
I'M... SEEING A COUNSELOR AND TAKING MEDICATION NOW.
C'MON WINSLOW, WE BOTH KNOW THAT'S...
S'NOT TRUE.
THERE'S BEEN SOME CUT-BACKS IN SOCIAL PROGRAMS.
EVEN NEEDED ONES.
WHAT'S THIS?
THE JOB I PROMISED.
I DIDN'T PROMISE I'D DO IT.
NO, BUT YOU JUST COULDN'T HELP YOURSELF COMING TO SEE WHAT IT IS.
INTERESTING.
THIS ALL CHECKS OUT?
EVERY SPARKLING BIT OF IT.
I'D NEED SOME UPFRONT--

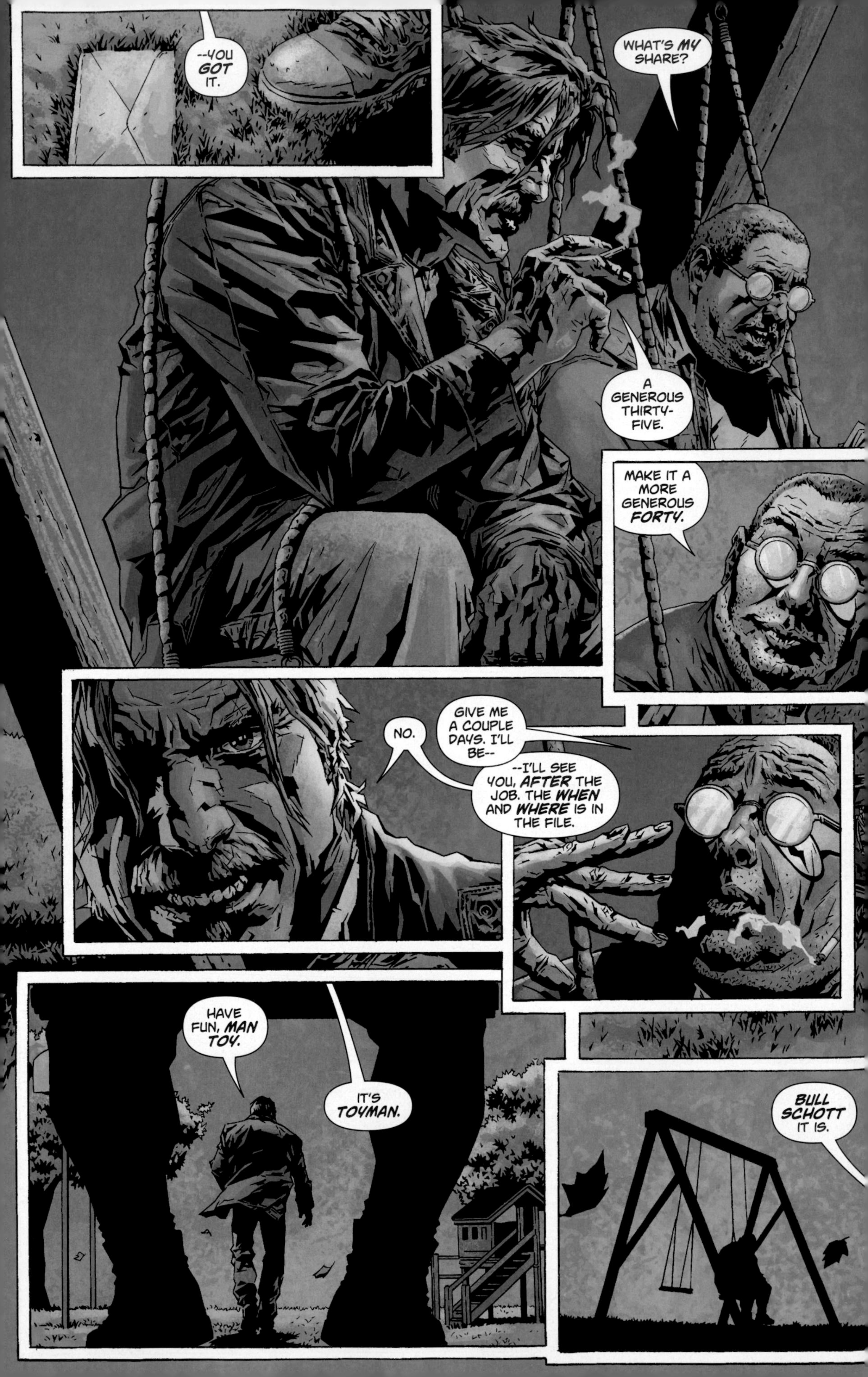
--YOU GOT IT.
WHAT'S MY SHARE?
A GENEROUS THIRTY-FIVE.
MAKE IT A MORE GENEROUS FORTY.
NO.
GIVE ME A COUPLE DAYS. I'LL BE--
--I'LL SEE YOU, AFTER THE JOB. THE WHEN AND WHERE IS IN THE FILE.
HAVE FUN, MAN TOY.
IT'S TOYMAN.
BULL SCHOTT IT IS.

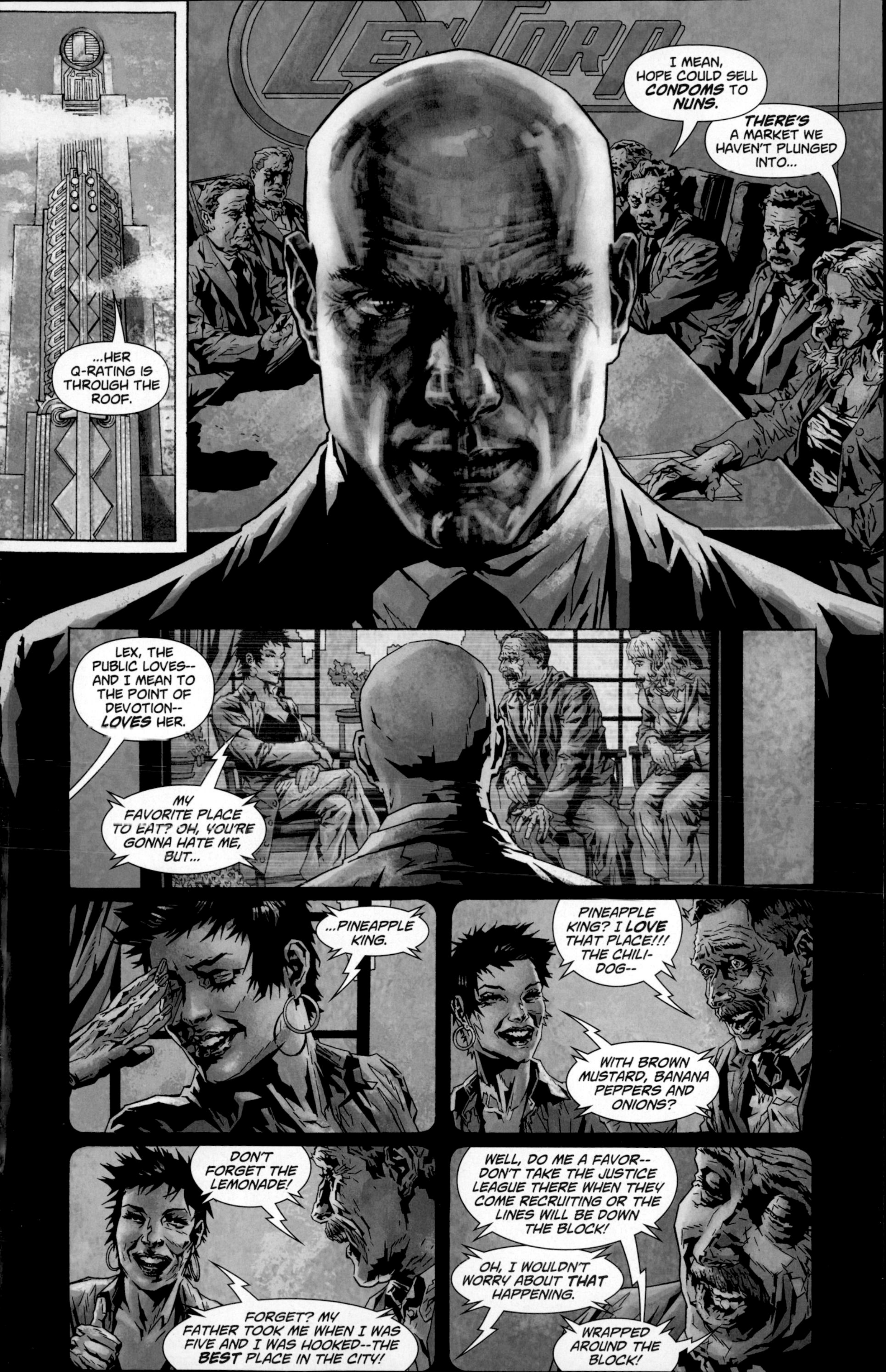
...HER Q-RATING IS THROUGH THE ROOF.
I MEAN, HOPE COULD SELL CONDOMS TO NUNS.
THERE'S A MARKET WE HAVEN'T PLUNGED INTO...
LEX, THE PUBLIC LOVES-- AND I MEAN TO THE POINT OF DEVOTION-- LOVES HER.
MY FAVORITE PLACE TO EAT? OH, YOU'RE GONNA HATE ME, BUT...
...PINEAPPLE KING.
PINEAPPLE KING? I LOVE THAT PLACE!!! THE CHILI-DOG--
WITH BROWN MUSTARD, BANANA PEPPERS AND ONIONS?
DON'T FORGET THE LEMONADE!
FORGET? MY FATHER TOOK ME WHEN I WAS FIVE AND I WAS HOOKED--THE BEST PLACE IN THE CITY!
WELL, DO ME A FAVOR-- DON'T TAKE THE JUSTICE LEAGUE THERE WHEN THEY COME RECRUITING OR THE LINES WILL BE DOWN THE BLOCK!
OH, I WOULDN'T WORRY ABOUT THAT HAPPENING.
WRAPPED AROUND THE BLOCK!

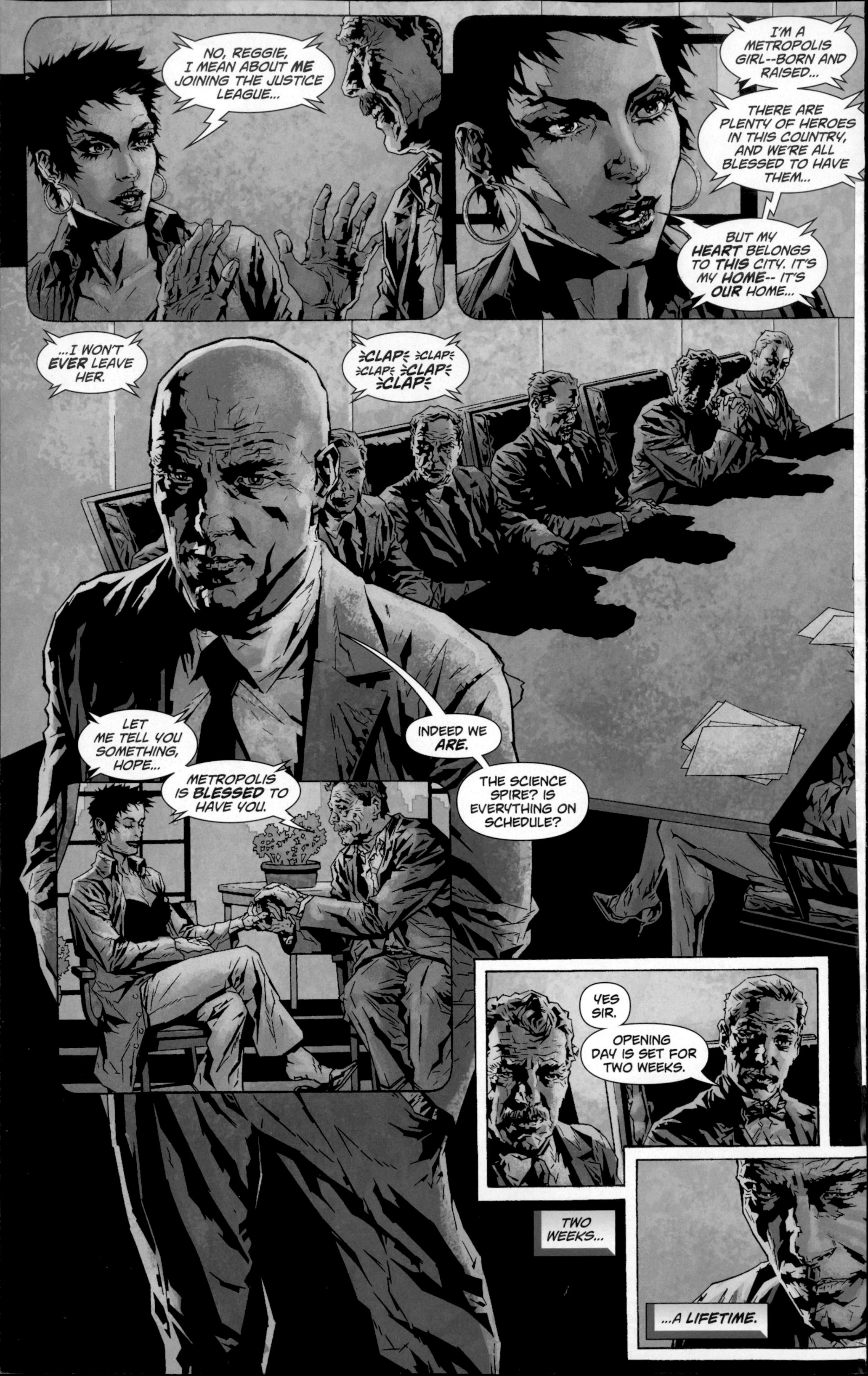

NO, REGGIE, I MEAN ABOUT **ME** JOINING THE JUSTICE LEAGUE...
I'M A METROPOLIS GIRL--BORN AND RAISED...
THERE ARE PLENTY OF HEROES IN THIS COUNTRY, AND WE'RE ALL BLESSED TO HAVE THEM...
BUT MY **HEART** BELONGS TO **THIS** CITY. IT'S MY **HOME**-- IT'S **OUR** HOME...
...I WON'T **EVER** LEAVE HER.
CLAP CLAP CLAP CLAP CLAP
LET ME TELL YOU SOMETHING, HOPE...
METROPOLIS IS **BLESSED** TO HAVE YOU.
INDEED WE **ARE**.
THE SCIENCE SPIRE? IS EVERYTHING ON SCHEDULE?
YES SIR.
OPENING DAY IS SET FOR TWO WEEKS.
TWO WEEKS...
...A **LIFETIME**.

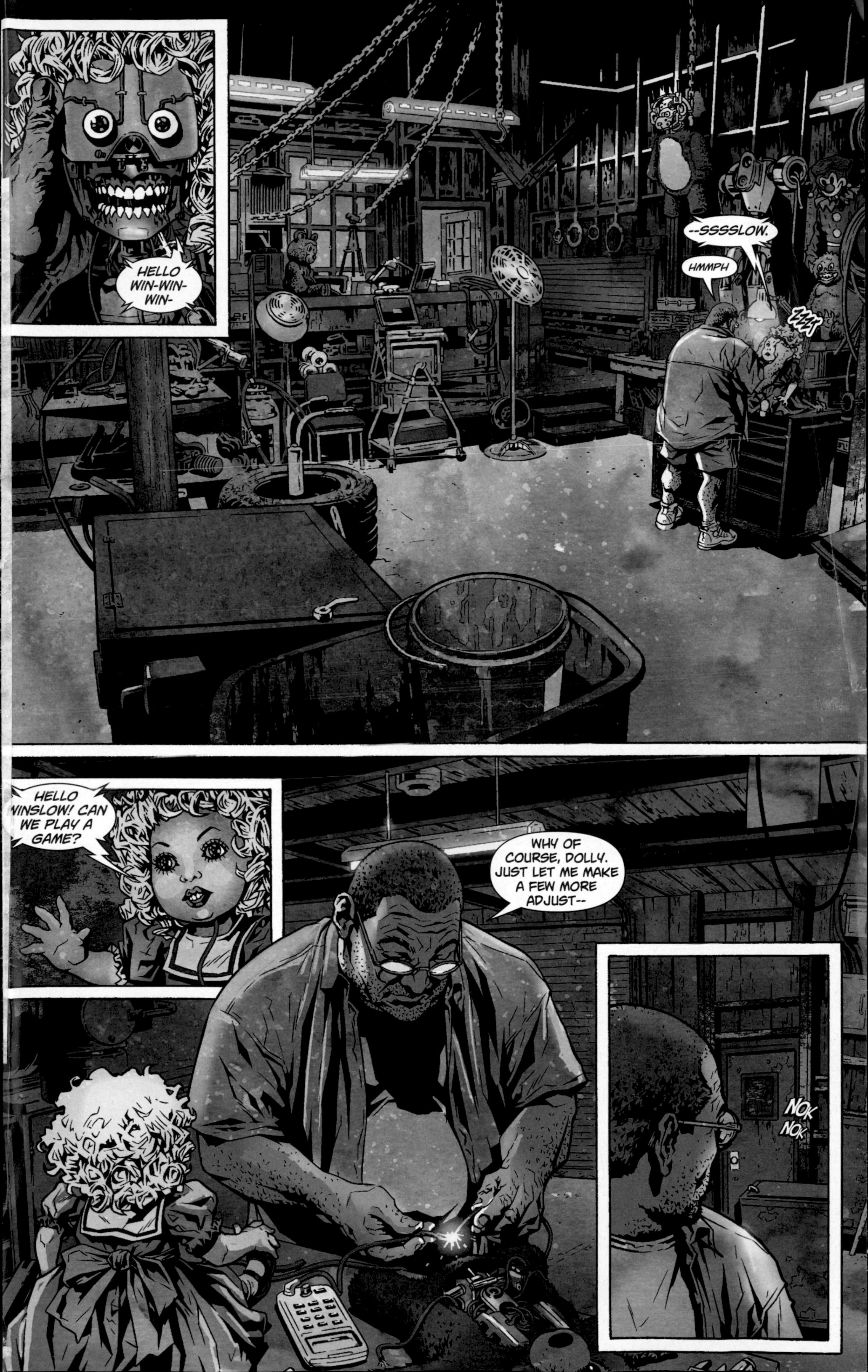
HELLO WIN-WIN-WIN-
--SSSSLOW.
HMMPH
ZZZT
HELLO WINSLOW! CAN WE PLAY A GAME?
WHY OF COURSE, DOLLY. JUST LET ME MAKE A FEW MORE ADJUST--
NOK NOK

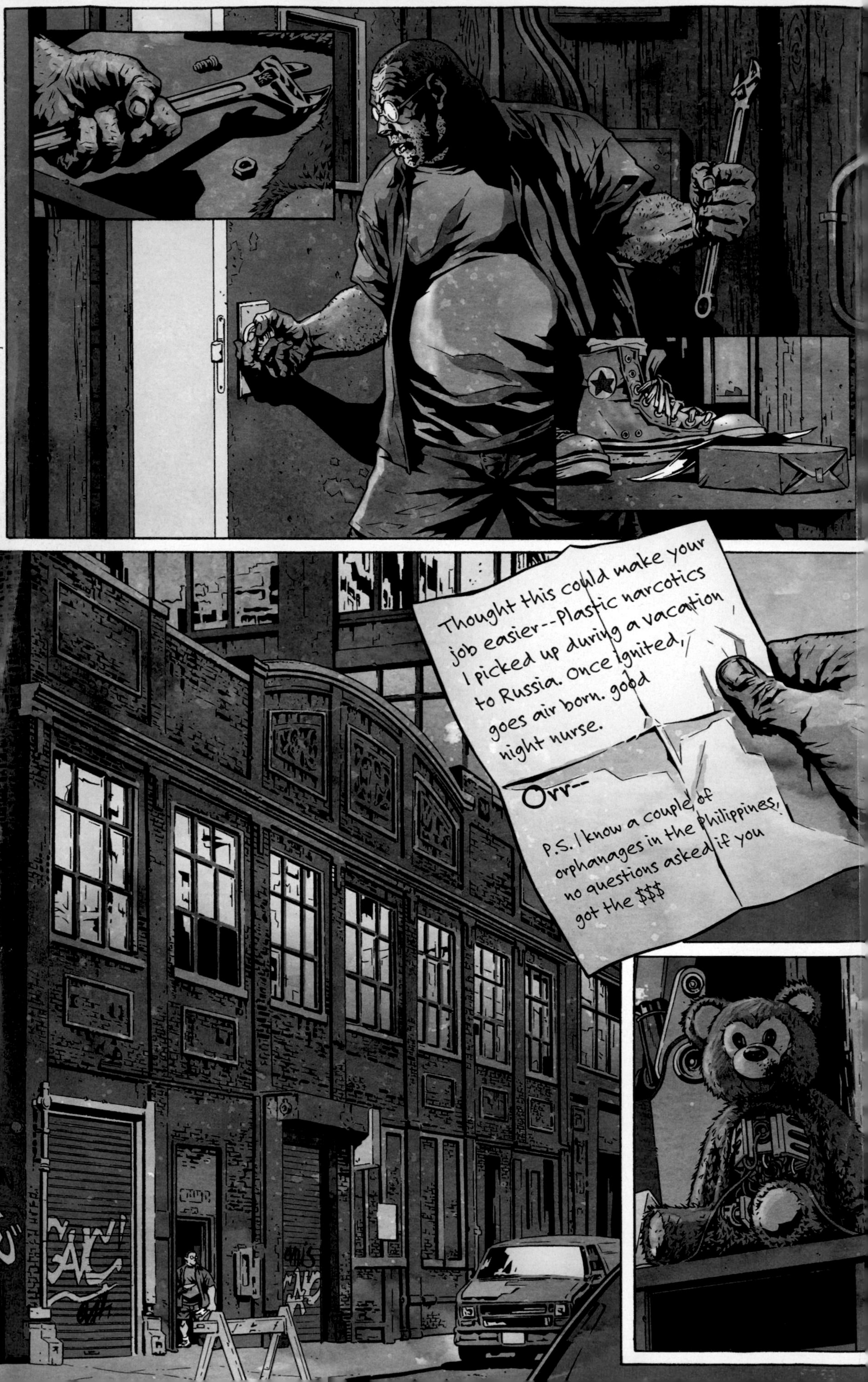
Thought this could make your job easier--Plastic narcotics I picked up during a vacation to Russia. Once ignited, goes air born. good night nurse.
Orr--
P.S. I know a couple of orphanages in the Philippines, no questions asked if you got the $$$

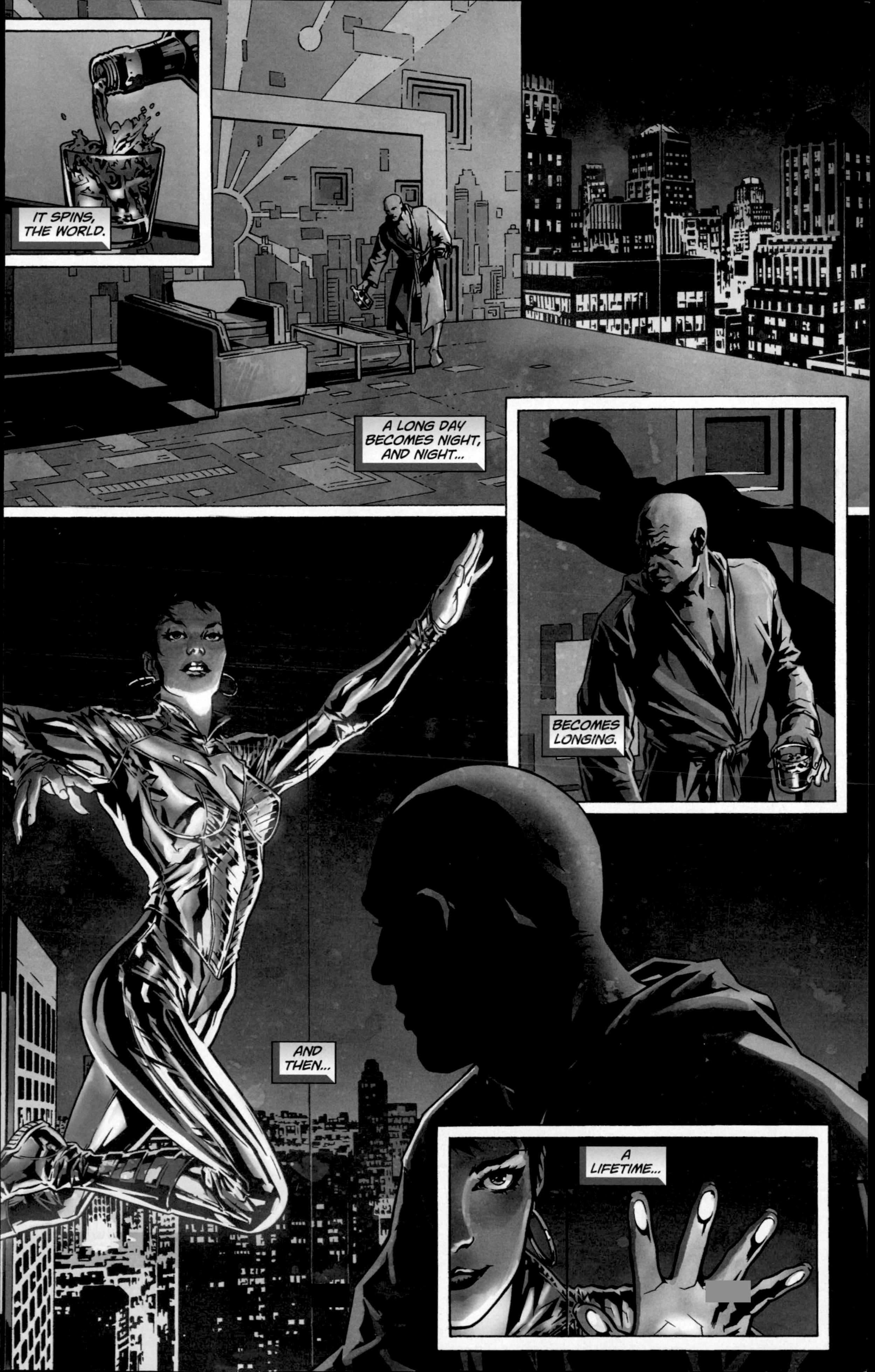
IT SPINS, THE WORLD.
A LONG DAY BECOMES NIGHT, AND NIGHT...
BECOMES LONGING.
AND THEN...
A LIFETIME...

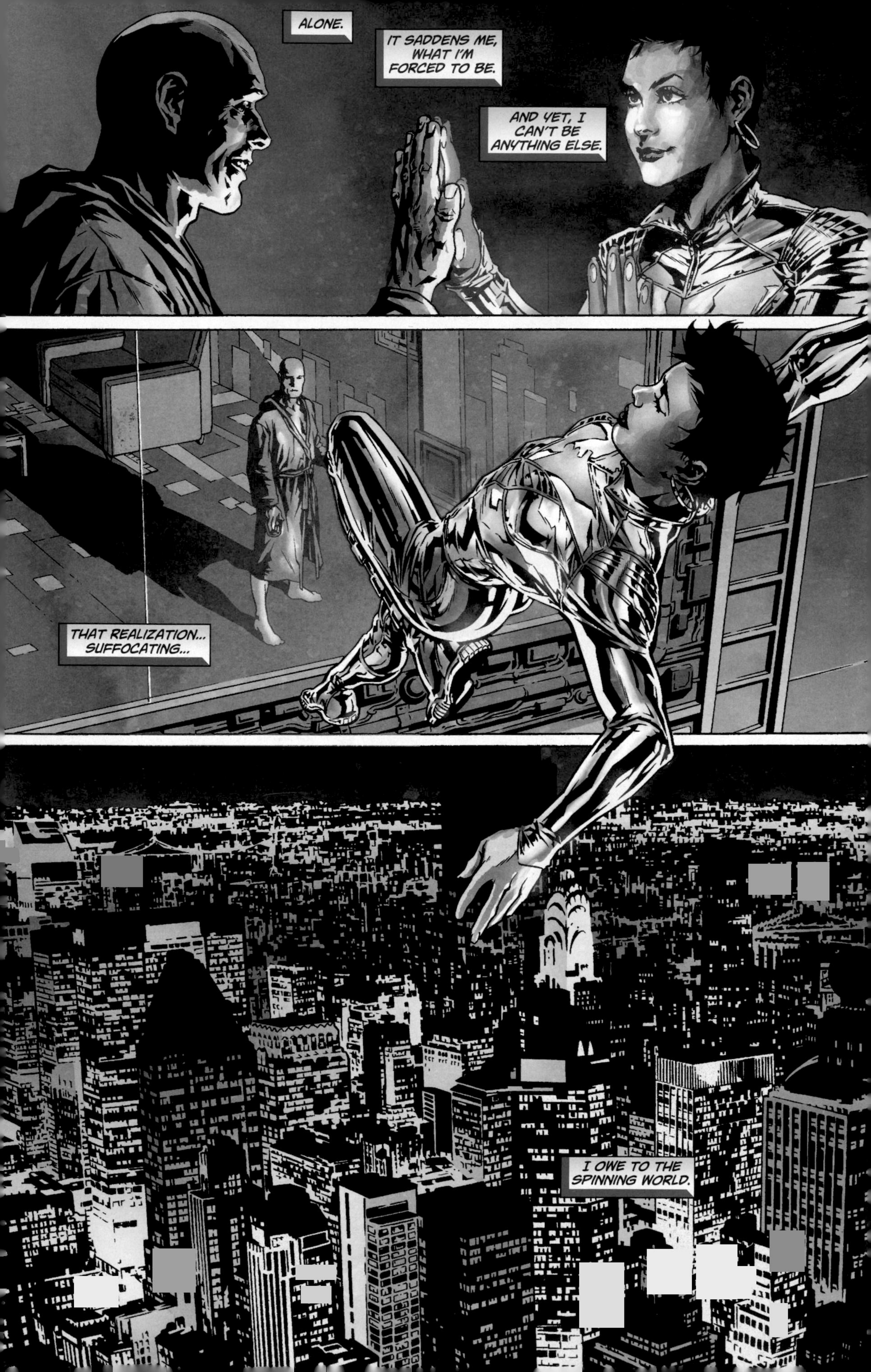
ALONE.
IT SADDENS ME, WHAT I'M FORCED TO BE.
AND YET, I CAN'T BE ANYTHING ELSE.
THAT REALIZATION... SUFFOCATING...
I OWE TO THE SPINNING WORLD.

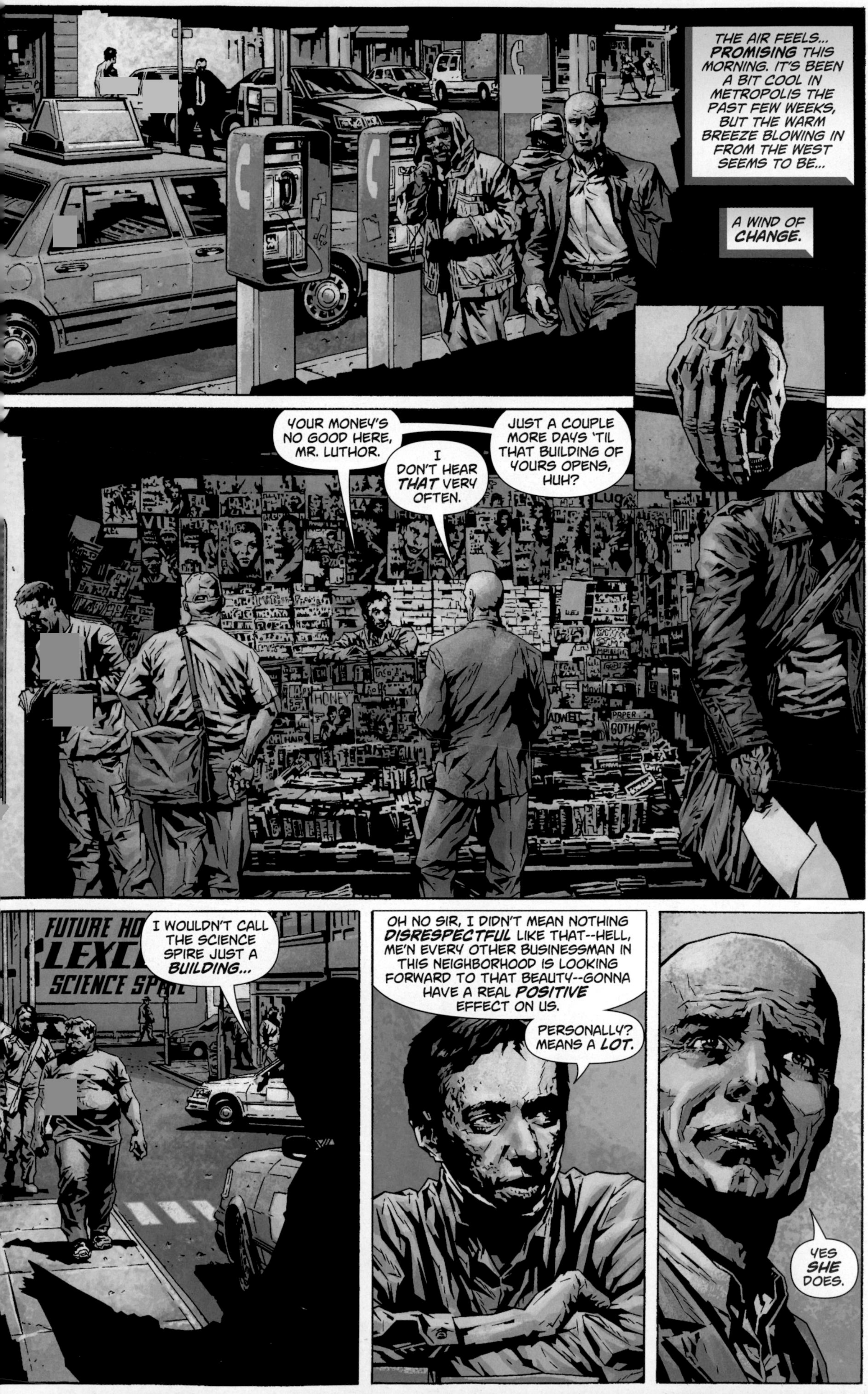
THE AIR FEELS... PROMISING THIS MORNING. IT'S BEEN A BIT COOL IN METROPOLIS THE PAST FEW WEEKS, BUT THE WARM BREEZE BLOWING IN FROM THE WEST SEEMS TO BE...
A WIND OF CHANGE.
YOUR MONEY'S NO GOOD HERE, MR. LUTHOR.
I DON'T HEAR THAT VERY OFTEN.
JUST A COUPLE MORE DAYS 'TIL THAT BUILDING OF YOURS OPENS, HUH?
I WOULDN'T CALL THE SCIENCE SPIRE JUST A BUILDING...
OH NO SIR, I DIDN'T MEAN NOTHING DISRESPECTFUL LIKE THAT--HELL, ME'N EVERY OTHER BUSINESSMAN IN THIS NEIGHBORHOOD IS LOOKING FORWARD TO THAT BEAUTY--GONNA HAVE A REAL POSITIVE EFFECT ON US.
PERSONALLY? MEANS A LOT.
YES SHE DOES.

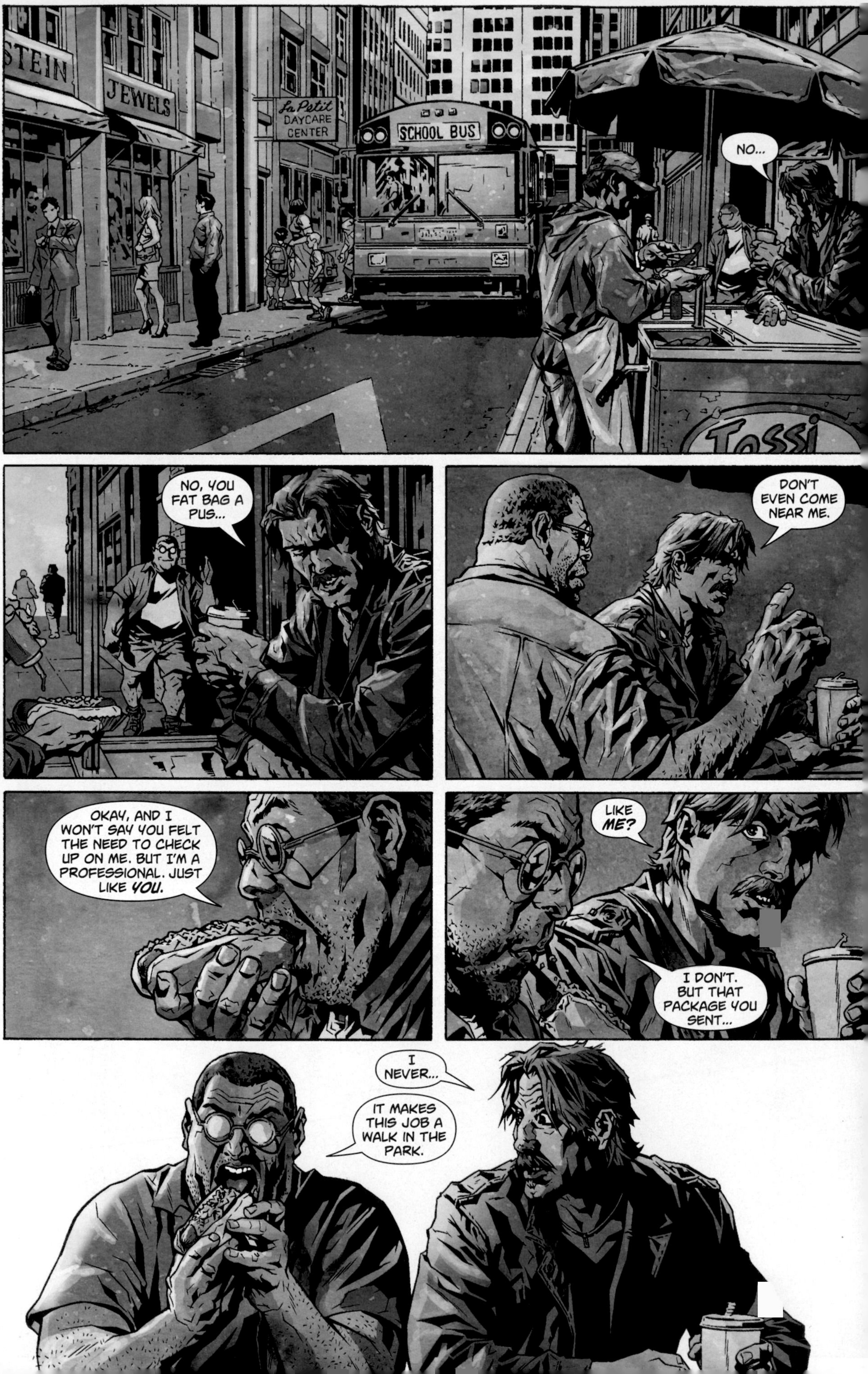
STEIN
JEWELS
La Petit DAYCARE CENTER
SCHOOL BUS
NO...
Tossi
NO, YOU FAT BAG A PUS...
DON'T EVEN COME NEAR ME.
OKAY, AND I WON'T SAY YOU FELT THE NEED TO CHECK UP ON ME. BUT I'M A PROFESSIONAL. JUST LIKE *YOU*.
LIKE *ME*?
I DON'T. BUT THAT PACKAGE YOU SENT...
I NEVER...
IT MAKES THIS JOB A WALK IN THE PARK.

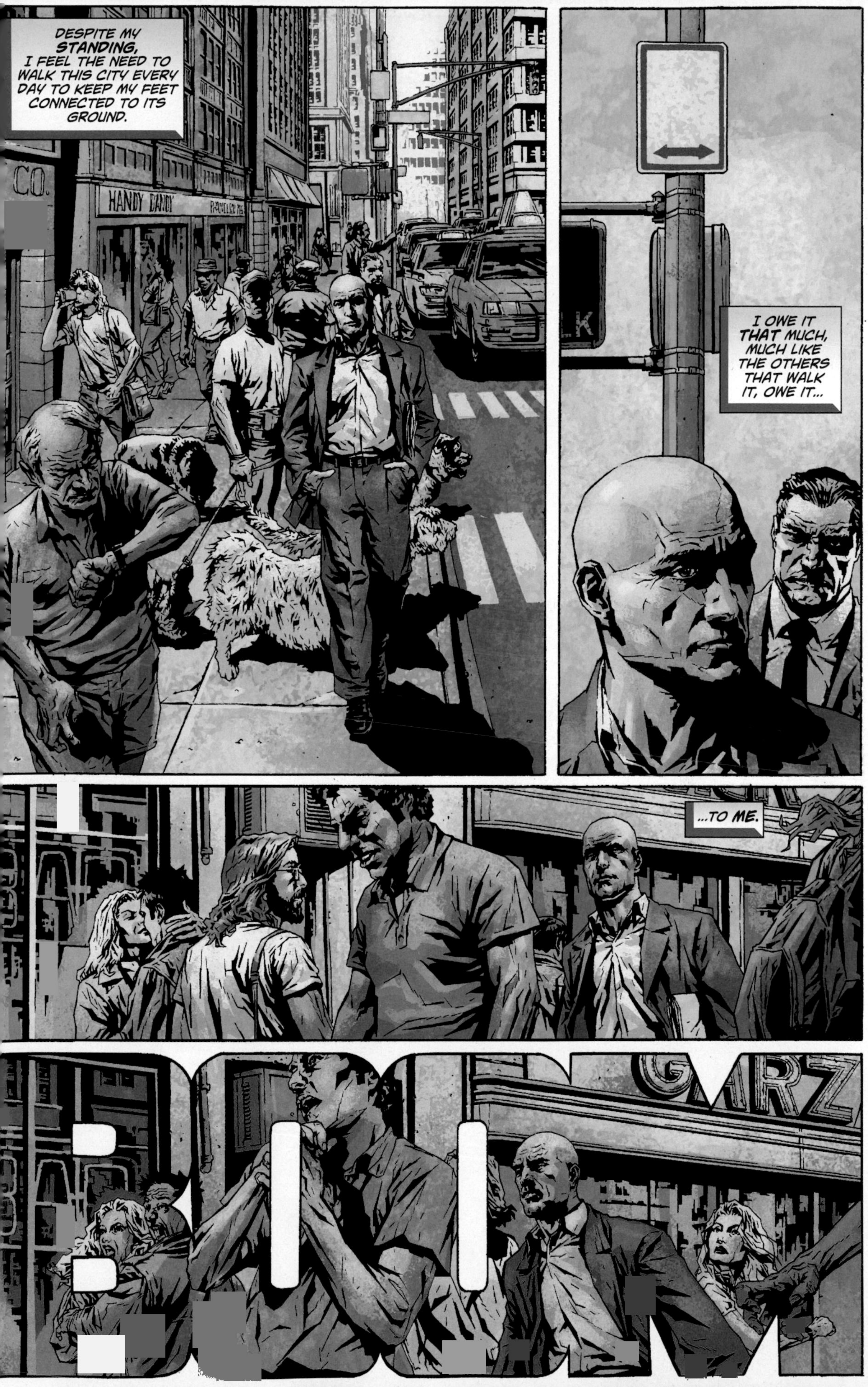
DESPITE MY STANDING, I FEEL THE NEED TO WALK THIS CITY EVERY DAY TO KEEP MY FEET CONNECTED TO ITS GROUND.
CO.
HANDY DANDY
I OWE IT THAT MUCH, MUCH LIKE THE OTHERS THAT WALK IT, OWE IT...
...TO ME.
GARZ
BOOM

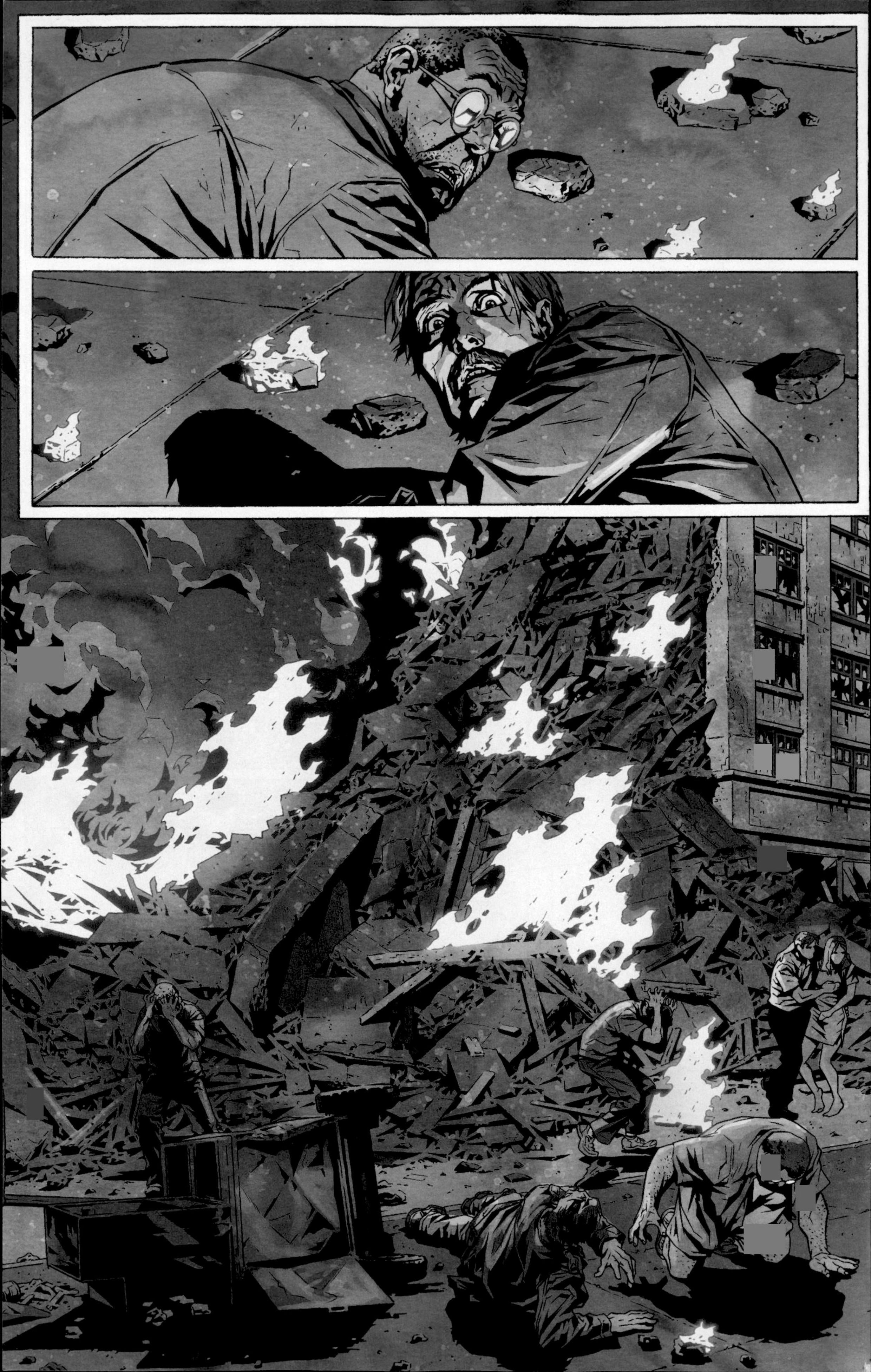

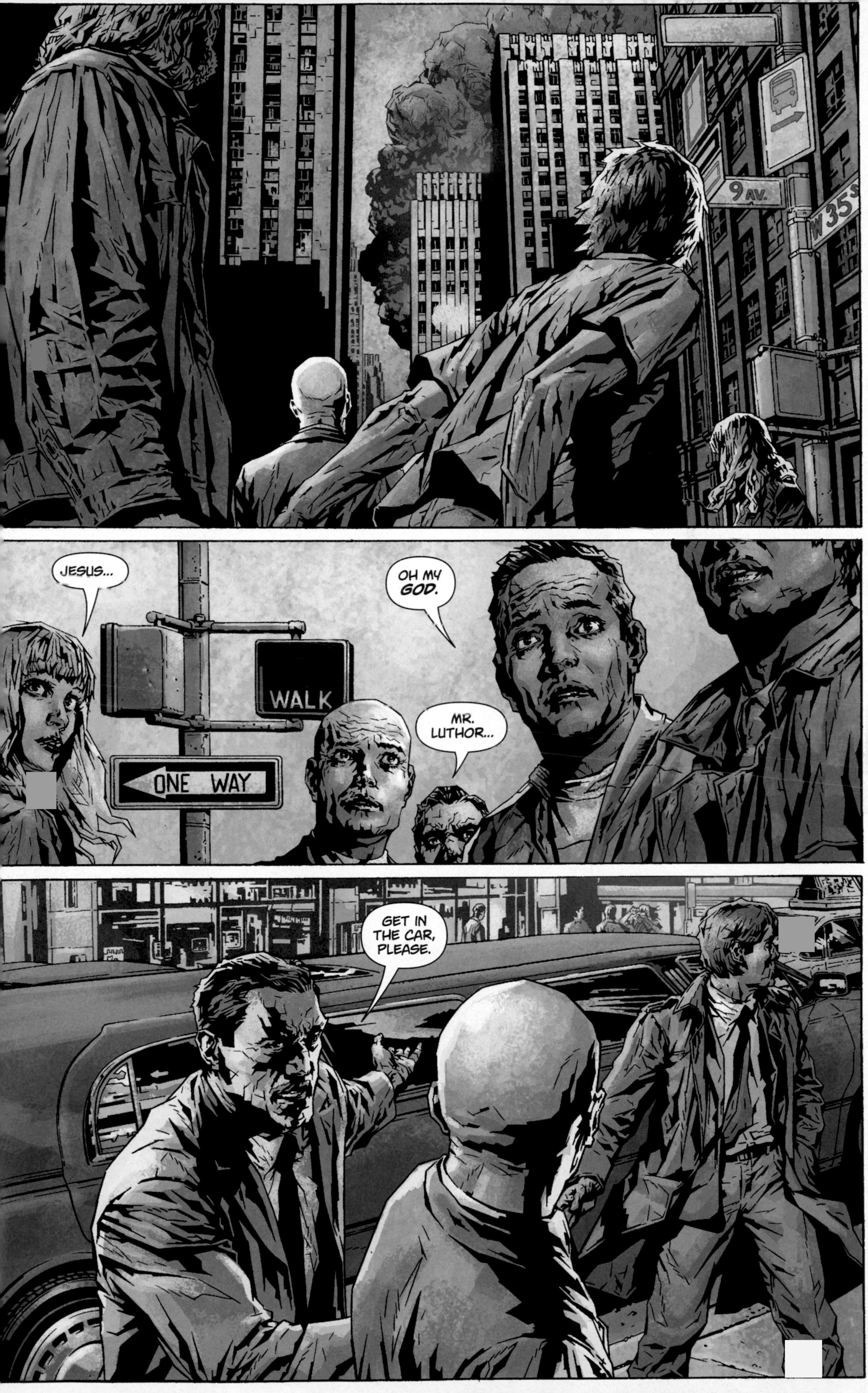
9 AV.
W 35 S
JESUS...
OH MY GOD.
WALK
ONE WAY
MR. LUTHOR...
GET IN THE CAR, PLEASE.

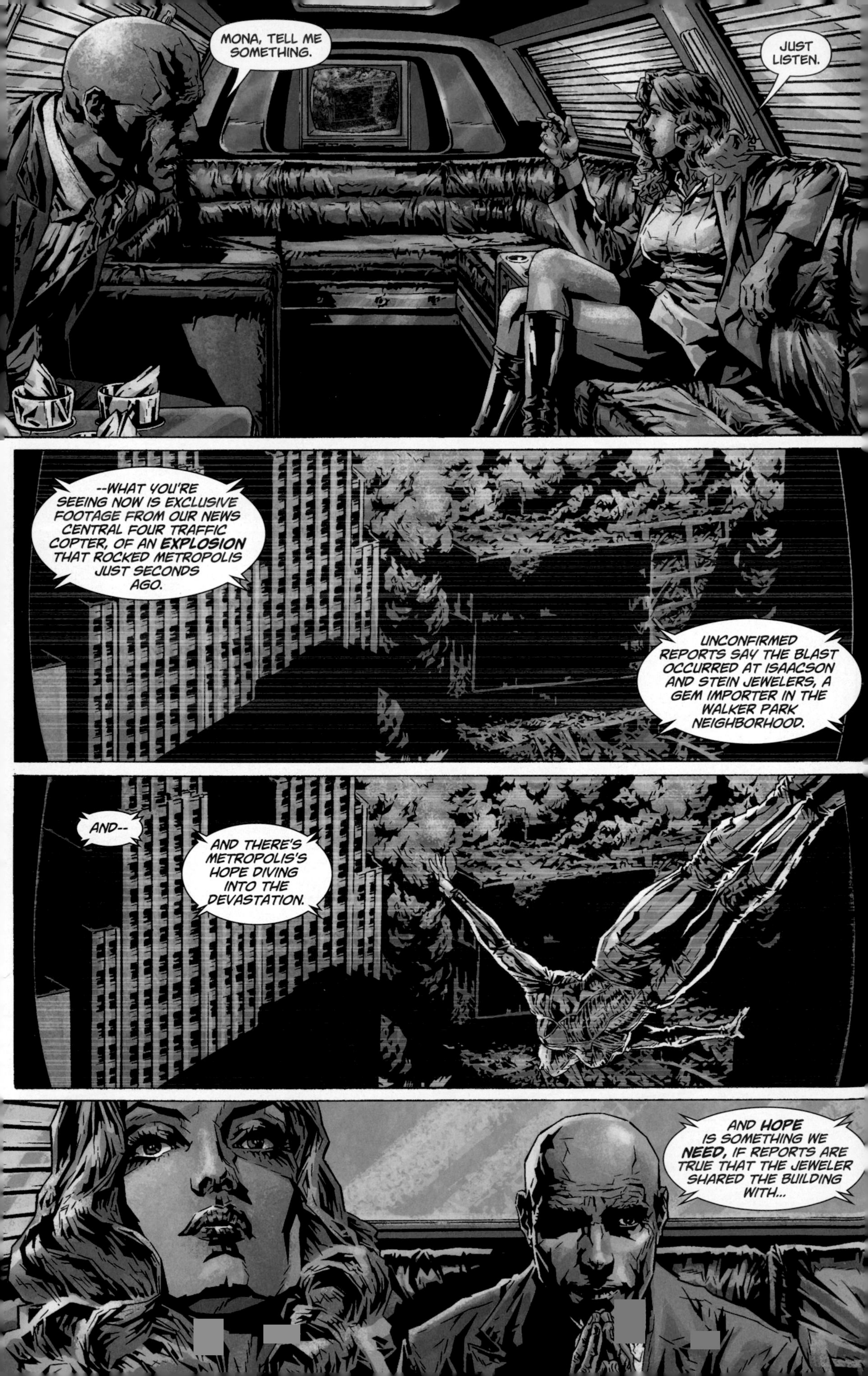
MONA, TELL ME SOMETHING.
JUST LISTEN.
--WHAT YOU'RE SEEING NOW IS EXCLUSIVE FOOTAGE FROM OUR NEWS CENTRAL FOUR TRAFFIC COPTER, OF AN **EXPLOSION** THAT ROCKED METROPOLIS JUST SECONDS AGO.
UNCONFIRMED REPORTS SAY THE BLAST OCCURRED AT ISAACSON AND STEIN JEWELERS, A GEM IMPORTER IN THE WALKER PARK NEIGHBORHOOD.
AND--
AND THERE'S METROPOLIS'S HOPE DIVING INTO THE DEVASTATION.
AND **HOPE** IS SOMETHING WE **NEED,** IF REPORTS ARE TRUE THAT THE JEWELER SHARED THE BUILDING WITH...

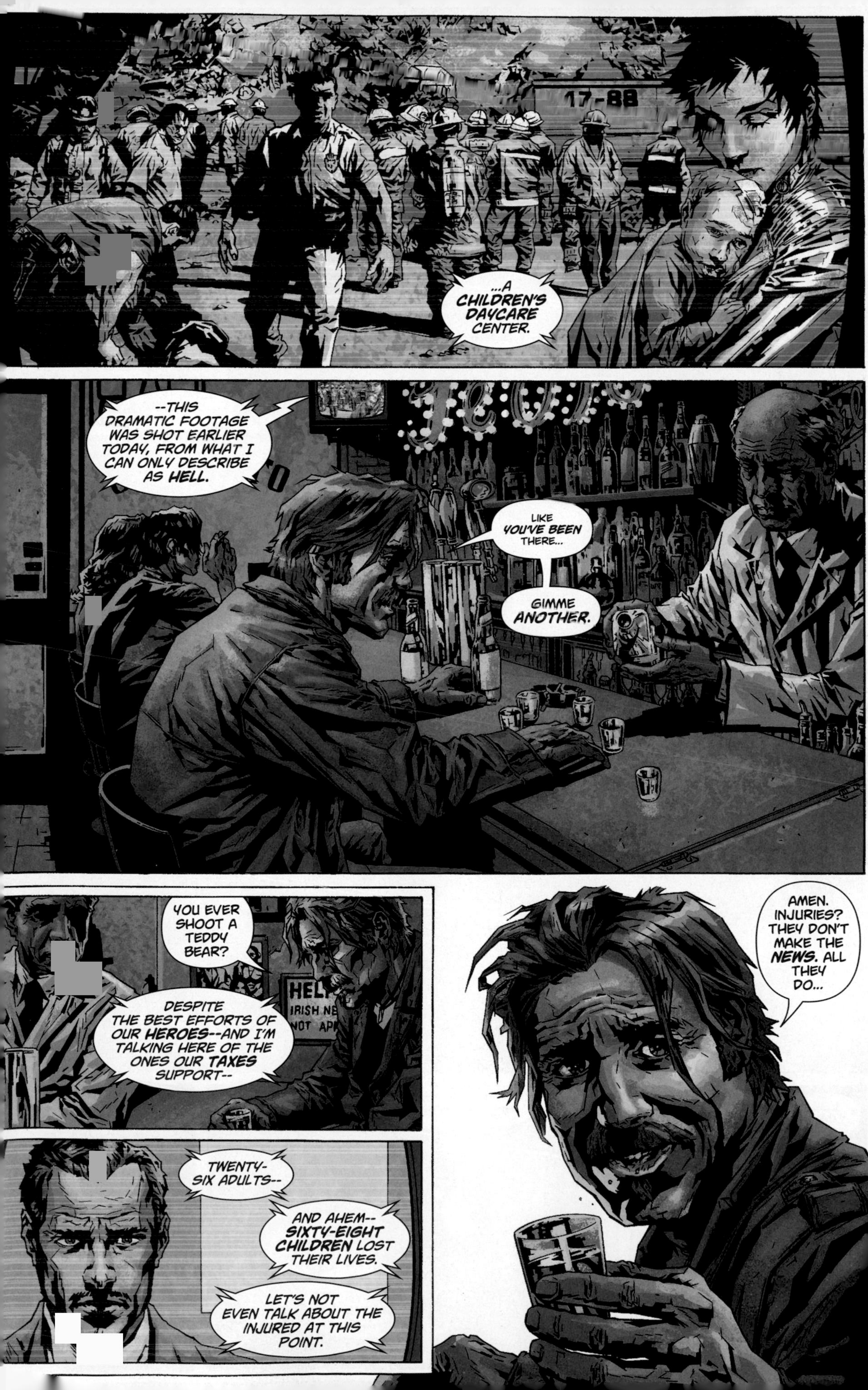
17-88
...A CHILDREN'S DAYCARE CENTER.
--THIS DRAMATIC FOOTAGE WAS SHOT EARLIER TODAY, FROM WHAT I CAN ONLY DESCRIBE AS HELL.
LIKE YOU'VE BEEN THERE...
GIMME ANOTHER.
YOU EVER SHOOT A TEDDY BEAR?
DESPITE THE BEST EFFORTS OF OUR HEROES--AND I'M TALKING HERE OF THE ONES OUR TAXES SUPPORT--
TWENTY-SIX ADULTS--
AND AHEM--SIXTY-EIGHT CHILDREN LOST THEIR LIVES.
LET'S NOT EVEN TALK ABOUT THE INJURED AT THIS POINT.
AMEN. INJURIES? THEY DON'T MAKE THE NEWS. ALL THEY DO...

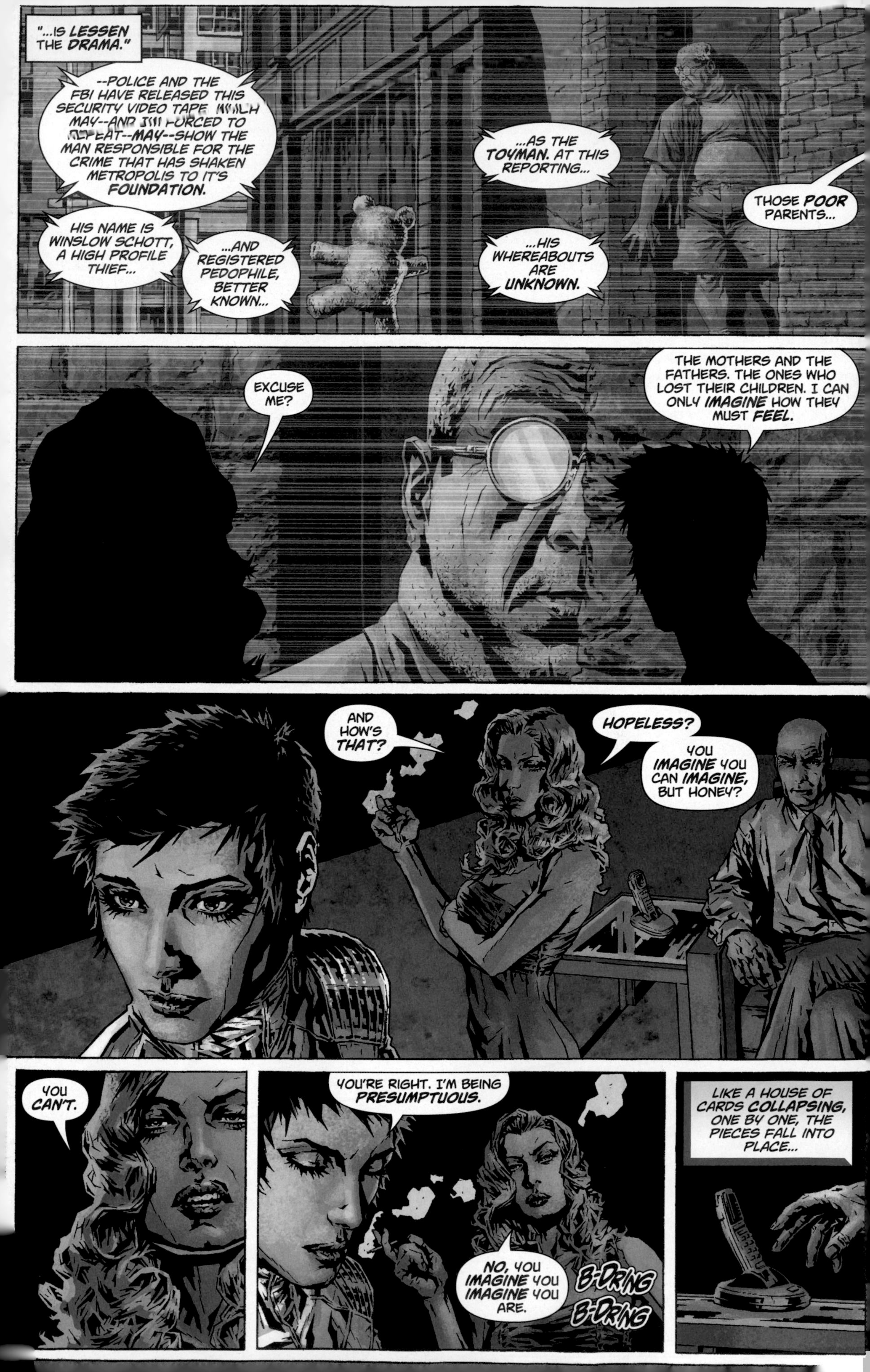
"...IS LESSEN THE DRAMA."
--POLICE AND THE FBI HAVE RELEASED THIS SECURITY VIDEO TAPE WHICH MAY--AND I'M FORCED TO REPEAT--MAY--SHOW THE MAN RESPONSIBLE FOR THE CRIME THAT HAS SHAKEN METROPOLIS TO IT'S FOUNDATION.
HIS NAME IS WINSLOW SCHOTT, A HIGH PROFILE THIEF...
...AND REGISTERED PEDOPHILE, BETTER KNOWN...
...AS THE TOYMAN. AT THIS REPORTING...
...HIS WHEREABOUTS ARE UNKNOWN.
THOSE POOR PARENTS...
EXCUSE ME?
THE MOTHERS AND THE FATHERS. THE ONES WHO LOST THEIR CHILDREN. I CAN ONLY IMAGINE HOW THEY MUST FEEL.
AND HOW'S THAT?
HOPELESS?
YOU IMAGINE YOU CAN IMAGINE, BUT HONEY?
YOU CAN'T.
YOU'RE RIGHT. I'M BEING PRESUMPTUOUS.
NO, YOU IMAGINE YOU IMAGINE YOU ARE.
B-DRING
B-DRING
LIKE A HOUSE OF CARDS COLLAPSING, ONE BY ONE, THE PIECES FALL INTO PLACE...

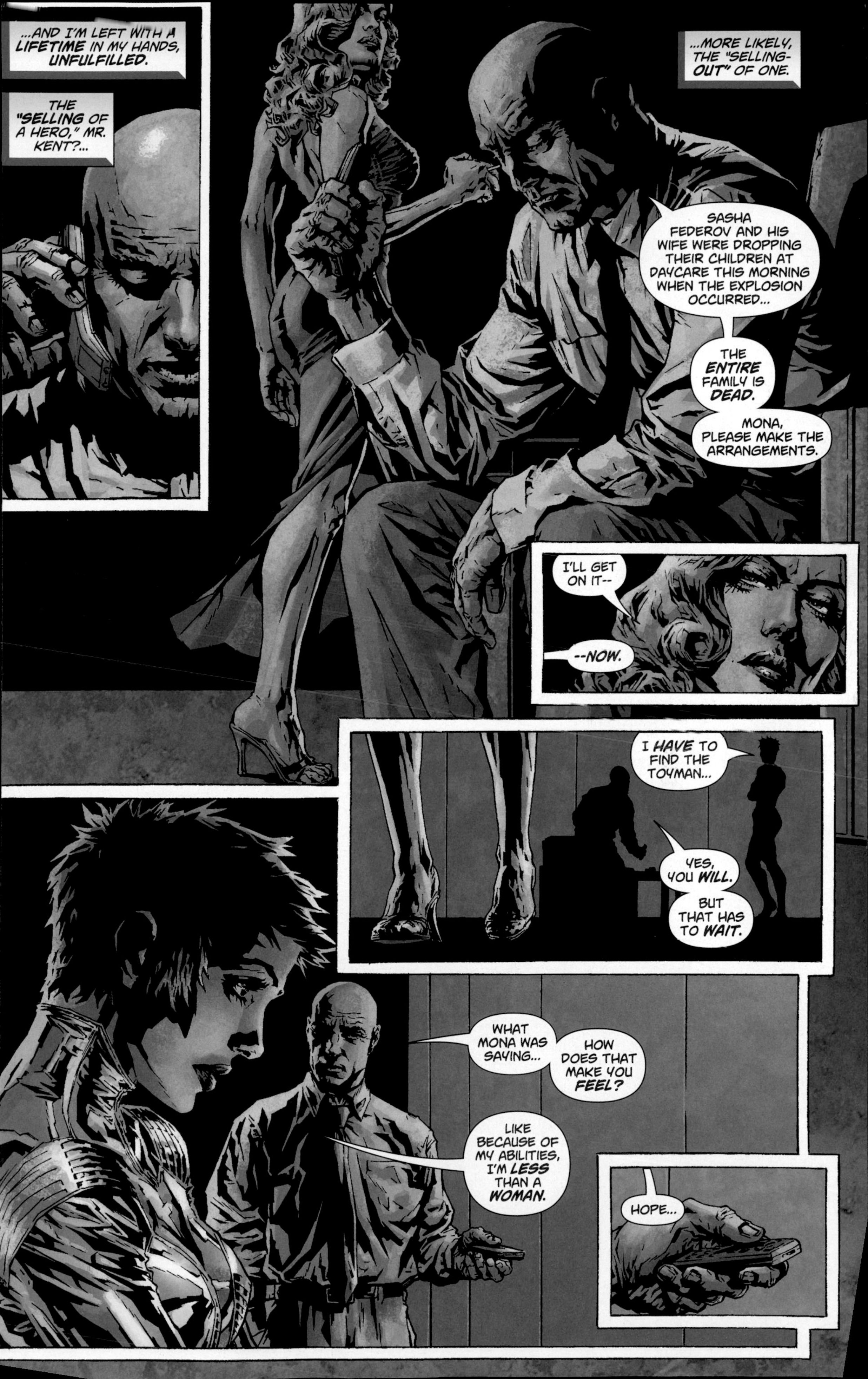
...AND I'M LEFT WITH A LIFETIME IN MY HANDS, UNFULFILLED.
THE "SELLING OF A HERO," MR. KENT?...
...MORE LIKELY, THE "SELLING-OUT" OF ONE.
SASHA FEDEROV AND HIS WIFE WERE DROPPING THEIR CHILDREN AT DAYCARE THIS MORNING WHEN THE EXPLOSION OCCURRED...
THE ENTIRE FAMILY IS DEAD.
MONA, PLEASE MAKE THE ARRANGEMENTS.
I'LL GET ON IT--
--NOW.
I HAVE TO FIND THE TOYMAN...
YES, YOU WILL.
BUT THAT HAS TO WAIT.
WHAT MONA WAS SAYING...
HOW DOES THAT MAKE YOU FEEL?
LIKE BECAUSE OF MY ABILITIES, I'M LESS THAN A WOMAN.
HOPE...

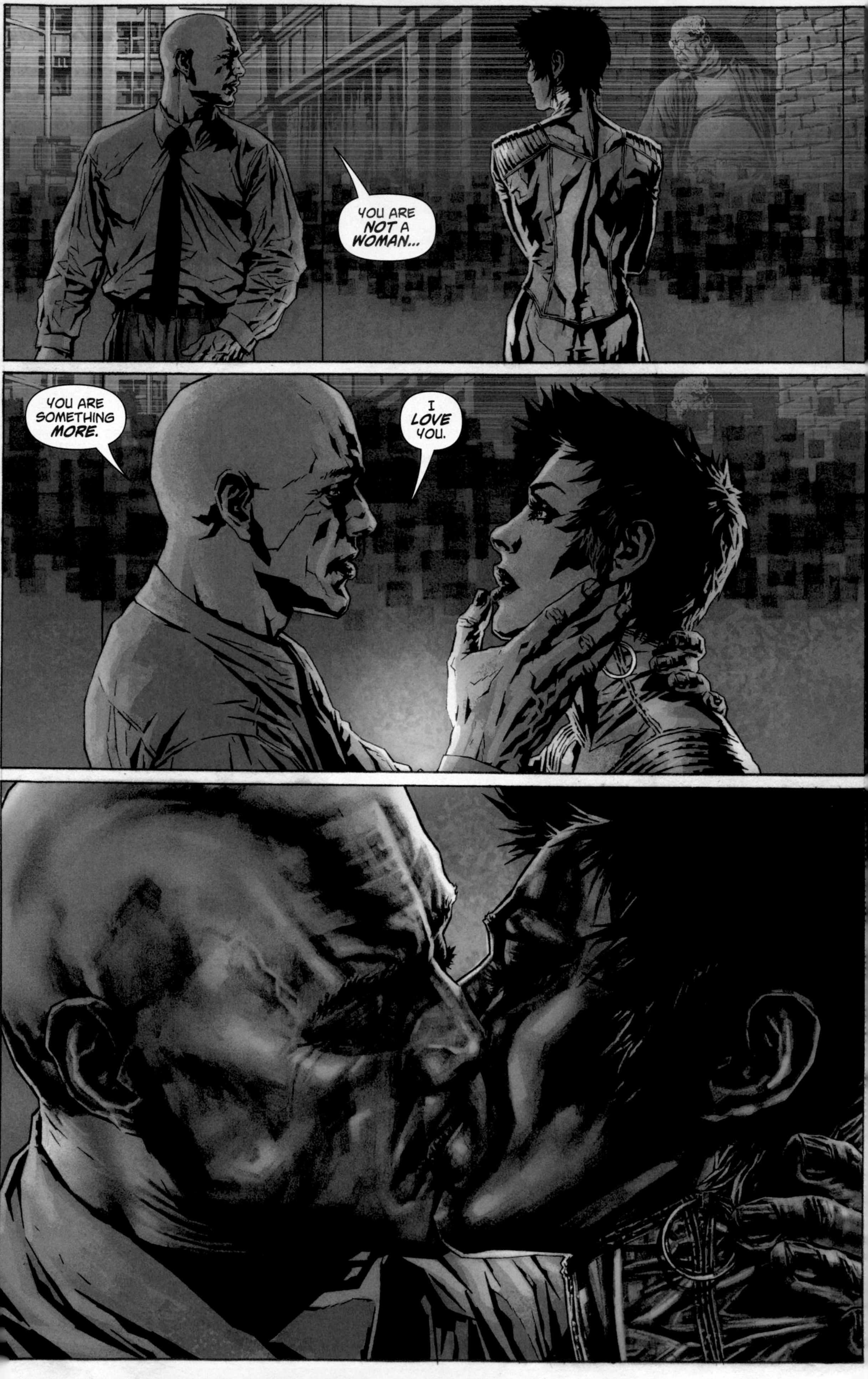
YOU ARE NOT A WOMAN...
YOU ARE SOMETHING MORE.
I LOVE YOU.

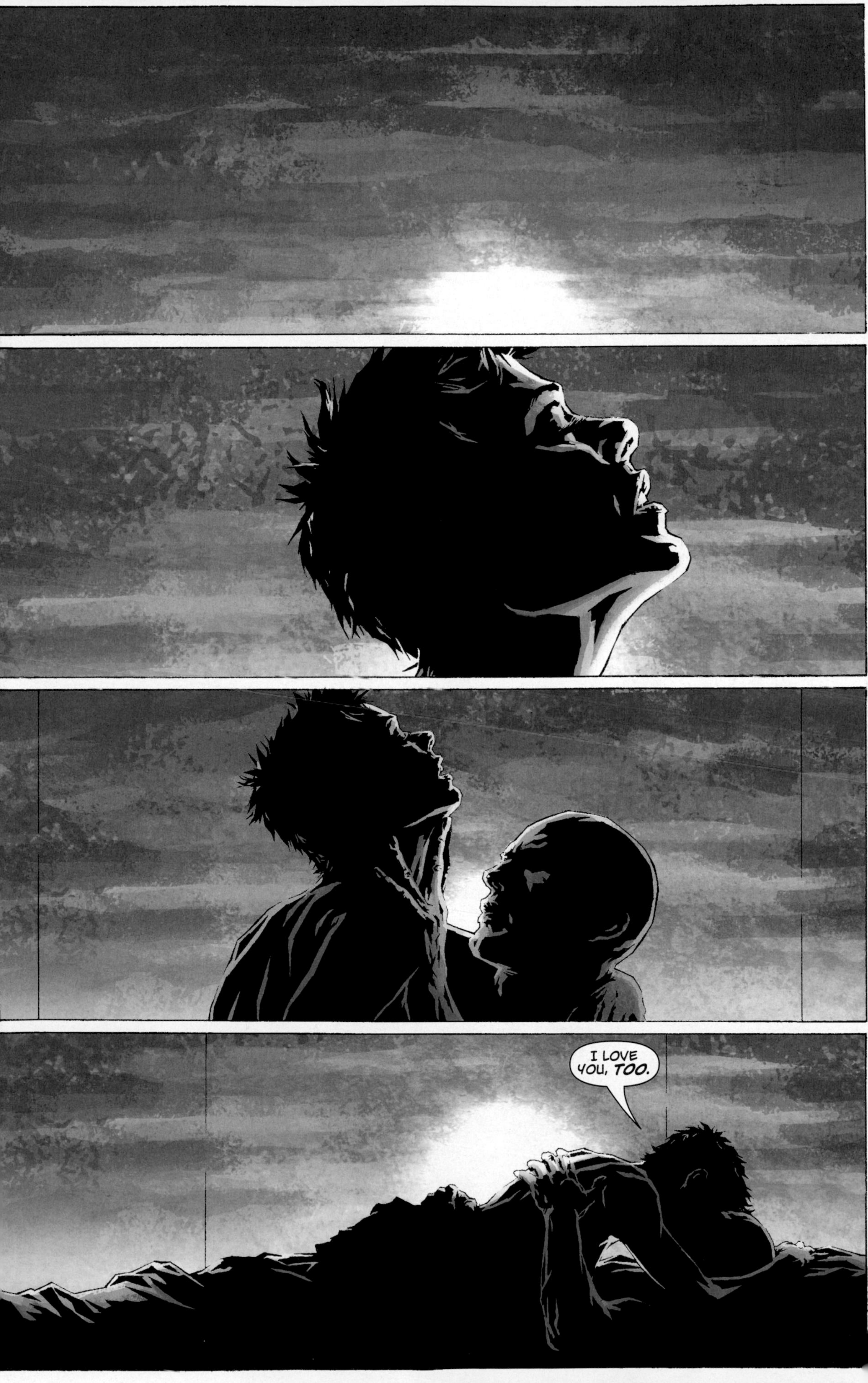
I LOVE YOU, TOO.

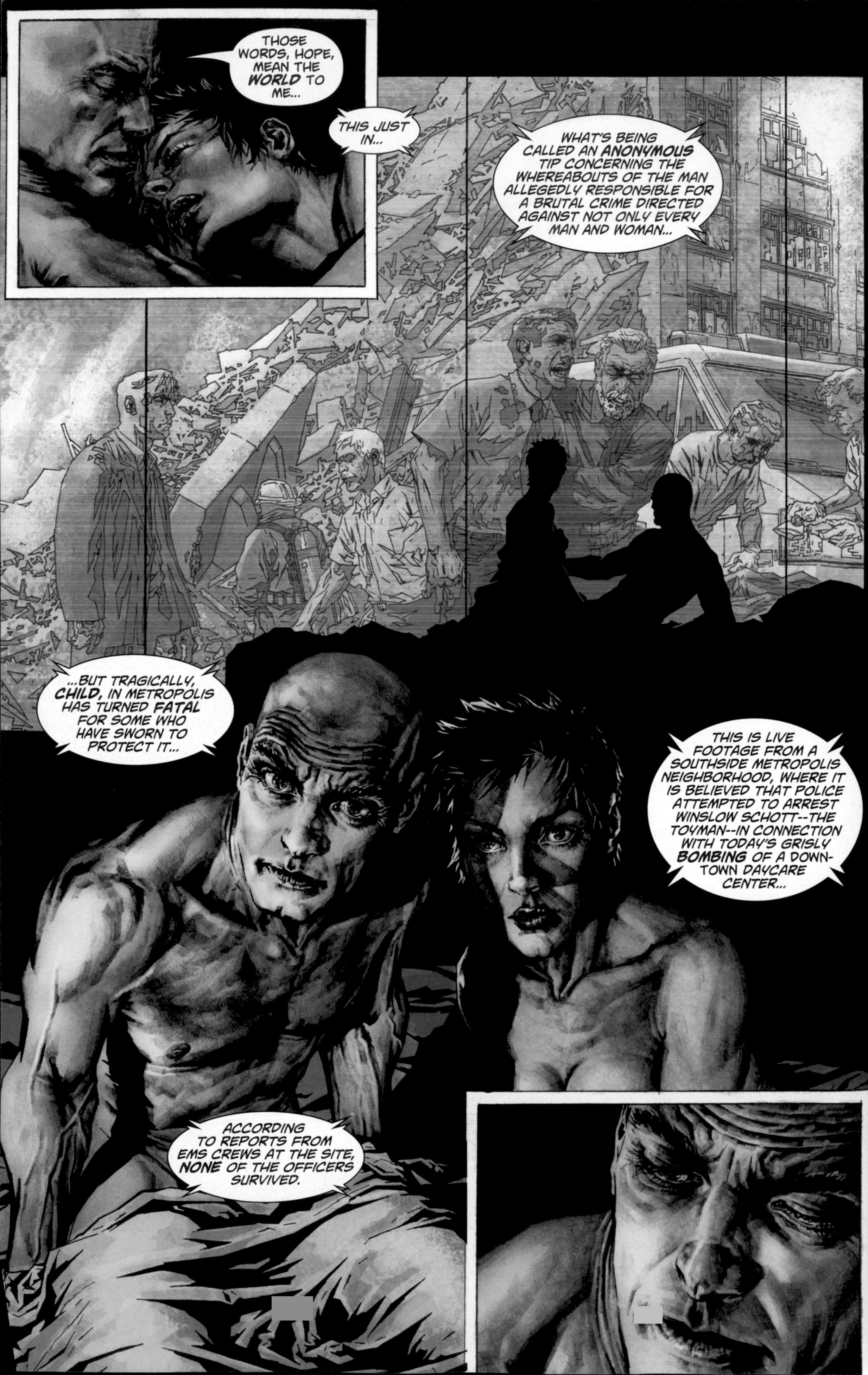
THOSE WORDS, HOPE, MEAN THE WORLD TO ME...
THIS JUST IN...
WHAT'S BEING CALLED AN ANONYMOUS TIP CONCERNING THE WHEREABOUTS OF THE MAN ALLEGEDLY RESPONSIBLE FOR A BRUTAL CRIME DIRECTED AGAINST NOT ONLY EVERY MAN AND WOMAN...
...BUT TRAGICALLY, CHILD, IN METROPOLIS HAS TURNED FATAL FOR SOME WHO HAVE SWORN TO PROTECT IT...
THIS IS LIVE FOOTAGE FROM A SOUTHSIDE METROPOLIS NEIGHBORHOOD, WHERE IT IS BELIEVED THAT POLICE ATTEMPTED TO ARREST WINSLOW SCHOTT--THE TOYMAN--IN CONNECTION WITH TODAY'S GRISLY BOMBING OF A DOWN-TOWN DAYCARE CENTER...
ACCORDING TO REPORTS FROM EMS CREWS AT THE SITE, NONE OF THE OFFICERS SURVIVED.

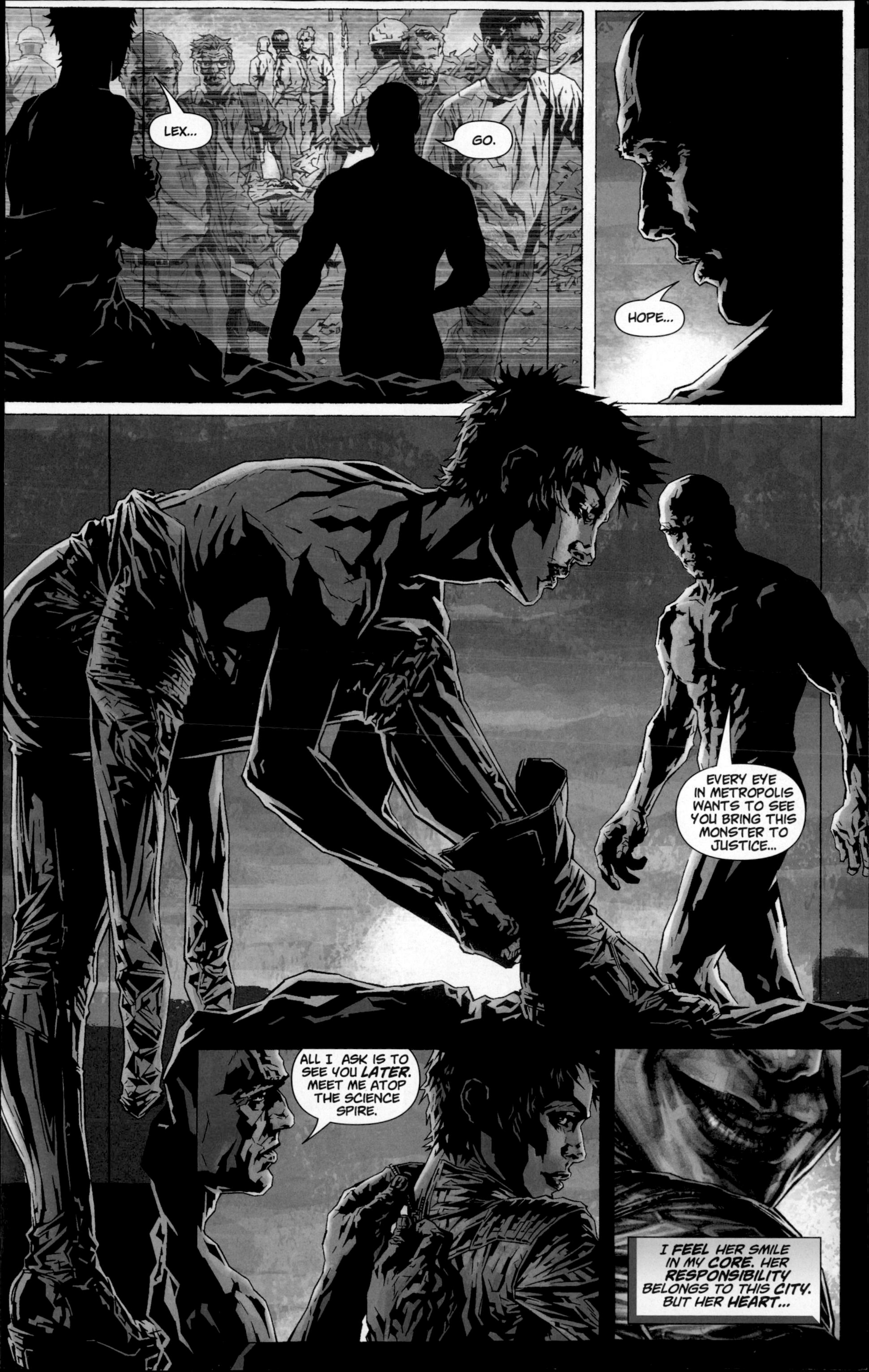
LEX...
GO.
HOPE...
EVERY EYE IN METROPOLIS WANTS TO SEE YOU BRING THIS MONSTER TO JUSTICE...
ALL I ASK IS TO SEE YOU LATER. MEET ME ATOP THE SCIENCE SPIRE.
I FEEL HER SMILE IN MY CORE. HER RESPONSIBILITY BELONGS TO THIS CITY. BUT HER HEART...

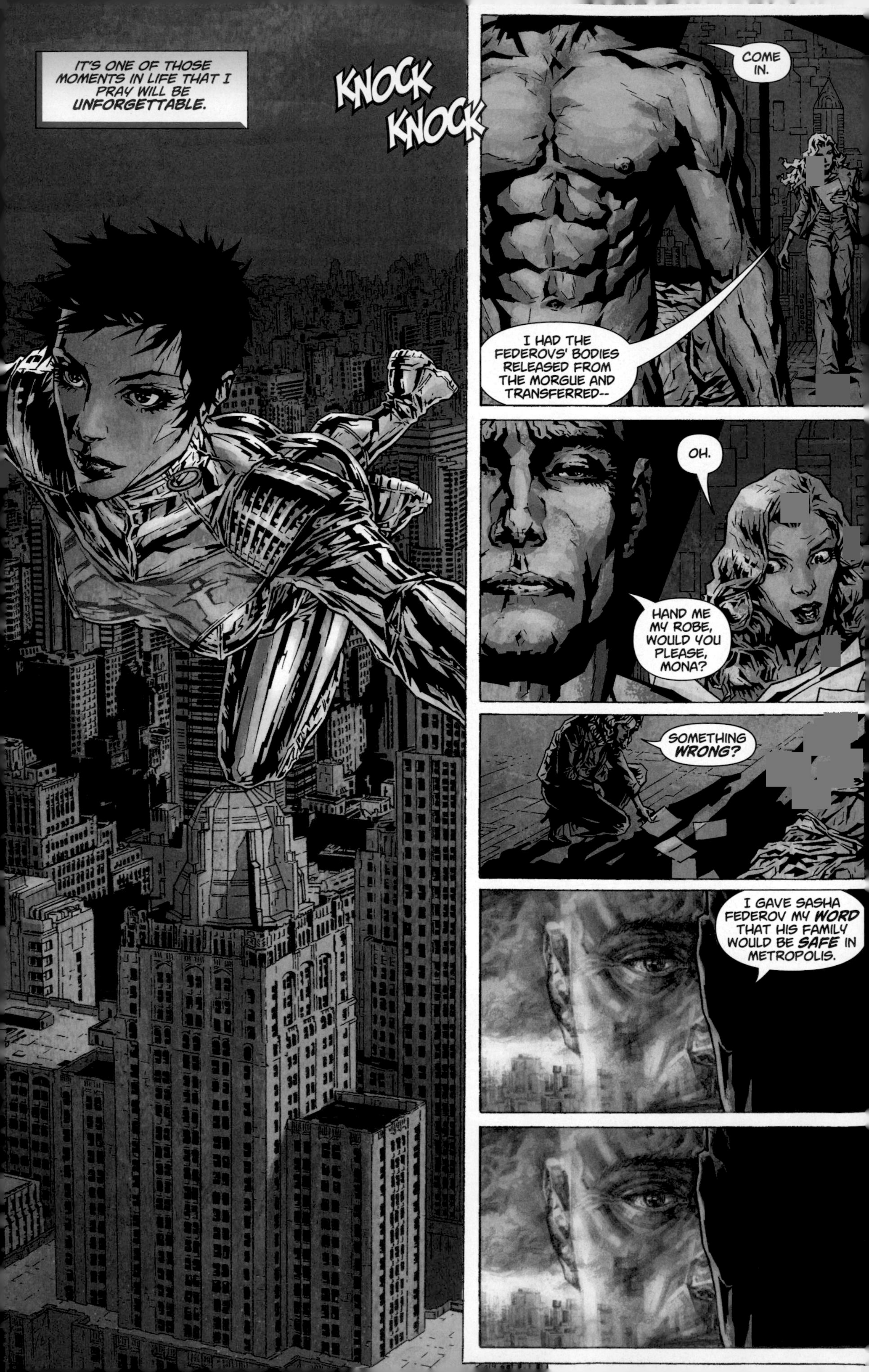
IT'S ONE OF THOSE MOMENTS IN LIFE THAT I PRAY WILL BE UNFORGETTABLE.
KNOCK KNOCK
COME IN.
I HAD THE FEDEROVS' BODIES RELEASED FROM THE MORGUE AND TRANSFERRED--
OH.
HAND ME MY ROBE, WOULD YOU PLEASE, MONA?
SOMETHING WRONG?
I GAVE SASHA FEDEROV MY WORD THAT HIS FAMILY WOULD BE SAFE IN METROPOLIS.

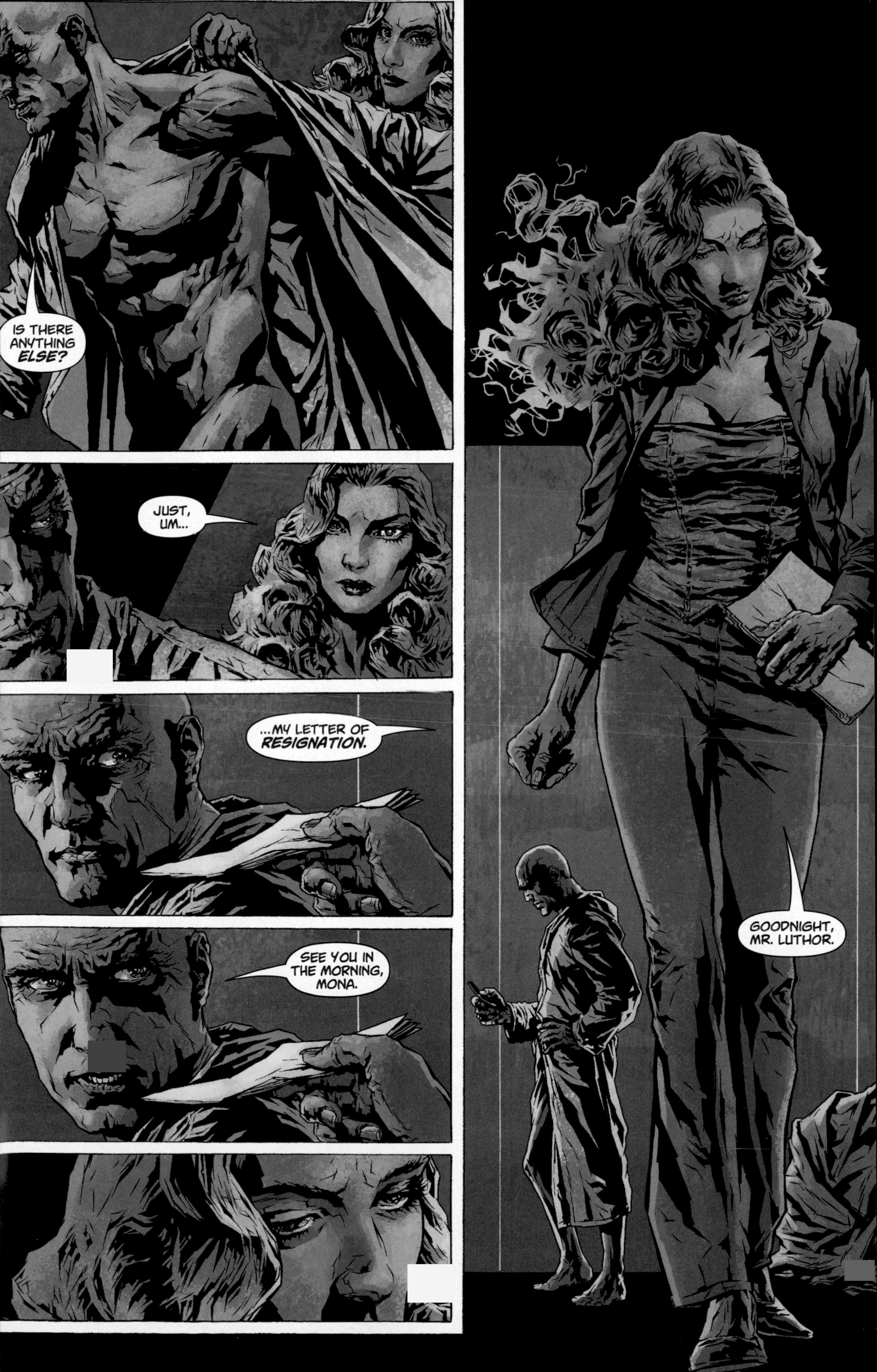
IS THERE ANYTHING ELSE?
JUST, UM...
...MY LETTER OF RESIGNATION.
SEE YOU IN THE MORNING, MONA.
GOODNIGHT, MR. LUTHOR.

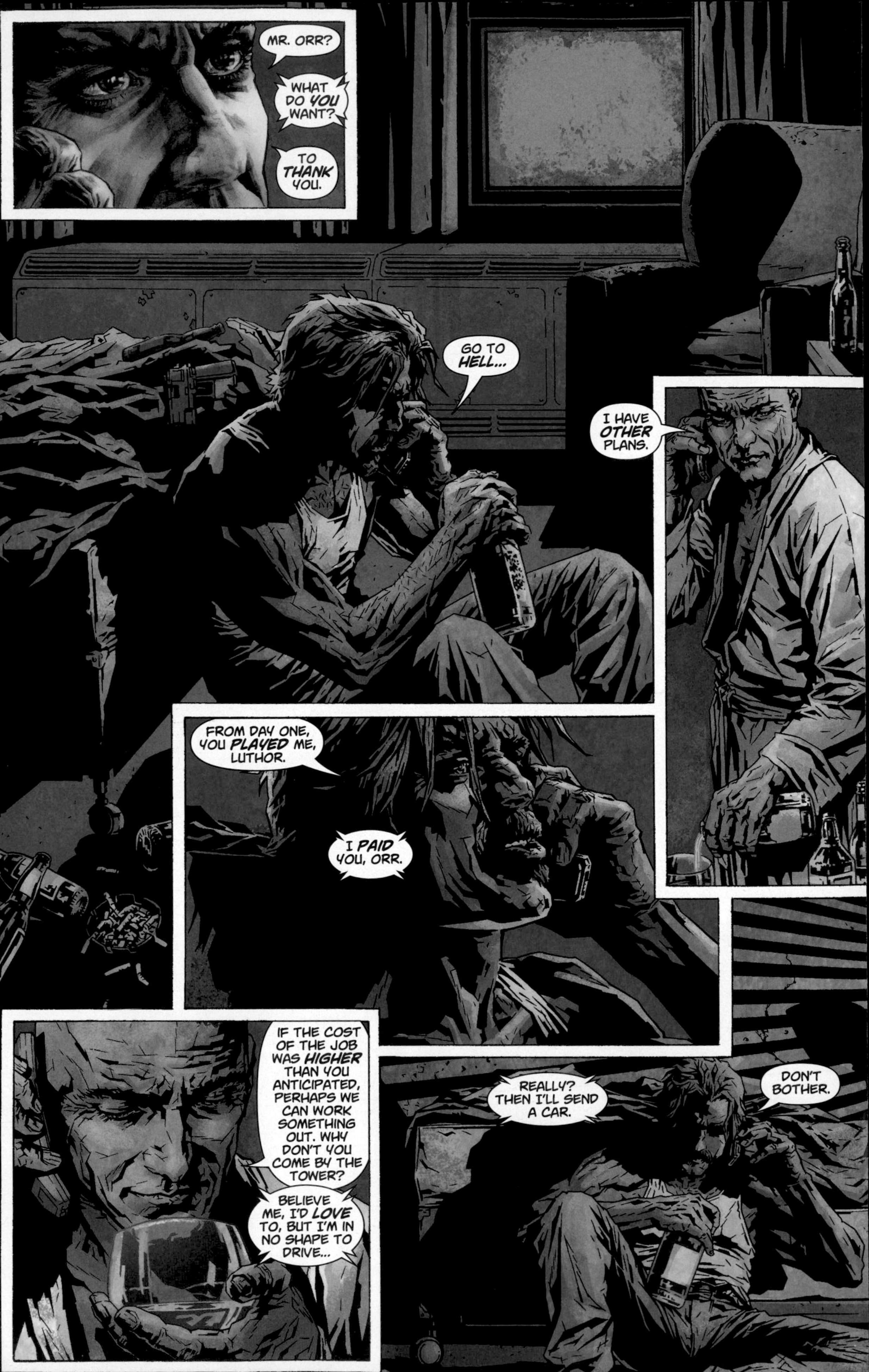
MR. ORR?
WHAT DO YOU WANT?
TO THANK YOU.
GO TO HELL...
I HAVE OTHER PLANS.
FROM DAY ONE, YOU PLAYED ME, LUTHOR.
I PAID YOU, ORR.
IF THE COST OF THE JOB WAS HIGHER THAN YOU ANTICIPATED, PERHAPS WE CAN WORK SOMETHING OUT. WHY DON'T YOU COME BY THE TOWER?
BELIEVE ME, I'D LOVE TO, BUT I'M IN NO SHAPE TO DRIVE...
REALLY? THEN I'LL SEND A CAR.
DON'T BOTHER.

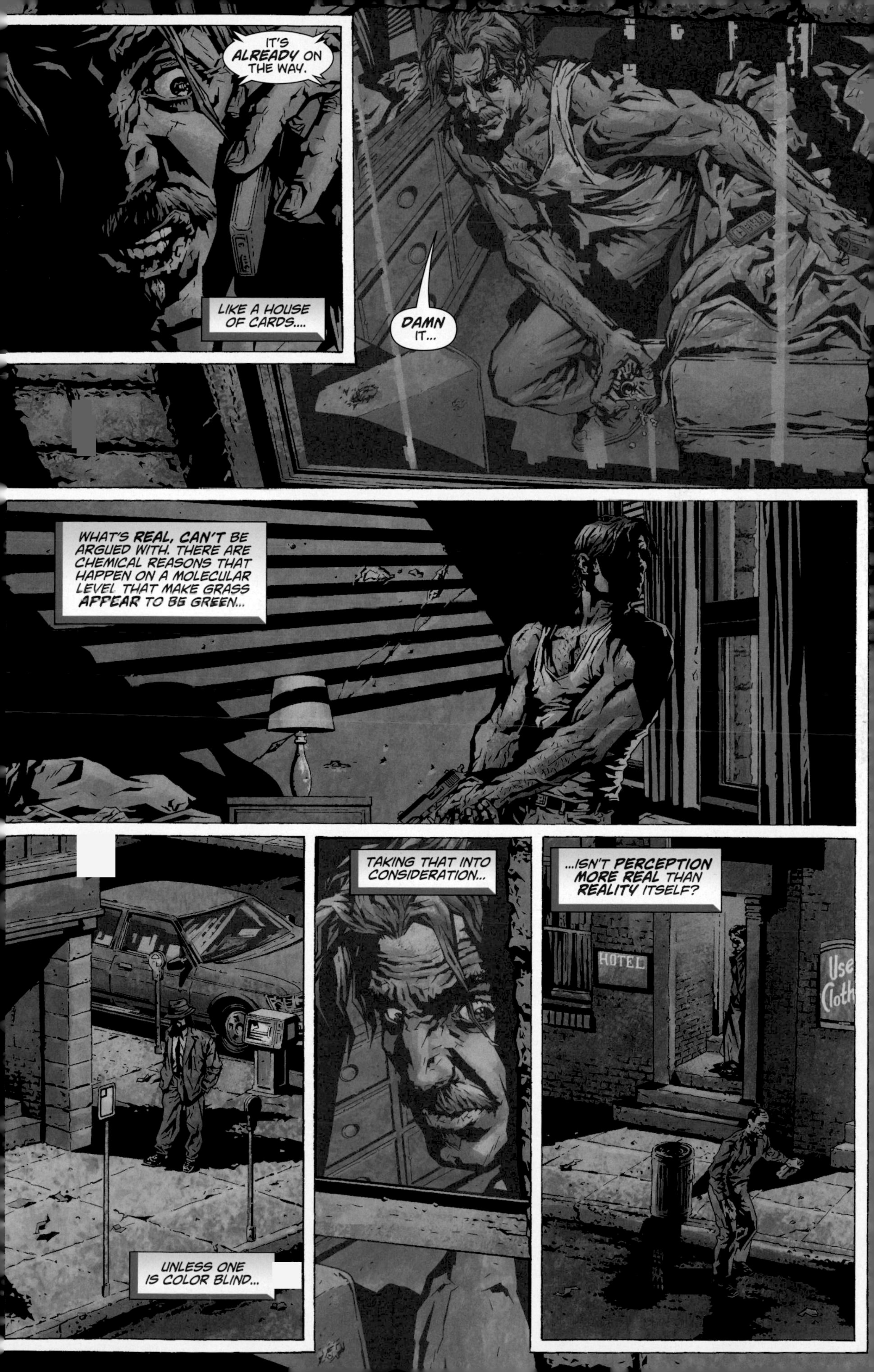
IT'S ALREADY ON THE WAY.
LIKE A HOUSE OF CARDS....
DAMN IT...
WHAT'S REAL, CAN'T BE ARGUED WITH. THERE ARE CHEMICAL REASONS THAT HAPPEN ON A MOLECULAR LEVEL THAT MAKE GRASS APPEAR TO BE GREEN...
UNLESS ONE IS COLOR BLIND...
TAKING THAT INTO CONSIDERATION...
...ISN'T PERCEPTION MORE REAL THAN REALITY ITSELF?
HOTEL

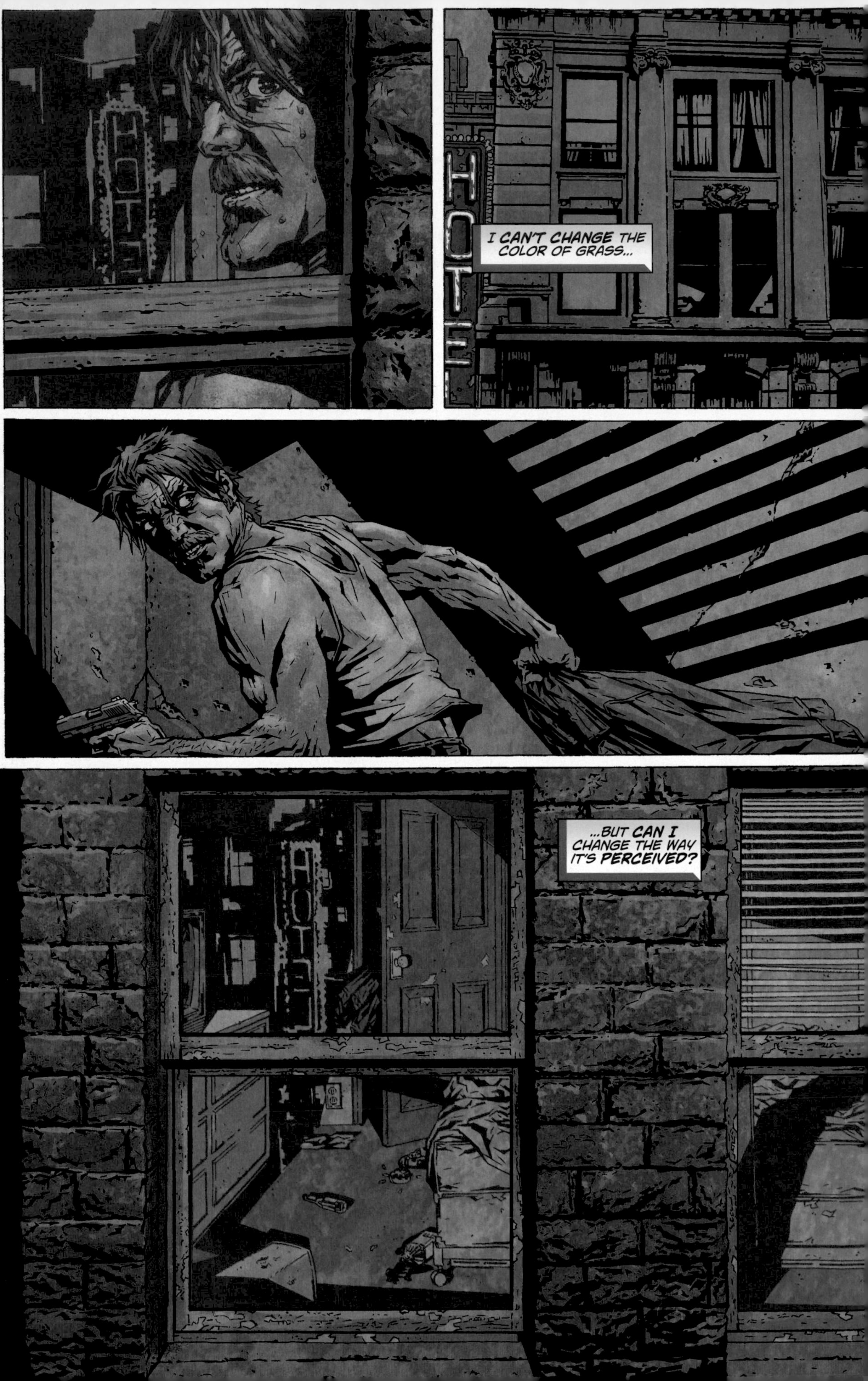

I CAN'T CHANGE THE COLOR OF GRASS...
...BUT CAN I CHANGE THE WAY IT'S PERCEIVED?

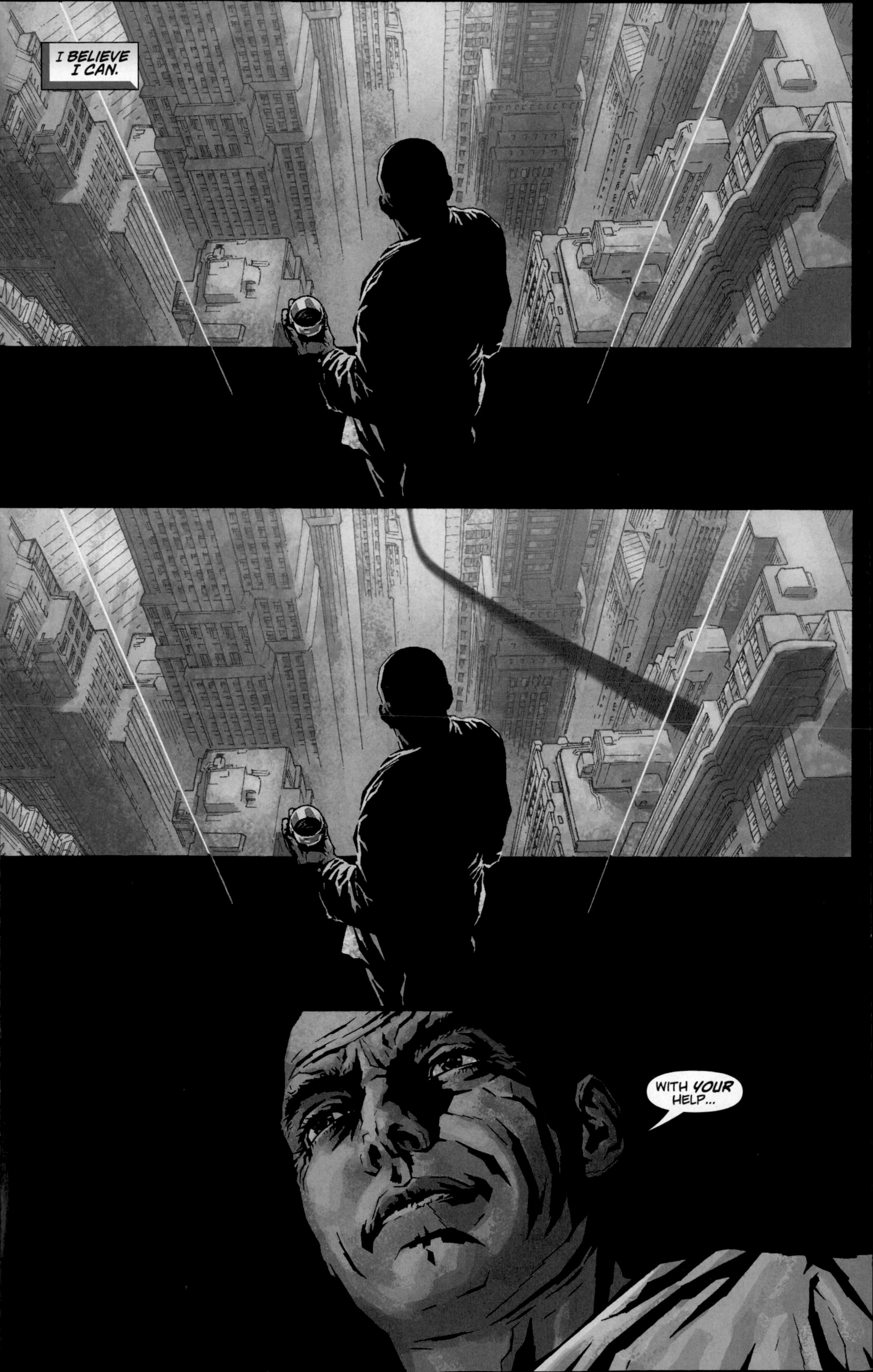
I BELIEVE I CAN.
WITH YOUR HELP...

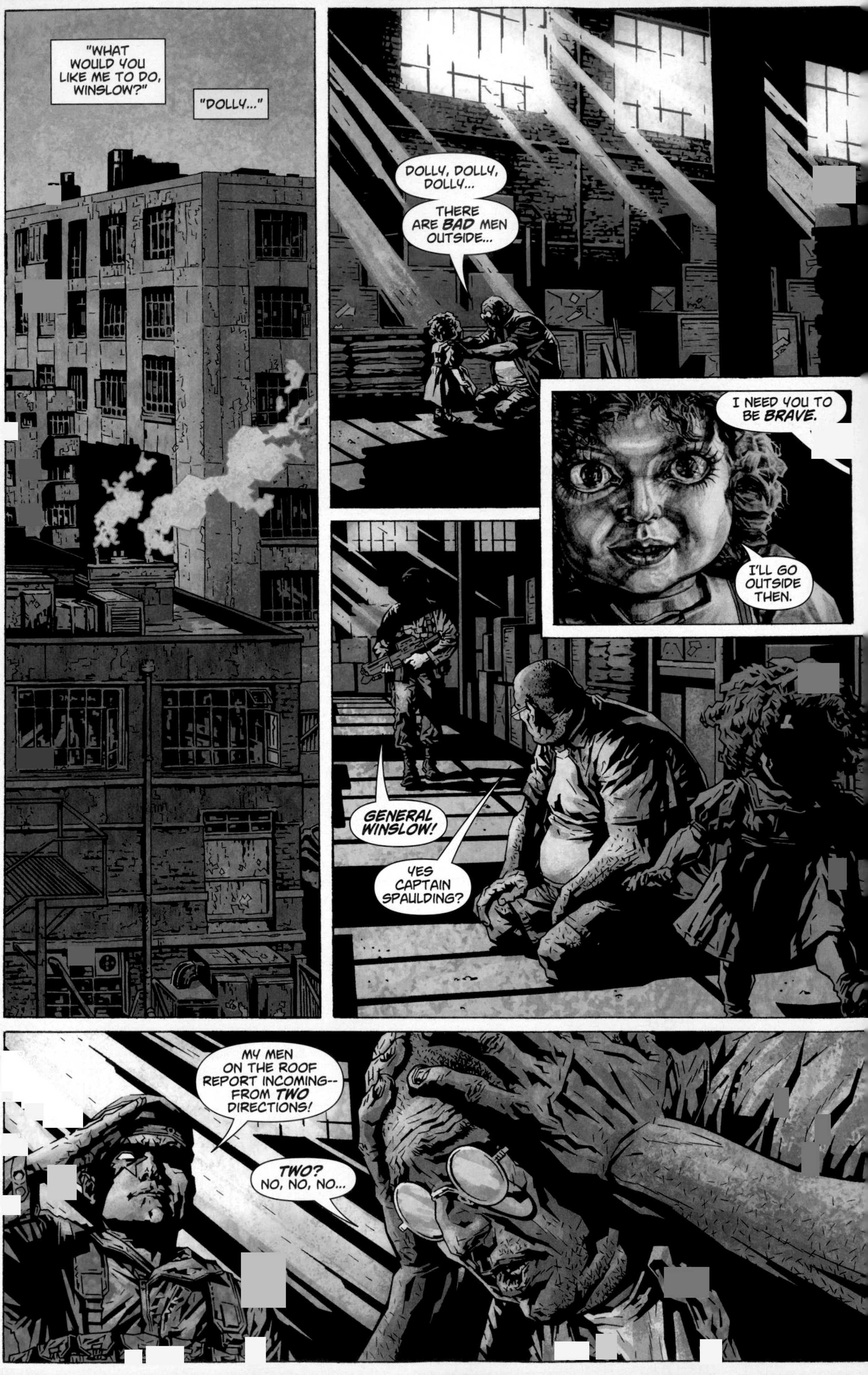
"WHAT WOULD YOU LIKE ME TO DO, WINSLOW?"
"DOLLY..."
DOLLY, DOLLY, DOLLY...
THERE ARE BAD MEN OUTSIDE...
I NEED YOU TO BE BRAVE.
I'LL GO OUTSIDE THEN.
GENERAL WINSLOW!
YES CAPTAIN SPAULDING?
MY MEN ON THE ROOF REPORT INCOMING-- FROM TWO DIRECTIONS!
TWO? NO, NO, NO...

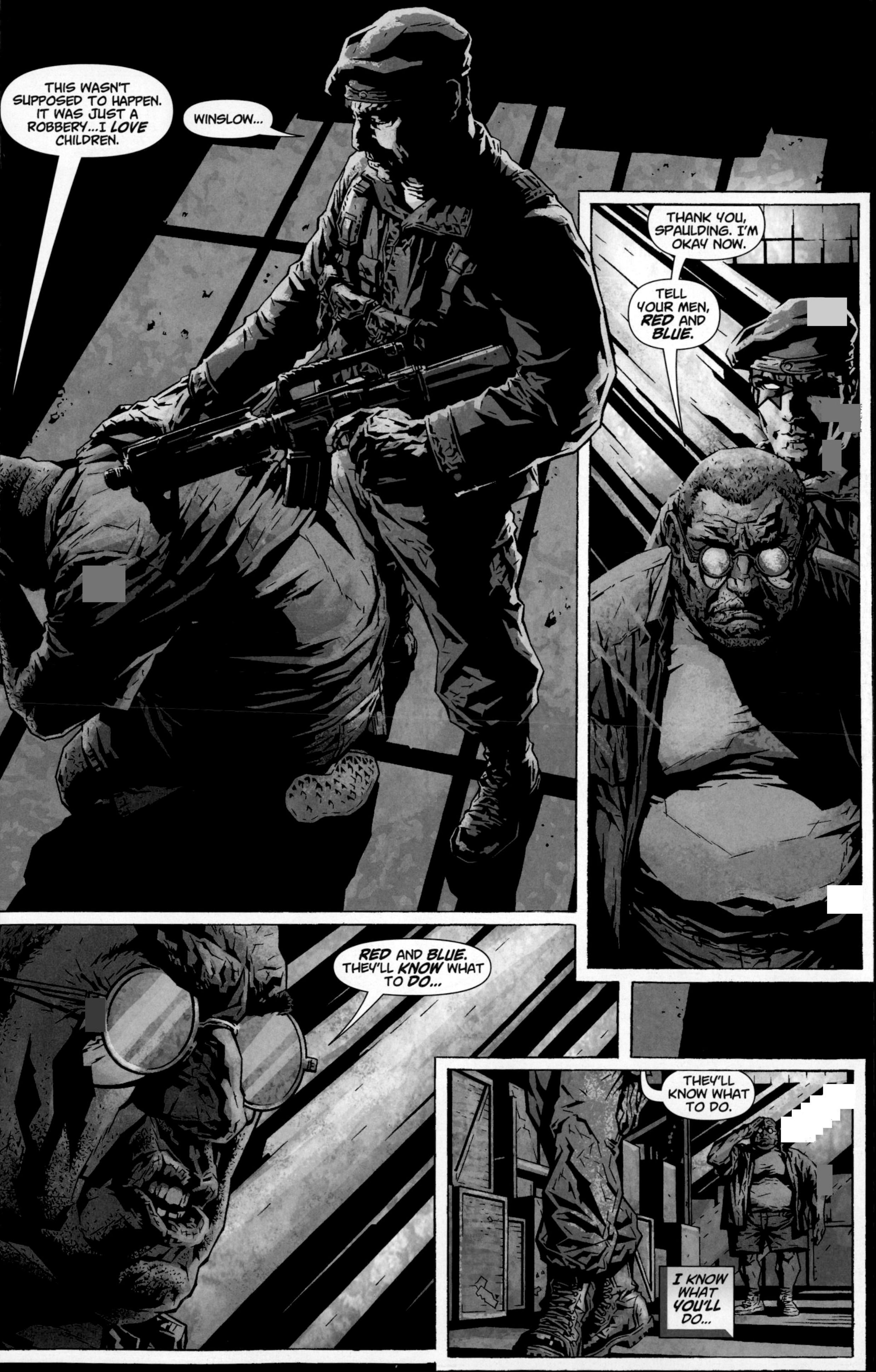
THIS WASN'T SUPPOSED TO HAPPEN. IT WAS JUST A ROBBERY...I LOVE CHILDREN.
WINSLOW...
THANK YOU, SPAULDING. I'M OKAY NOW.
TELL YOUR MEN, RED AND BLUE.
RED AND BLUE. THEY'LL KNOW WHAT TO DO...
THEY'LL KNOW WHAT TO DO.
I KNOW WHAT YOU'LL DO...

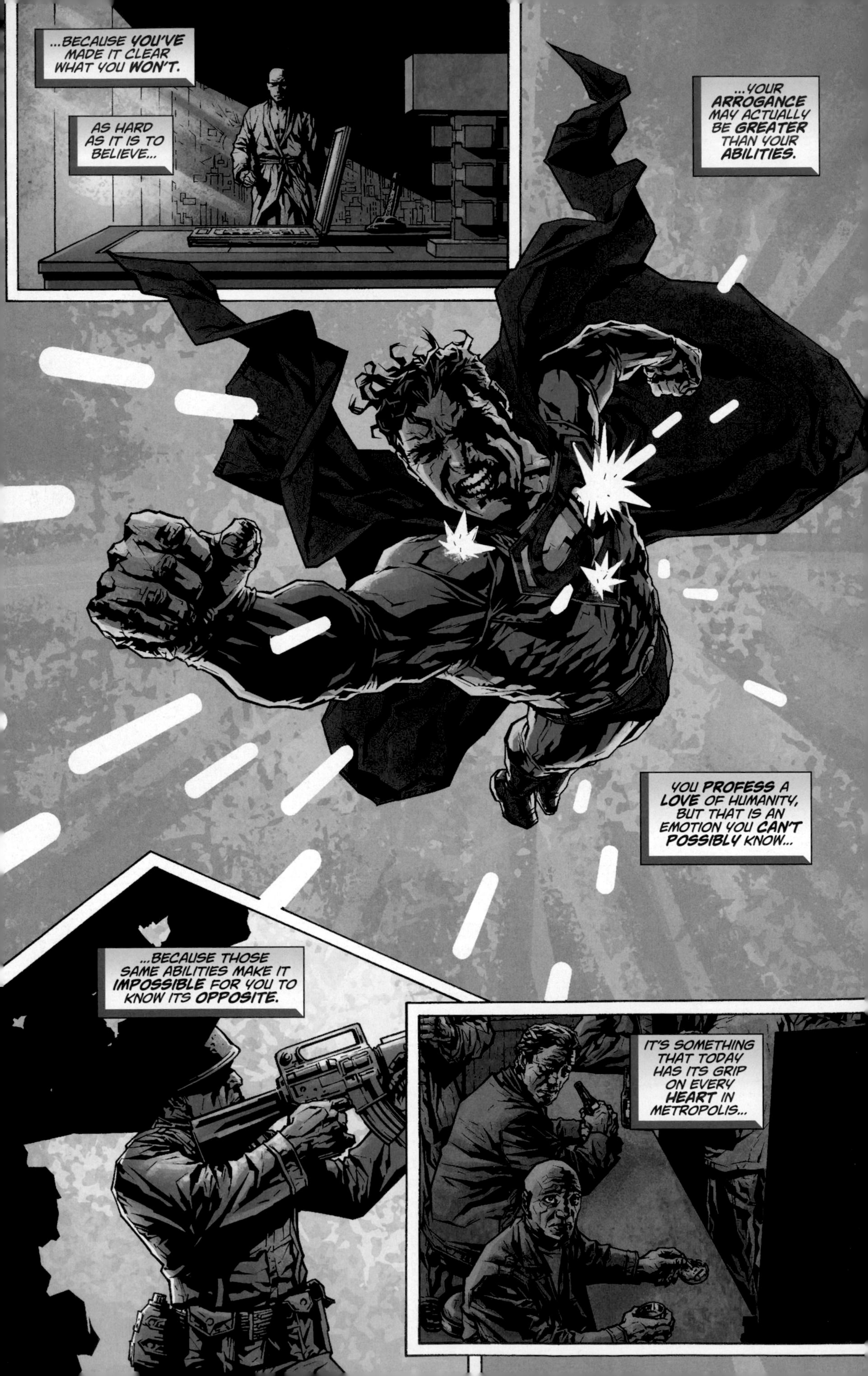
...BECAUSE YOU'VE MADE IT CLEAR WHAT YOU WON'T.
AS HARD AS IT IS TO BELIEVE...
...YOUR ARROGANCE MAY ACTUALLY BE GREATER THAN YOUR ABILITIES.
YOU PROFESS A LOVE OF HUMANITY, BUT THAT IS AN EMOTION YOU CAN'T POSSIBLY KNOW...
...BECAUSE THOSE SAME ABILITIES MAKE IT IMPOSSIBLE FOR YOU TO KNOW ITS OPPOSITE.
IT'S SOMETHING THAT TODAY HAS ITS GRIP ON EVERY HEART IN METROPOLIS...

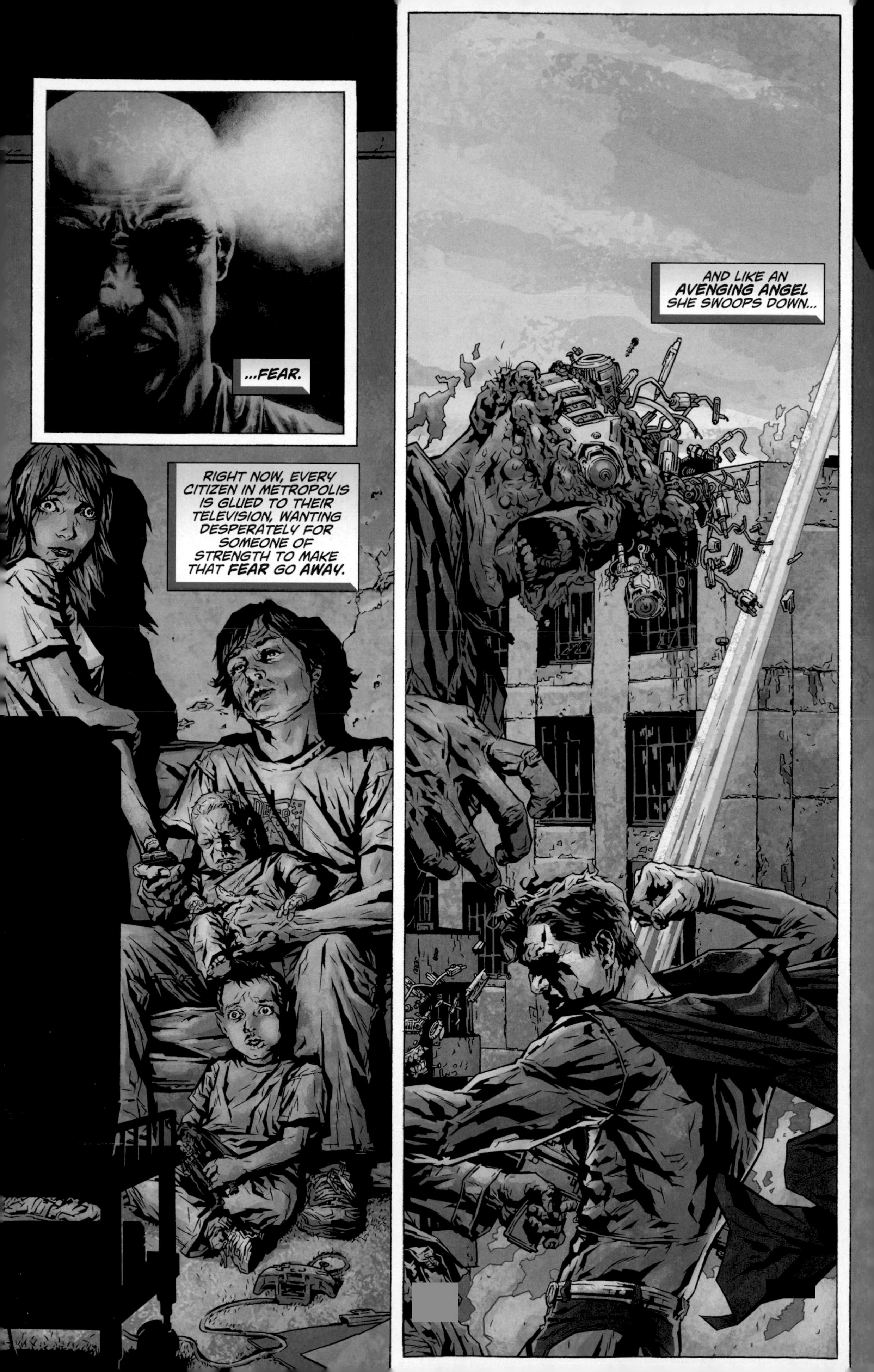
...FEAR.
RIGHT NOW, EVERY CITIZEN IN METROPOLIS IS GLUED TO THEIR TELEVISION, WANTING DESPERATELY FOR SOMEONE OF STRENGTH TO MAKE THAT FEAR GO AWAY.
AND LIKE AN AVENGING ANGEL SHE SWOOPS DOWN...

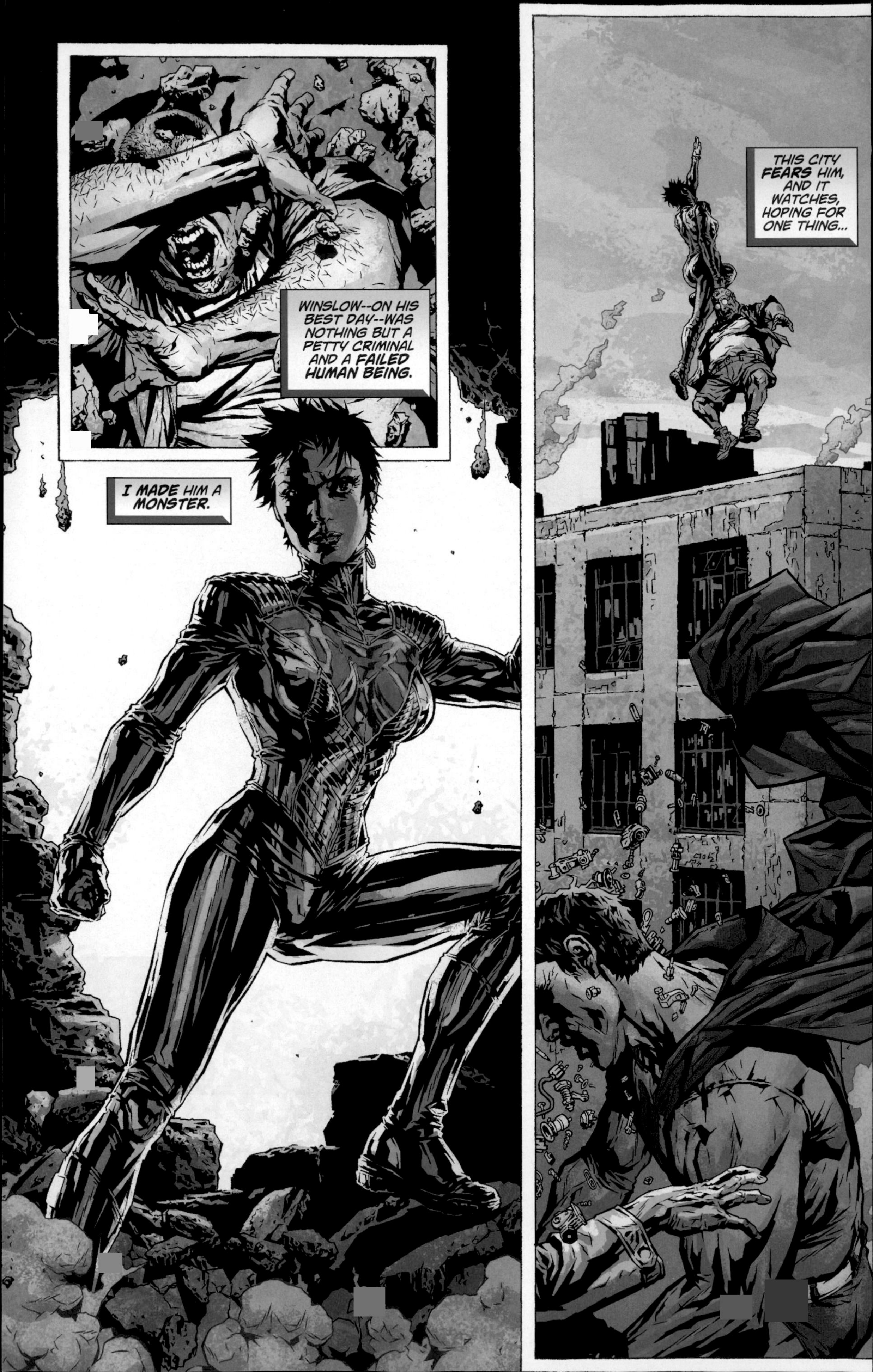
WINSLOW--ON HIS BEST DAY--WAS NOTHING BUT A PETTY CRIMINAL AND A FAILED HUMAN BEING.
I MADE HIM A MONSTER.
THIS CITY FEARS HIM, AND IT WATCHES, HOPING FOR ONE THING...

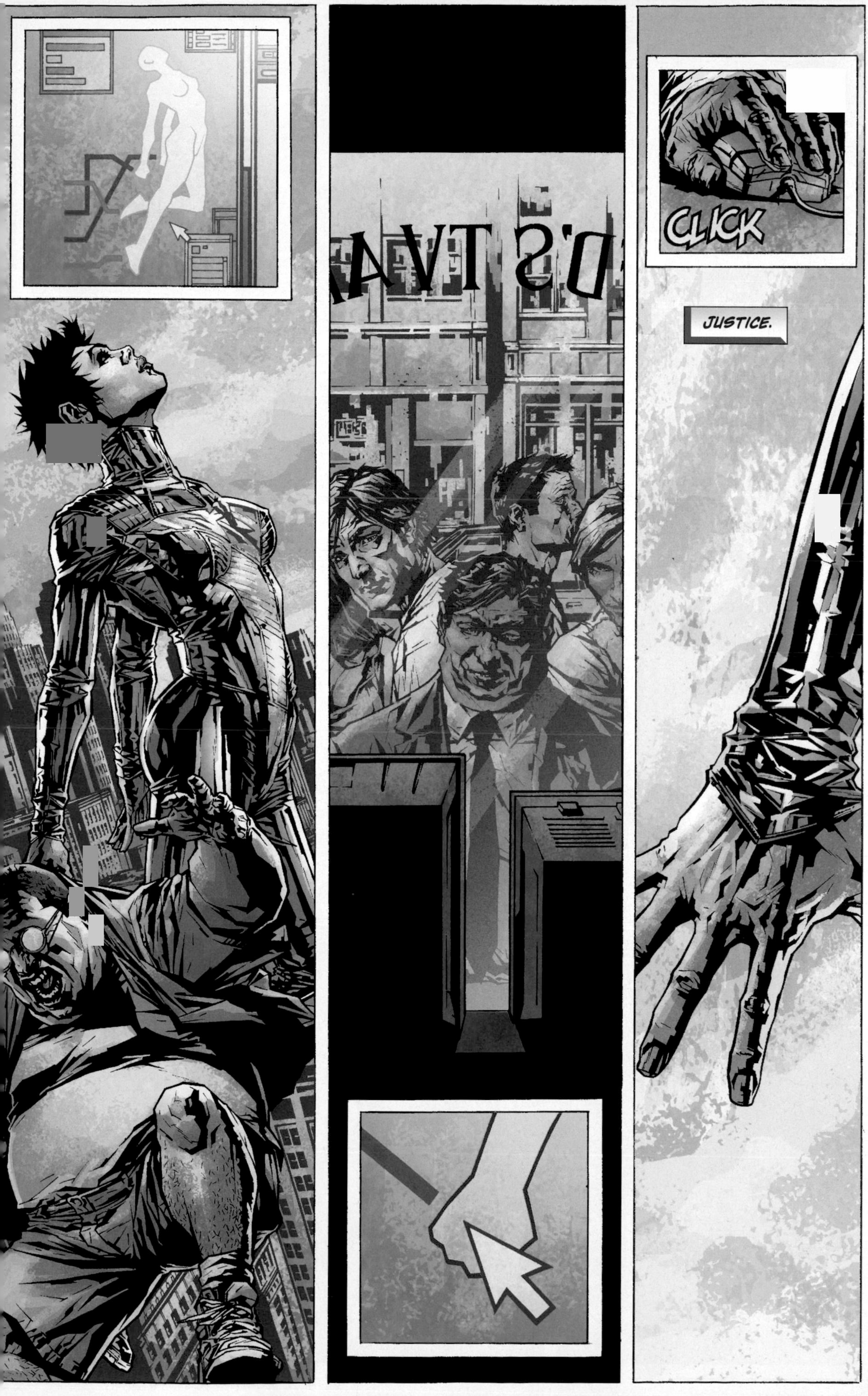
CLICK
JUSTICE.

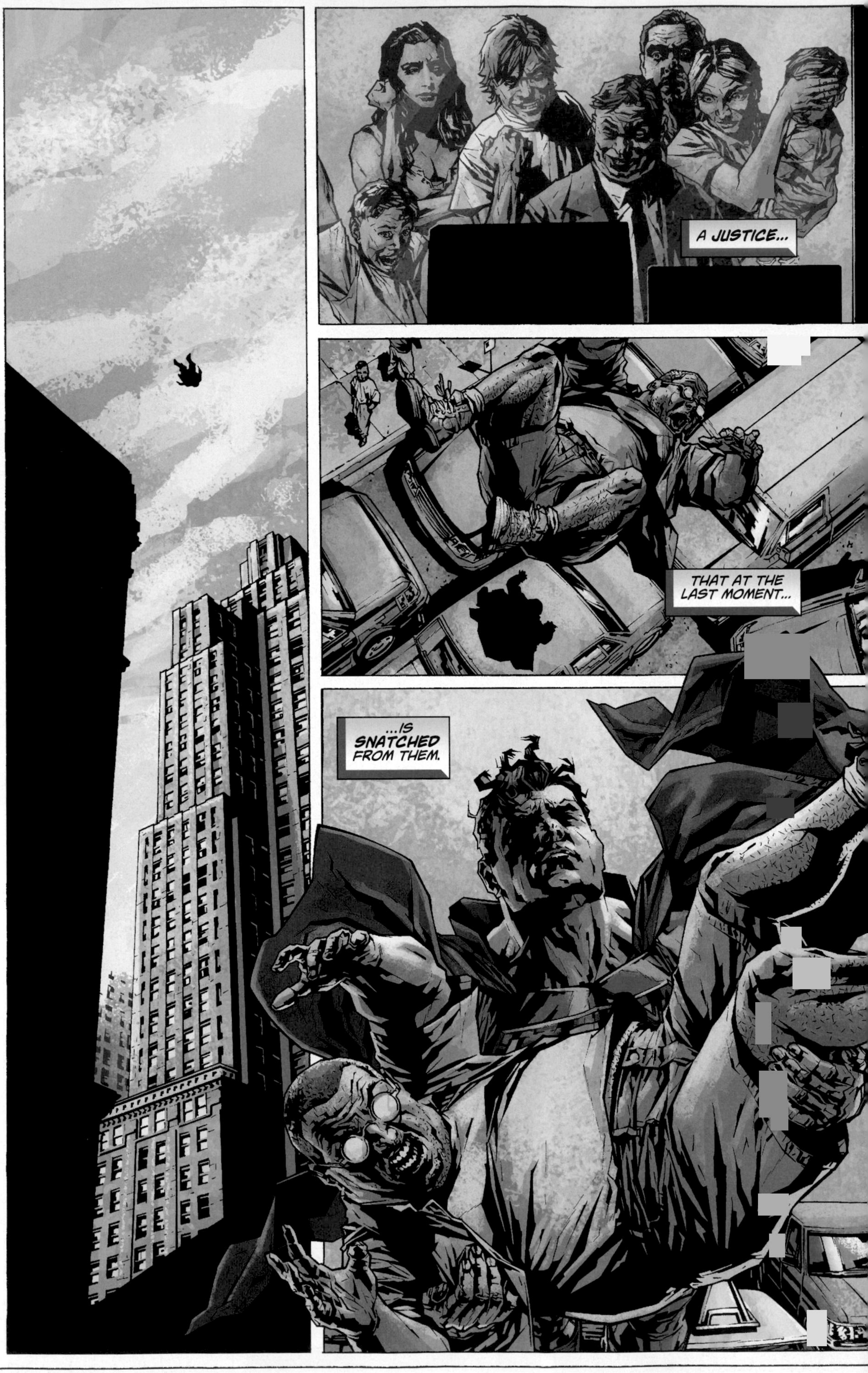
[redacted]
A JUSTICE...
[redacted]
THAT AT THE LAST MOMENT...
...IS SNATCHED FROM THEM.

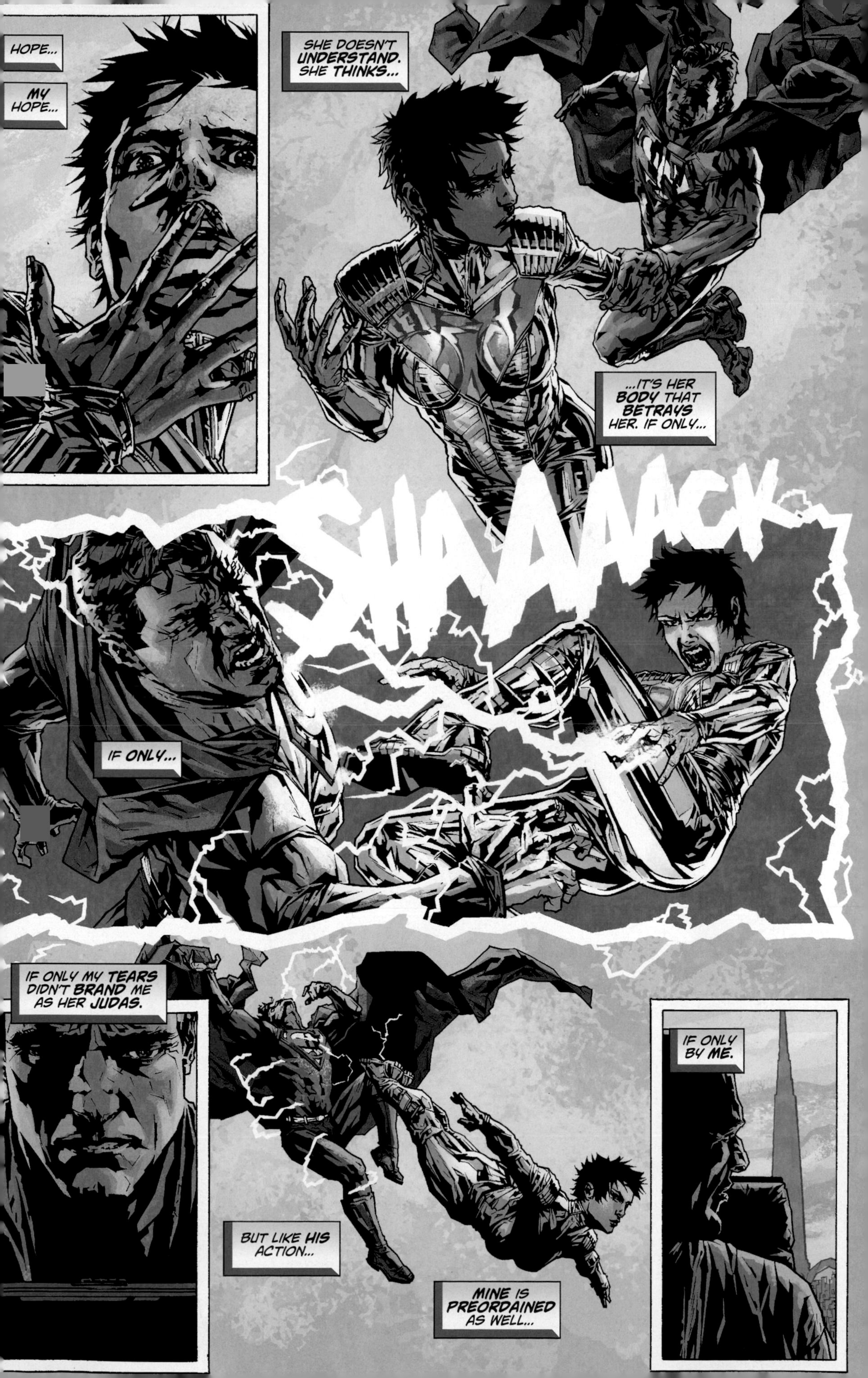
HOPE...
MY HOPE...
SHE DOESN'T UNDERSTAND. SHE THINKS...
...IT'S HER BODY THAT BETRAYS HER. IF ONLY...
SHAAAACK
IF ONLY...
IF ONLY MY TEARS DIDN'T BRAND ME AS HER JUDAS.
BUT LIKE HIS ACTION...
MINE IS PREORDAINED AS WELL...
IF ONLY BY ME.

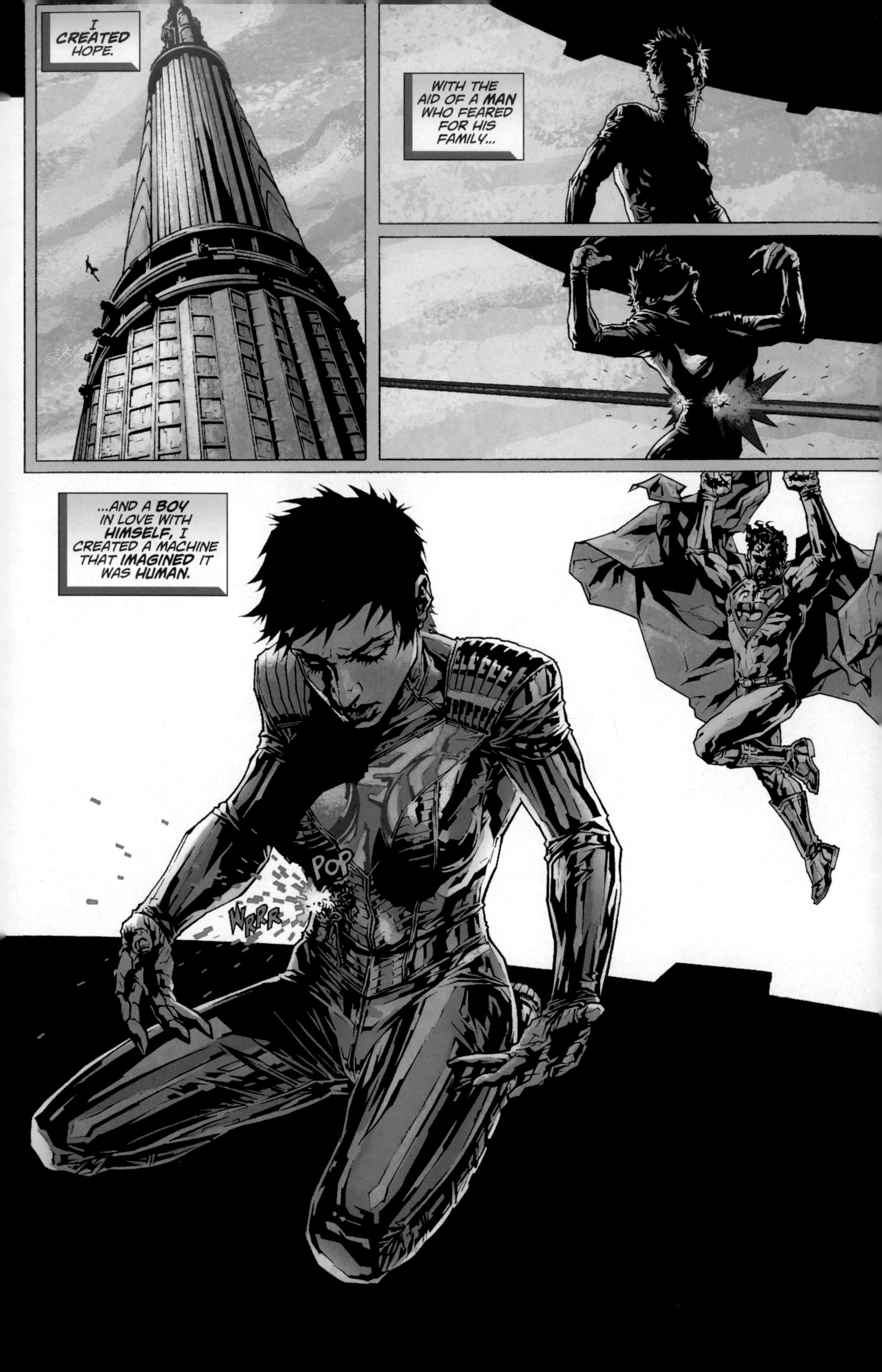
I CREATED HOPE.
WITH THE AID OF A MAN WHO FEARED FOR HIS FAMILY...
...AND A BOY IN LOVE WITH HIMSELF, I CREATED A MACHINE THAT IMAGINED IT WAS HUMAN.
POP
WRRR

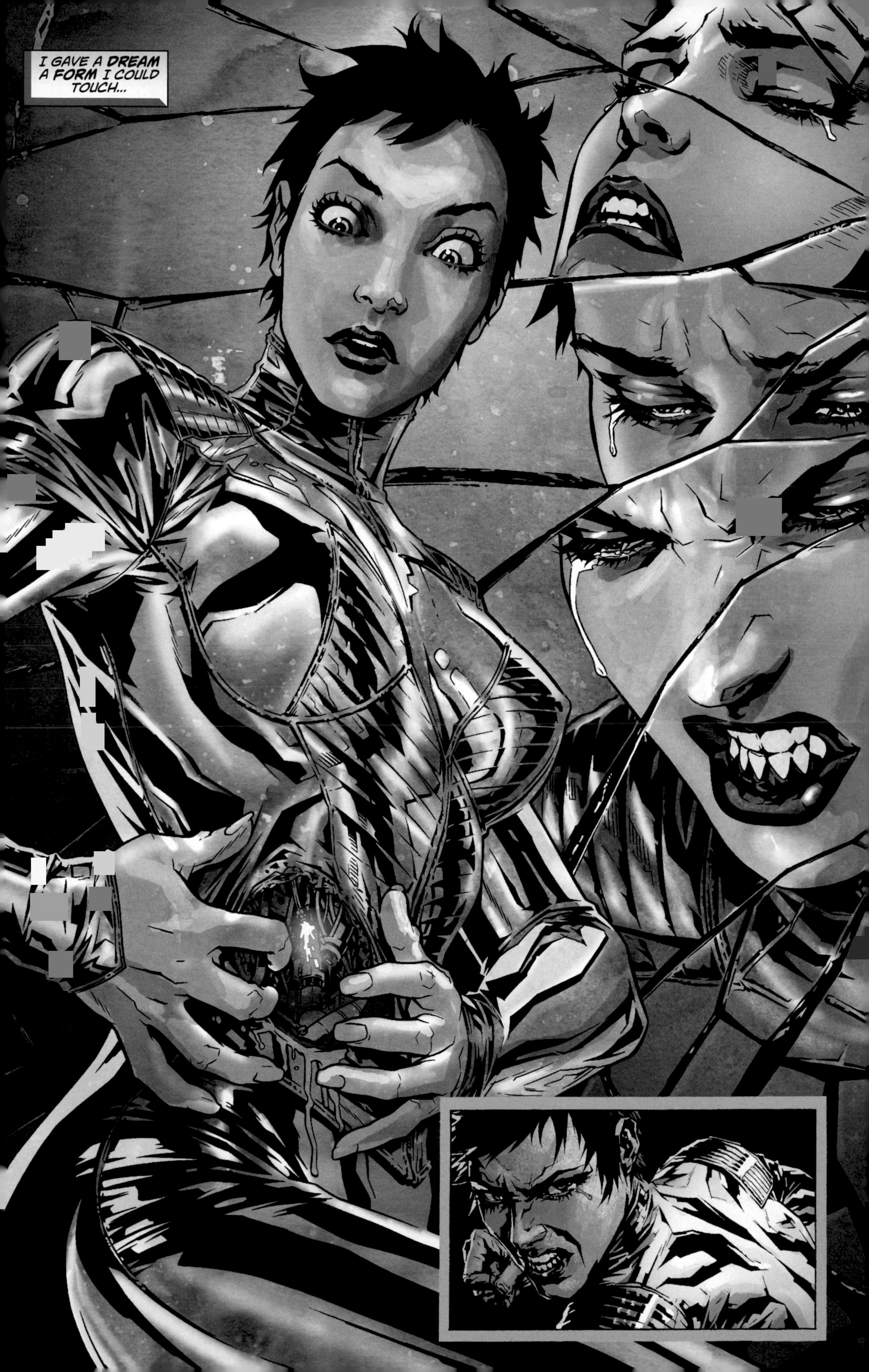
I GAVE A DREAM A FORM I COULD TOUCH...

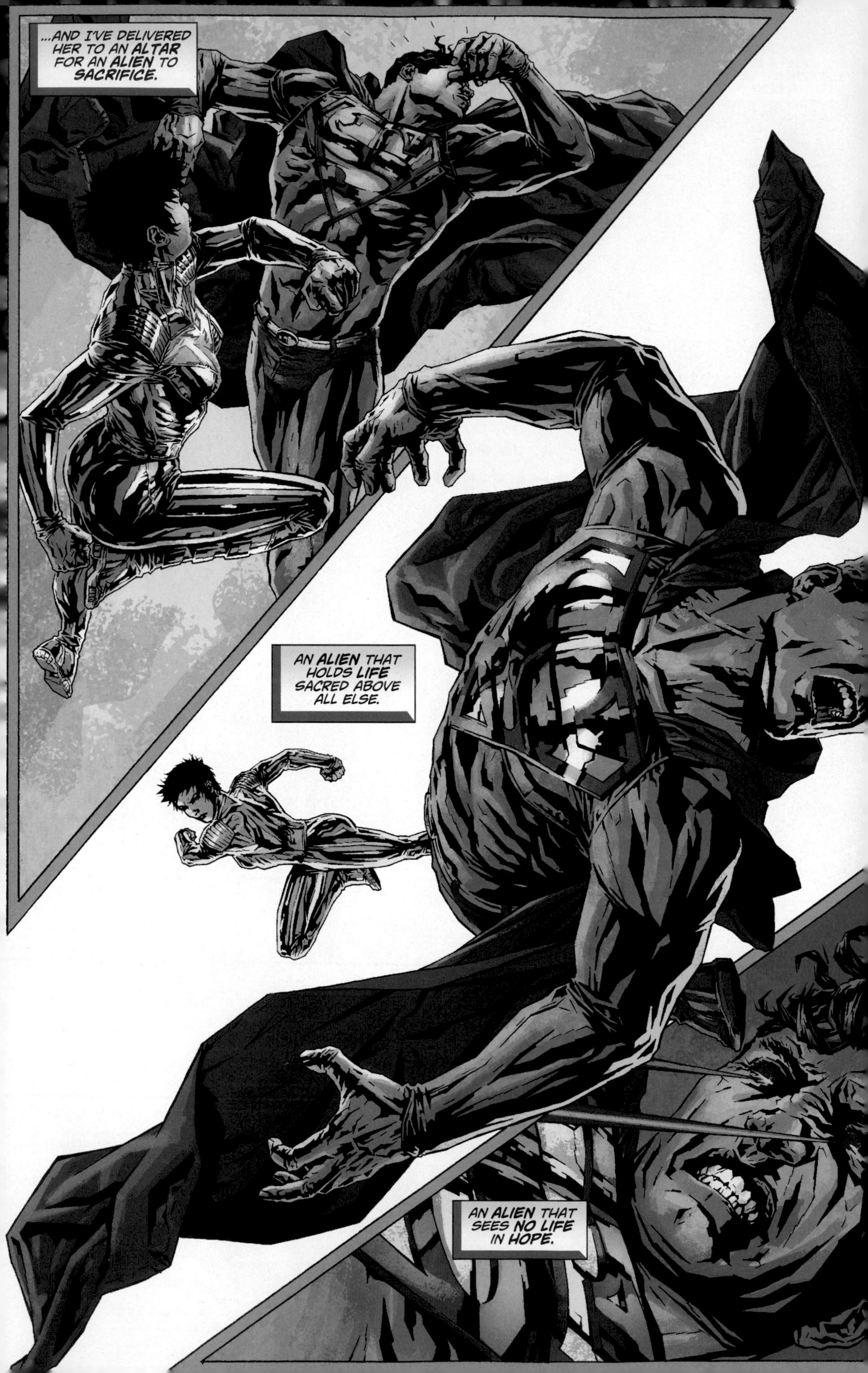
...AND I'VE DELIVERED HER TO AN ALTAR FOR AN ALIEN TO SACRIFICE.
AN ALIEN THAT HOLDS LIFE SACRED ABOVE ALL ELSE.
AN ALIEN THAT SEES NO LIFE IN HOPE.

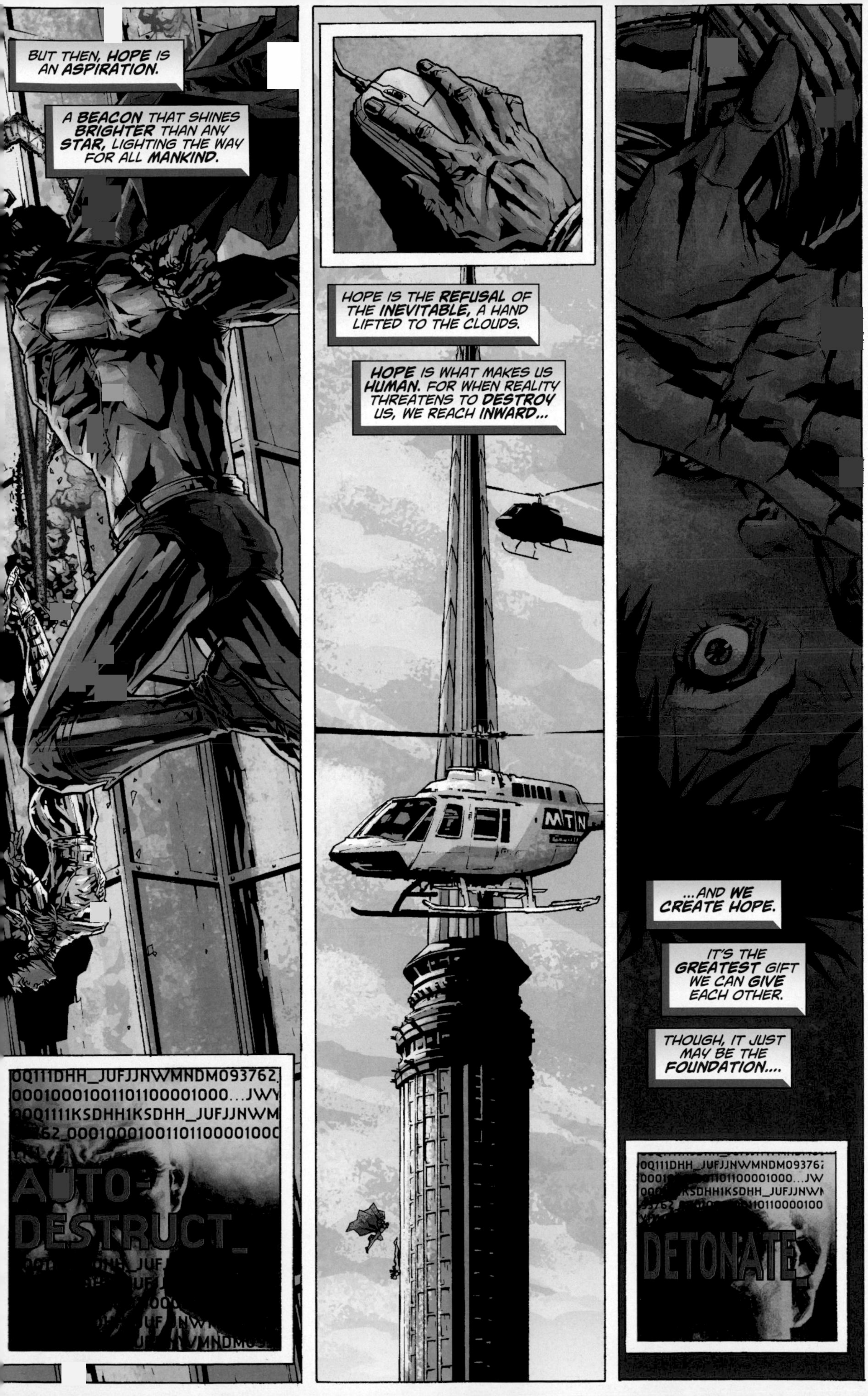
BUT THEN, HOPE IS AN ASPIRATION.
A BEACON THAT SHINES BRIGHTER THAN ANY STAR, LIGHTING THE WAY FOR ALL MANKIND.
0Q111DHH_JUFJJNWMNDM093762,
0001000100110110000100O...JWY
0001111KSDHH1KSDHH_JUFJJNWM
AUTO-DESTRUCT_
HOPE IS THE REFUSAL OF THE INEVITABLE, A HAND LIFTED TO THE CLOUDS.
HOPE IS WHAT MAKES US HUMAN. FOR WHEN REALITY THREATENS TO DESTROY US, WE REACH INWARD...
MTN
...AND WE CREATE HOPE.
IT'S THE GREATEST GIFT WE CAN GIVE EACH OTHER.
THOUGH, IT JUST MAY BE THE FOUNDATION....
0Q111DHH_JUFJJNWMNDM09376
DETONATE_

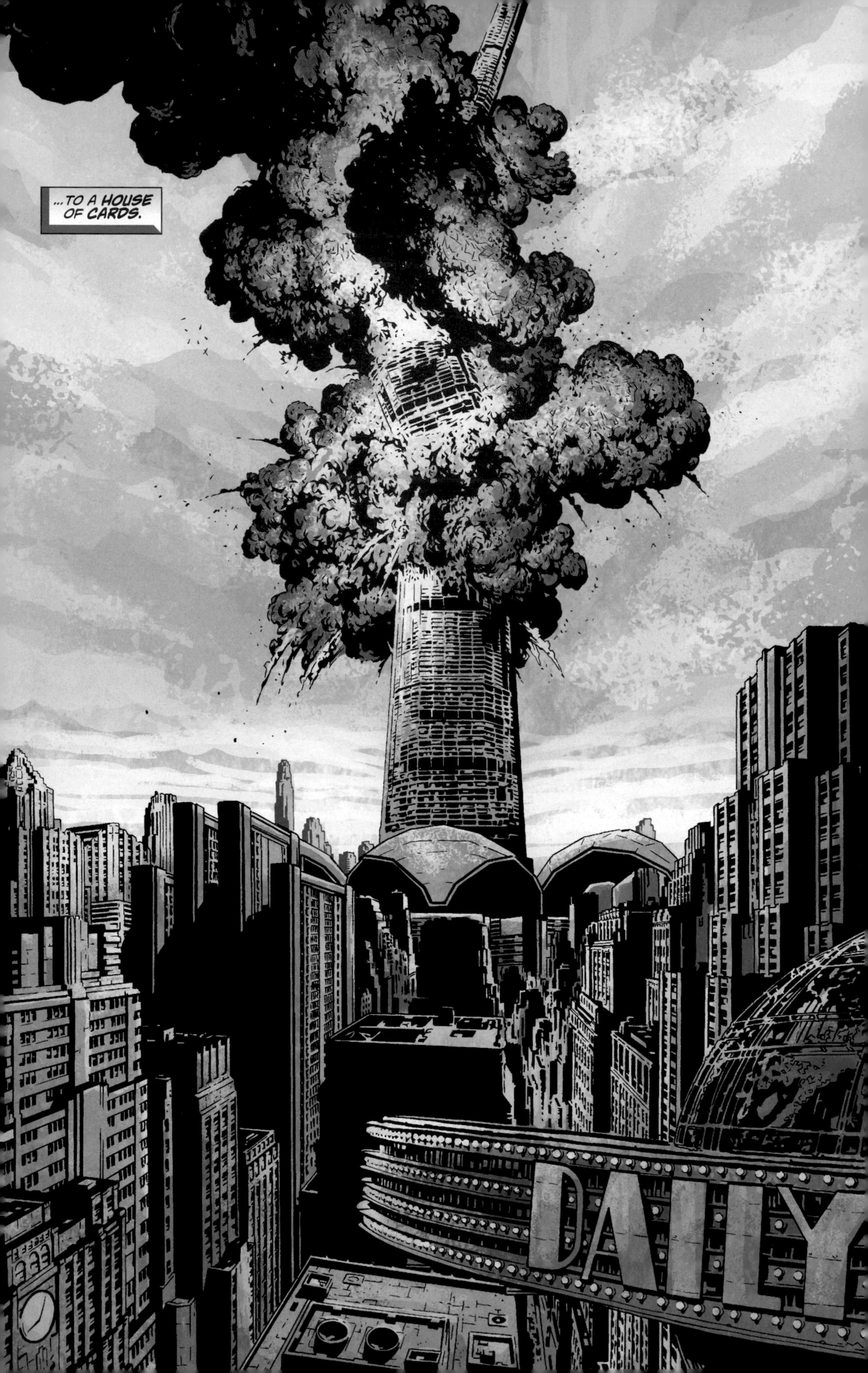
...TO A HOUSE OF CARDS.
DAILY

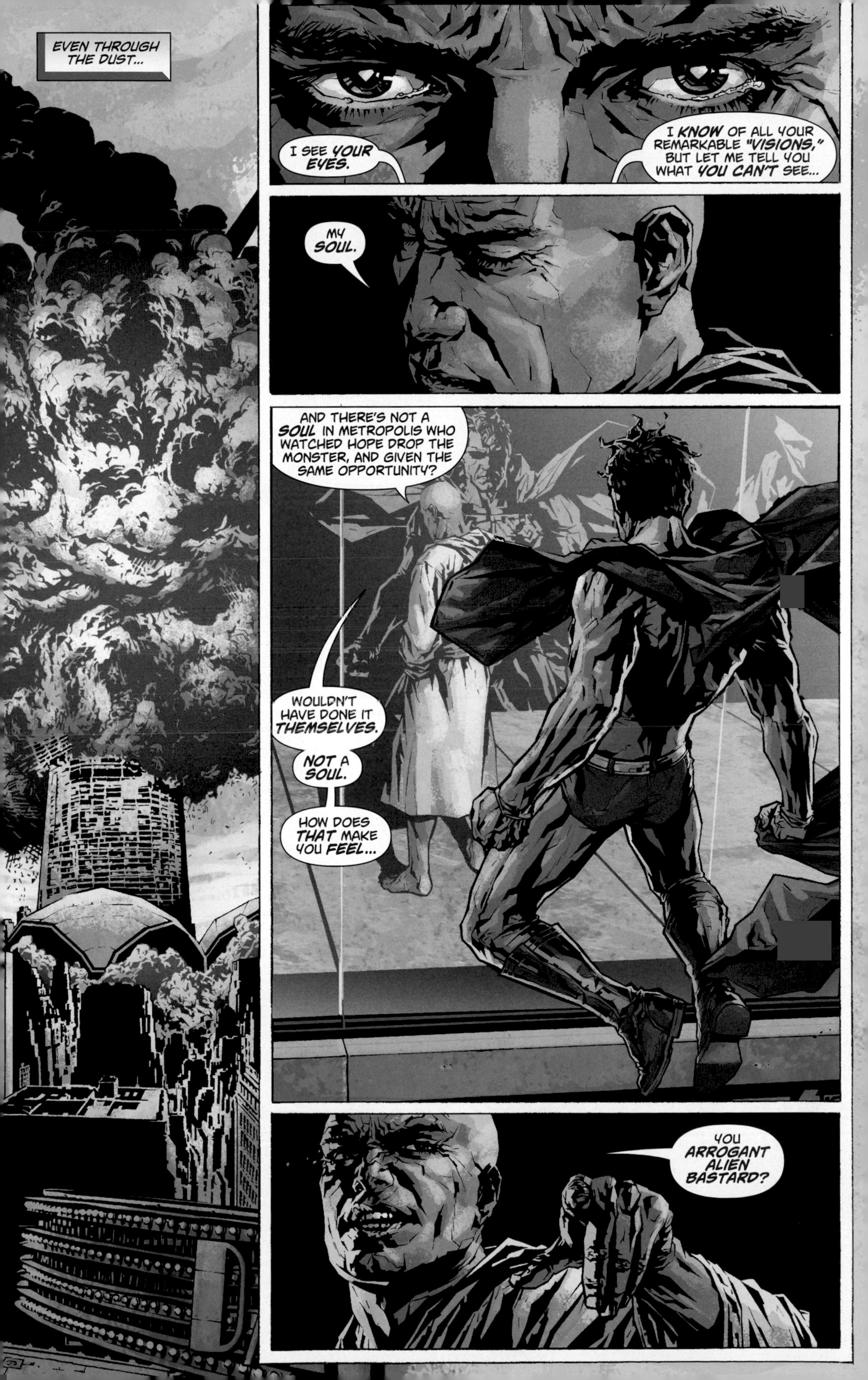
EVEN THROUGH THE DUST...
I SEE YOUR EYES.
I KNOW OF ALL YOUR REMARKABLE "VISIONS," BUT LET ME TELL YOU WHAT YOU CAN'T SEE...
MY SOUL.
AND THERE'S NOT A SOUL IN METROPOLIS WHO WATCHED HOPE DROP THE MONSTER, AND GIVEN THE SAME OPPORTUNITY?
WOULDN'T HAVE DONE IT THEMSELVES.
NOT A SOUL.
HOW DOES THAT MAKE YOU FEEL...
YOU ARROGANT ALIEN BASTARD?

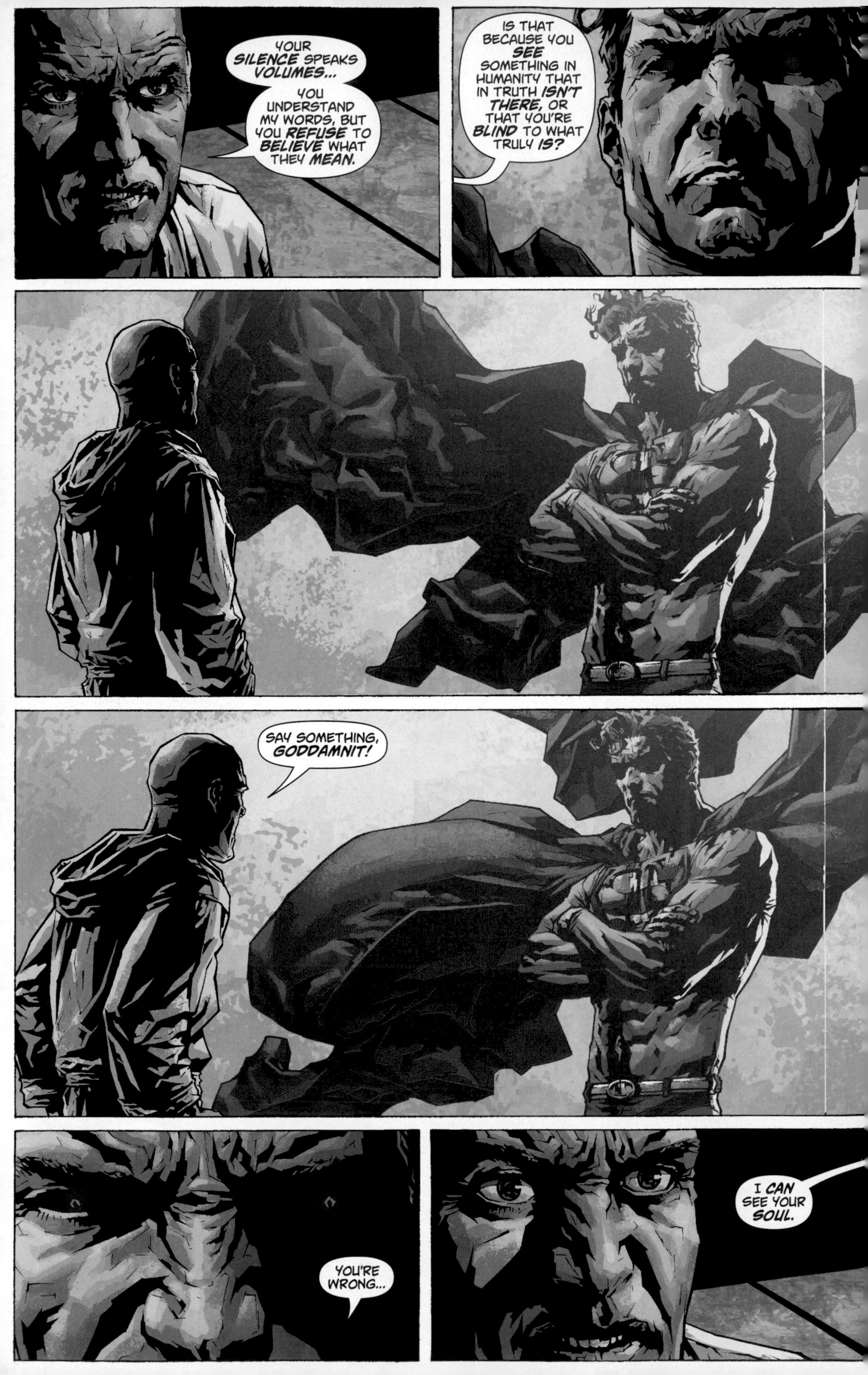
YOUR SILENCE SPEAKS VOLUMES...
YOU UNDERSTAND MY WORDS, BUT YOU REFUSE TO BELIEVE WHAT THEY MEAN.
IS THAT BECAUSE YOU SEE SOMETHING IN HUMANITY THAT IN TRUTH ISN'T THERE, OR THAT YOU'RE BLIND TO WHAT TRULY IS?
SAY SOMETHING, GODDAMNIT!
YOU'RE WRONG...
I CAN SEE YOUR SOUL.

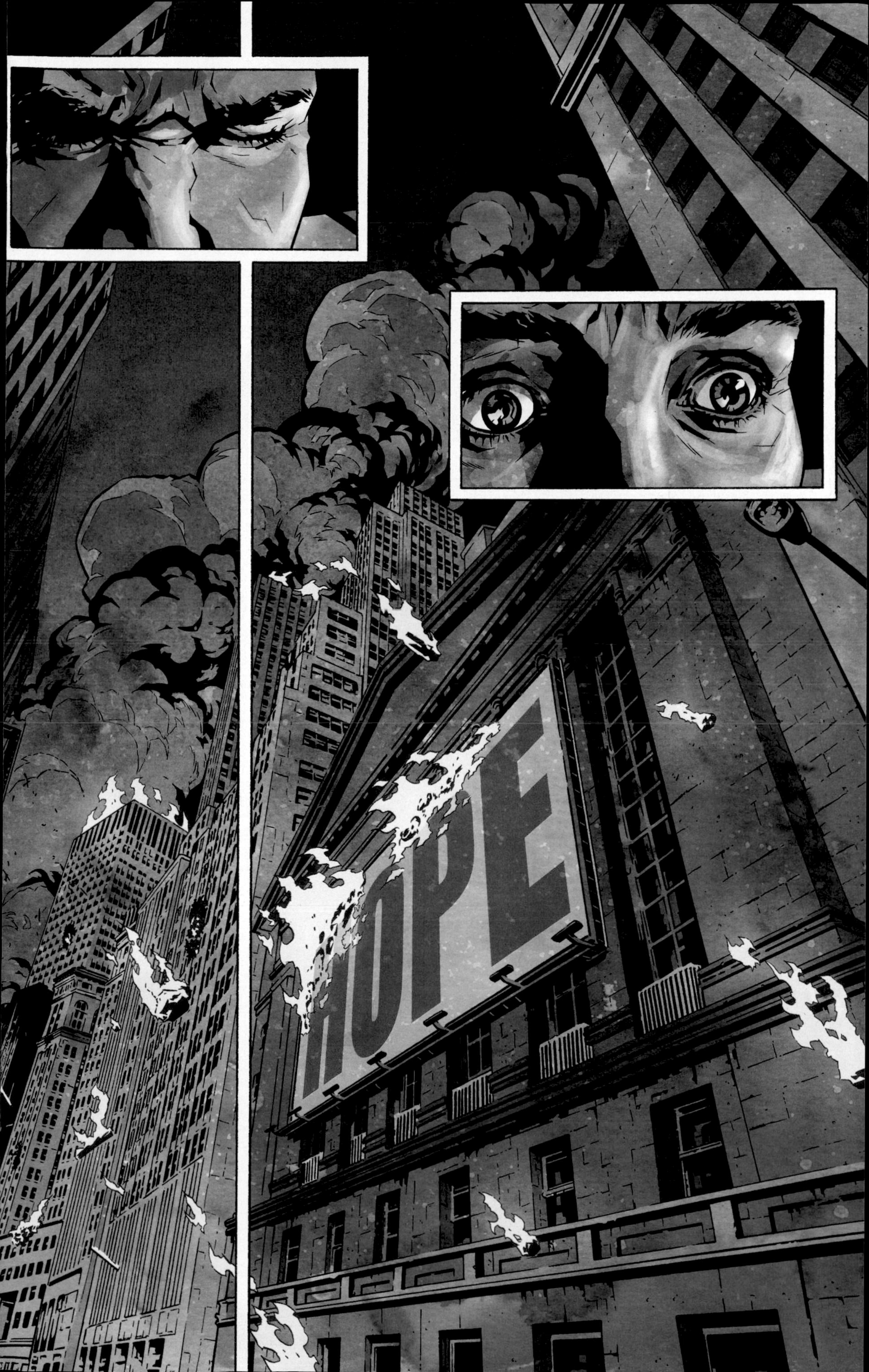
HOPE

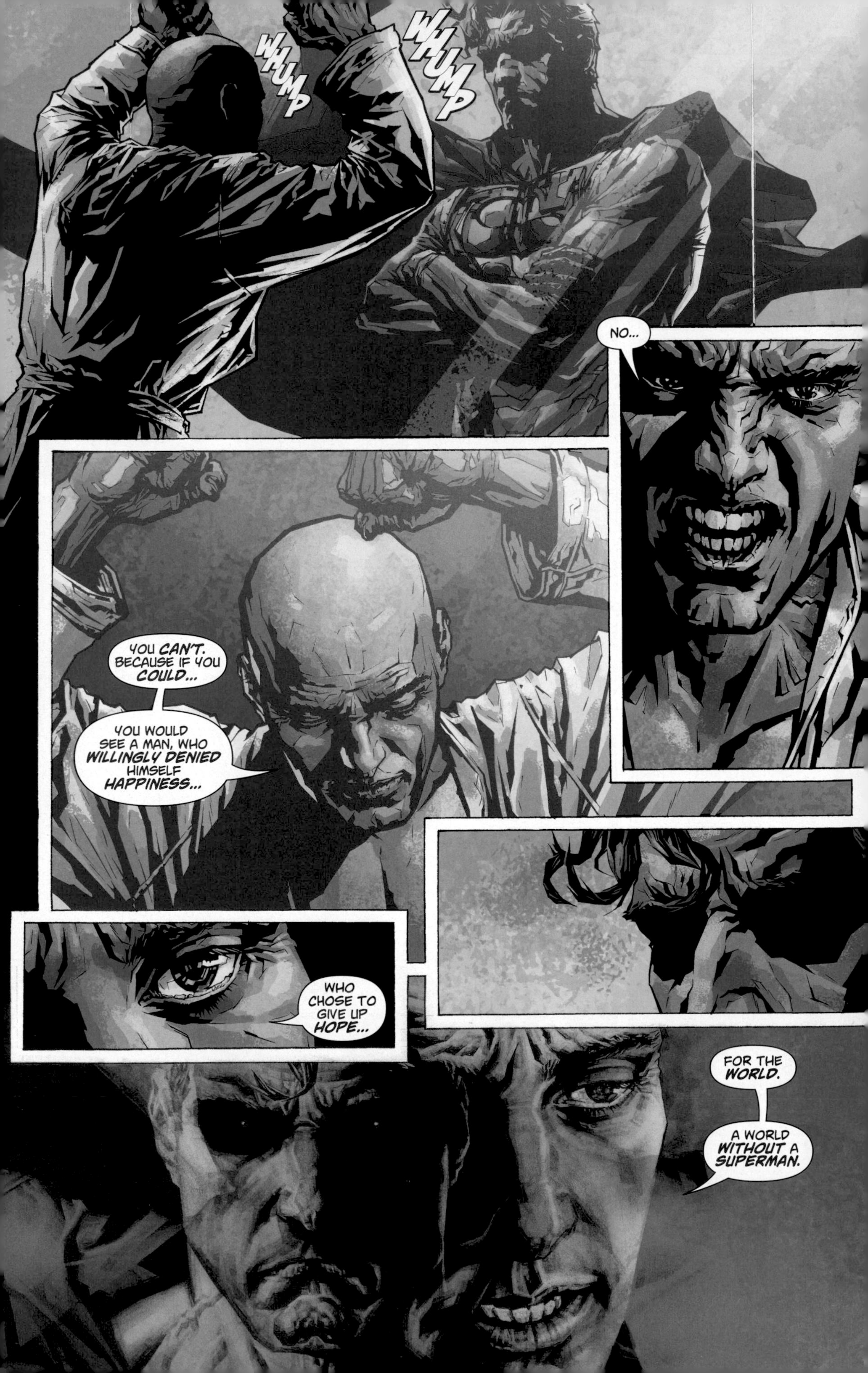
WHUMP
WHUMP
NO...
YOU CAN'T. BECAUSE IF YOU COULD...
YOU WOULD SEE A MAN, WHO WILLINGLY DENIED HIMSELF HAPPINESS...
WHO CHOSE TO GIVE UP HOPE...
FOR THE WORLD.
A WORLD WITHOUT A SUPERMAN.

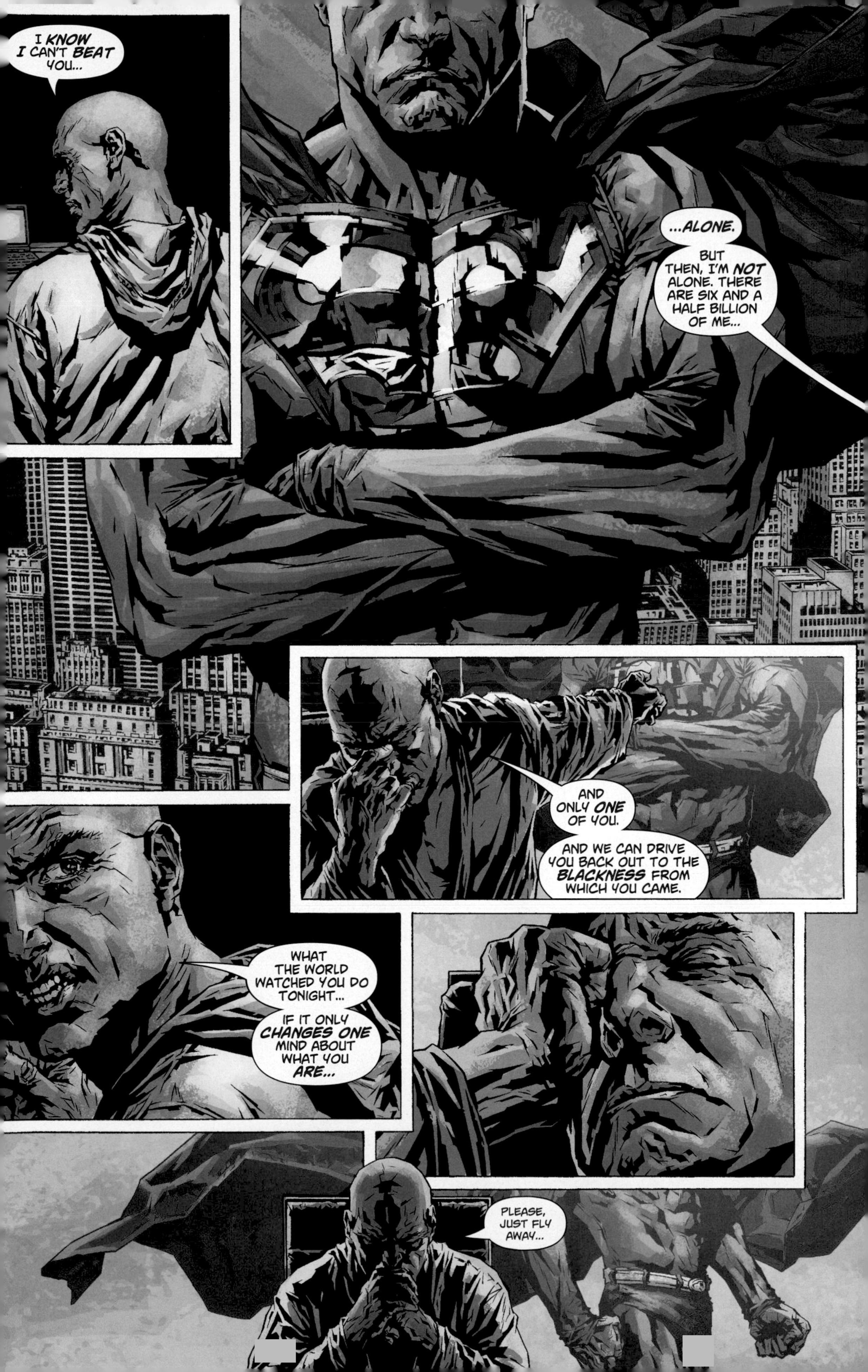
I KNOW I CAN'T BEAT YOU...
...ALONE.
BUT THEN, I'M NOT ALONE. THERE ARE SIX AND A HALF BILLION OF ME...
AND ONLY ONE OF YOU.
AND WE CAN DRIVE YOU BACK OUT TO THE BLACKNESS FROM WHICH YOU CAME.
WHAT THE WORLD WATCHED YOU DO TONIGHT...
IF IT ONLY CHANGES ONE MIND ABOUT WHAT YOU ARE...
PLEASE, JUST FLY AWAY...

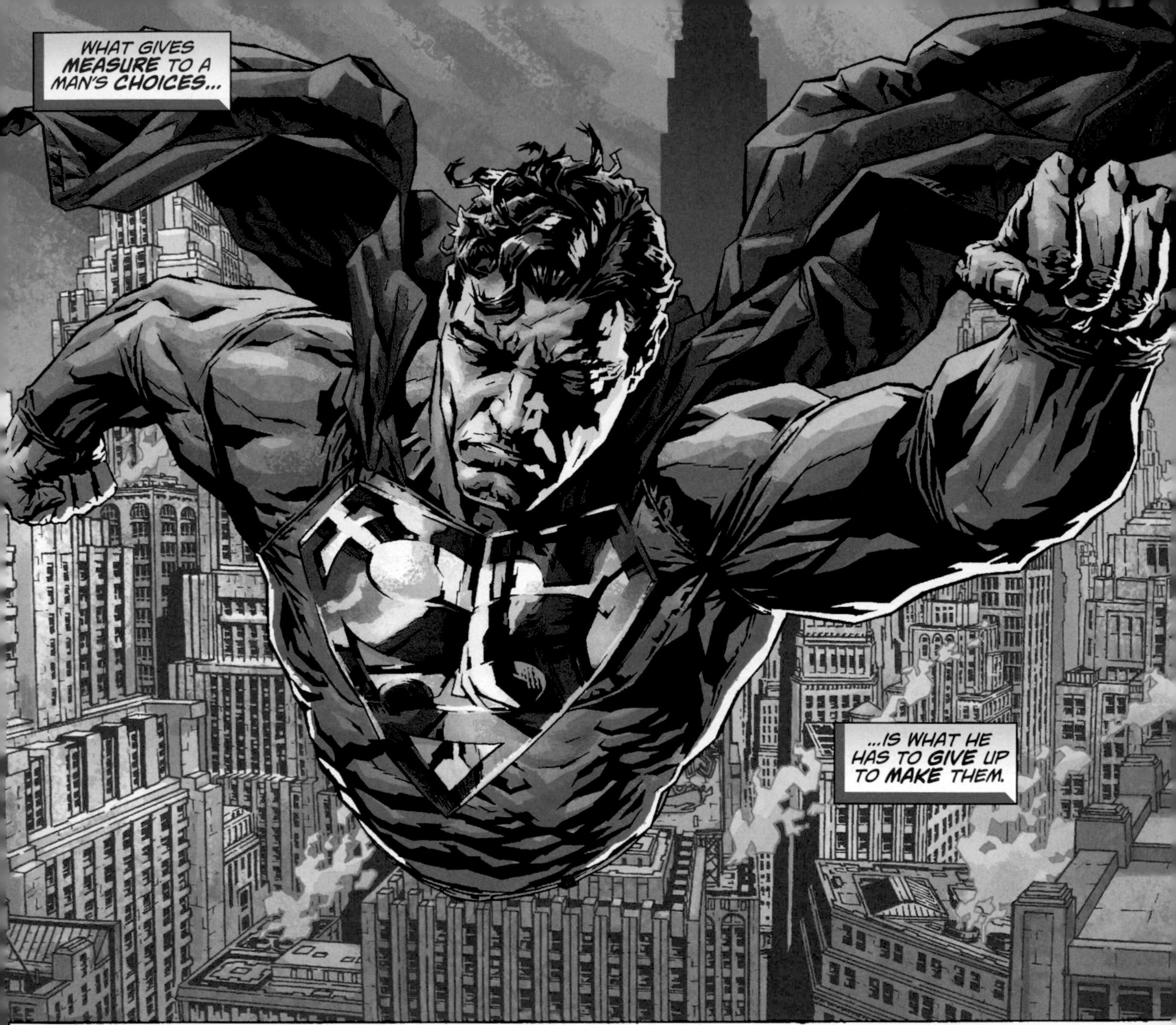
WHAT GIVES MEASURE TO A MAN'S CHOICES...
...IS WHAT HE HAS TO GIVE UP TO MAKE THEM.

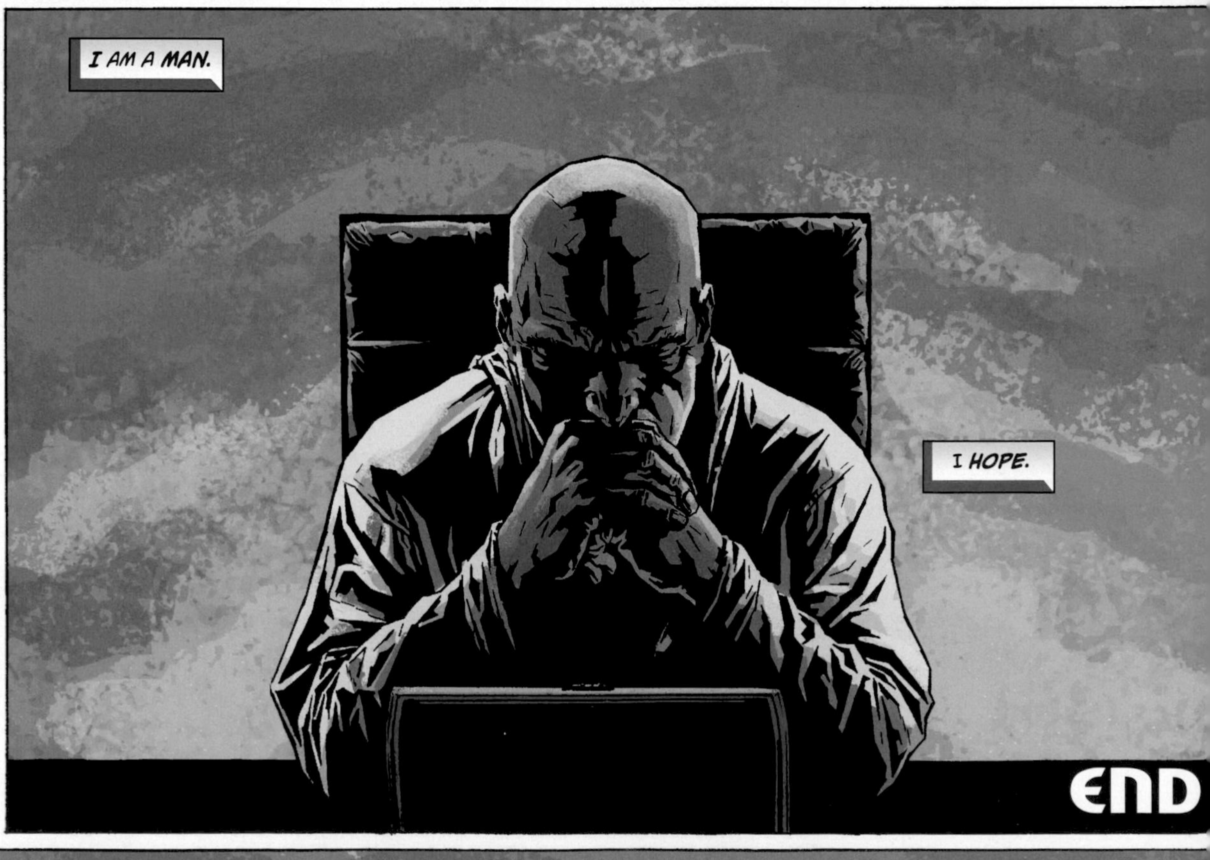
I AM A MAN.
I HOPE.
END

RESEARCH & DEVELOPMENT

Benchmarks from **Brian Azzarello** and **Lee Bermejo**

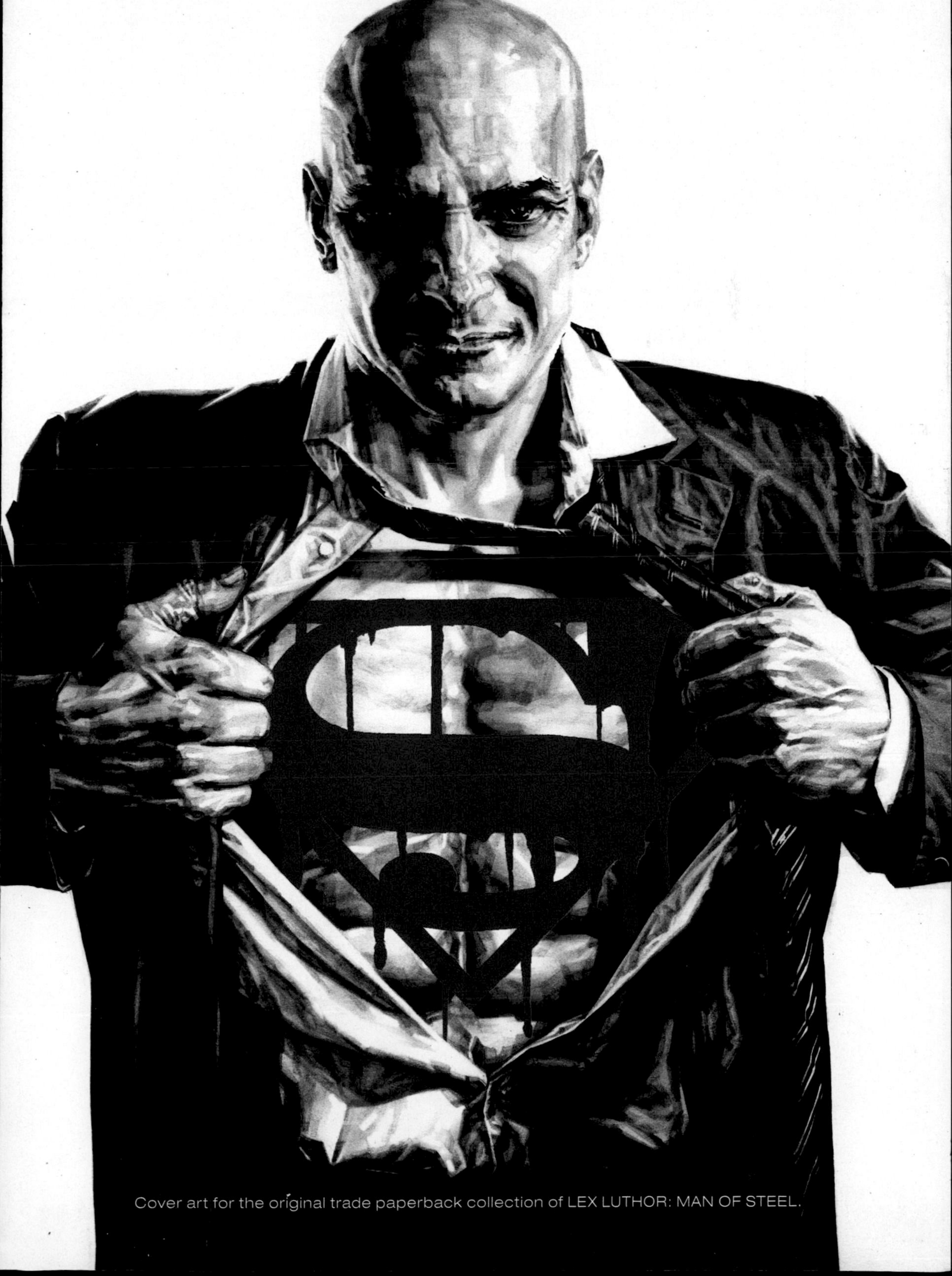

Cover art for the original trade paperback collection of LEX LUTHOR: MAN OF STEEL.

The original proposal for the five-issue LEX LUTHOR: MAN OF STEEL miniseries.

LEX LUTHOR: MAN OF STEEL

Proposal by Brian Azzarello & Lee Bermejo

Lex Luthor is arguably one of the most recognized comic book characters in mainstream culture, as well as a very vital part of the Superman myth. Evil genius. Billionaire industrialist. Superman's archenemy.

But who is Lex Luthor? More important—*why* is Lex Luthor?

This is the essence of MAN OF STEEL, a look at the Superman myth from Luthor's point of view — one that can't be as simply evil as it's been portrayed. I want to get at what motivates a man like Luthor—a self-made man who not only reached the mountaintop but maintains his lofty position there. The way the myth is structured now, Luthor feels threatened by Superman. But what if Luthor's actions are not based on his own personal insecurities, but on a recognition that Superman poses a threat to the world? What if Luthor's goal is not to bring Superman to his knees, but to save humanity before Superman brings it to *its* knees? What if Luthor understands that the only thing we have to prevent Superman from acting against humanity is his word? What if Luthor doesn't see the "man" part of Superman, but the alien? What if Luthor himself is a deeply religious man and sees Superman's status as a threat to the beliefs he shares with millions of people?

What if Luthor isn't motivated by petty evil, but by altruistic good? That would make Lex Luthor an extremely complex, rich, *human* character. It would also present a different, compelling view of the last son of Krypton, one that hasn't been touched on yet. It's been said that in any story, the villains are the most interesting characters. Well, in this story—according to Luthor—Superman is the villain. This could bring some of the vitality back to the character that has been missing for years. He wouldn't behave any differently than he has in the past, but through Luthor's eyes, Superman's actions are not those of a hero but the whims of an unstoppable force that could destroy Metropolis as easily as he could pluck a falling plane out of the sky. What if we've just been lucky so far that we've stayed on his good side?

And what if Luthor loves the human race more than Superman appears to? So much so that he chooses to sacrifice someone he loves personally and deeply, someone who has brought him a happiness he never dreamed he'd experience. Someone who will be lost to him forever.

The tragedy of the story is that Luthor cannot ever bring Superman down. Luthor is only human. He realizes the best he can possibly do is open people's eyes, and change the way they look at Superman. Give them pause, and have them say "Maybe he's not perfect..."

That's all we can hope to do as well.

← WHITE BACKGROUND →
HOPE'S UNIFORM IS LIKE A SHINY SILVER, LATEX LIKE MATERIAL.
COLOR SCHEME...
- FIGURES A BURNT UMBER, ORANGISH YELLOW.
A
B

LOGO SHOULD COVER HIS FACE
FOCUS SHOULD BE ON THE 'S' SHIELD WITH LUTHOR'S REFLECTI
AND THE CITY ON FIRE
THINK THE FIRST ISSUE COVER WITH MORE OF A WHOLE BODY SHOT OF LUTHOR
← BURNING CITY →

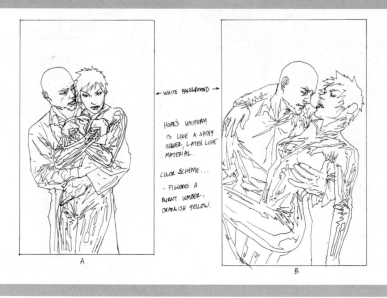

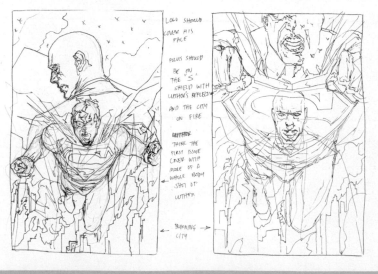

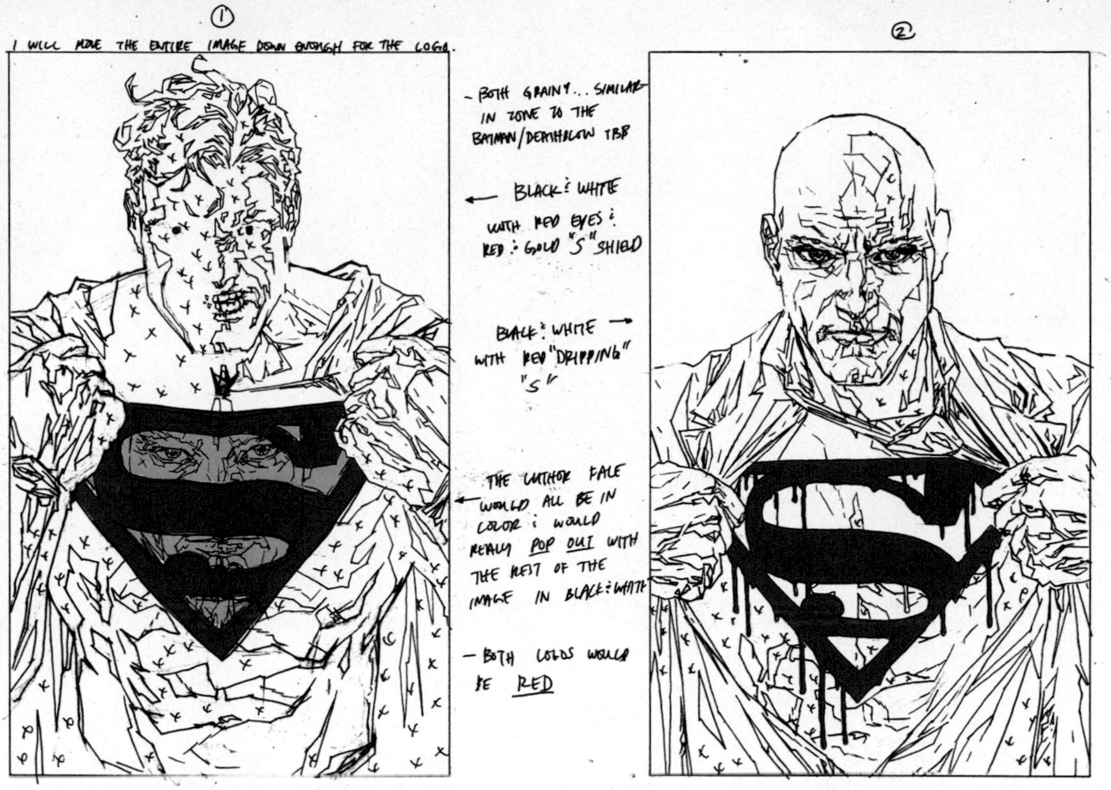
1
I WILL MOVE THE ENTIRE IMAGE DOWN ENOUGH FOR THE LOGO.
2
- BOTH GRAINY... SIMILAR IN ZONE TO THE BATMAN/DEATHBLOW TBB
BLACK & WHITE WITH RED EYES & RED & GOLD "S" SHIELD
BLACK & WHITE WITH RED "DRIPPING" "S"
THE LUTHOR FACE WOULD ALL BE IN COLOR & WOULD REALLY POP OUT WITH THE REST OF THE IMAGE IN BLACK & WHITE
- BOTH LOGOS WOULD BE RED

Cover sketches for issues 4 and 5 of the miniseries and the original trade paperback collection.

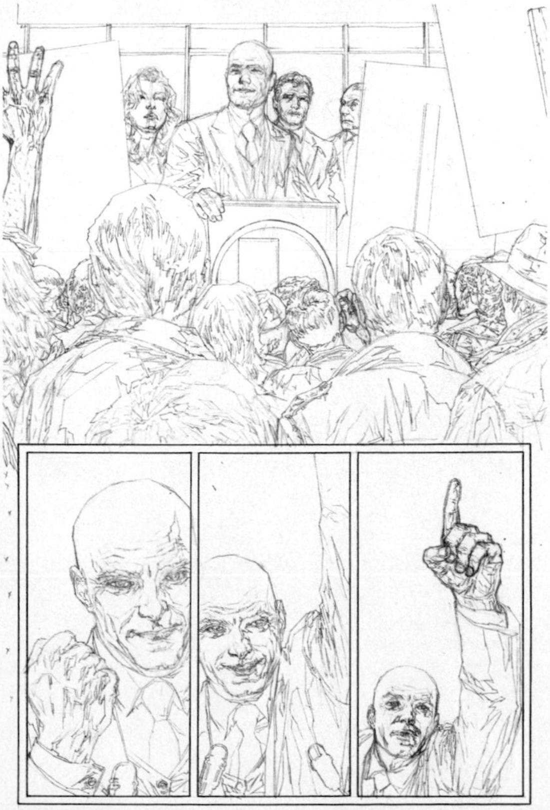

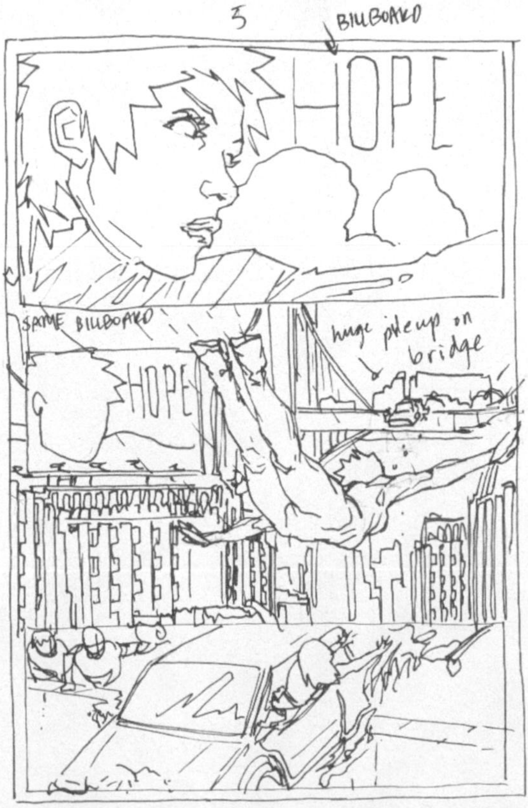
3
BILLBOARD
HOPE
SAME BILLBOARD
HOPE
huge pileup on bridge

Cover art for issue 1.

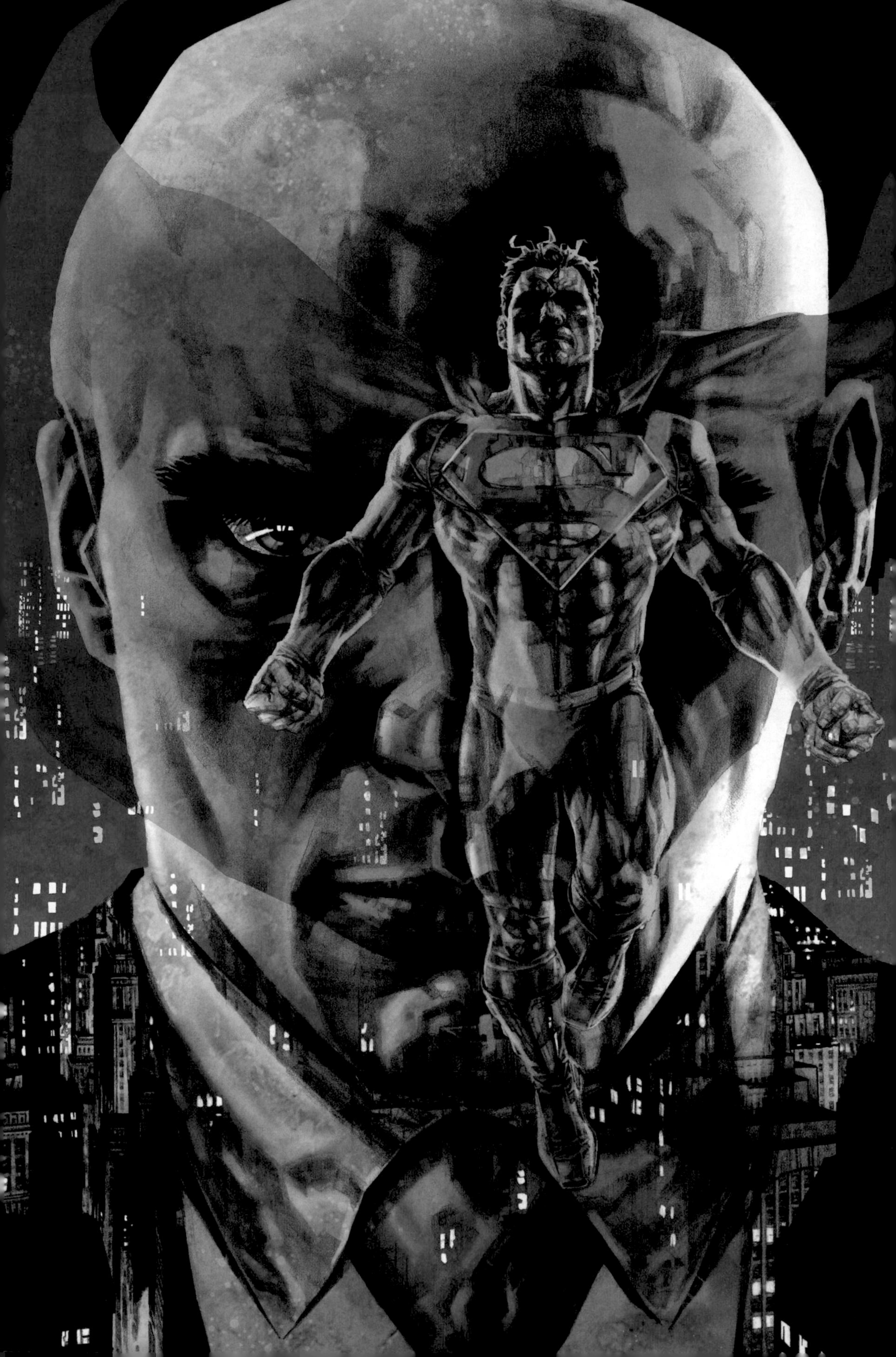

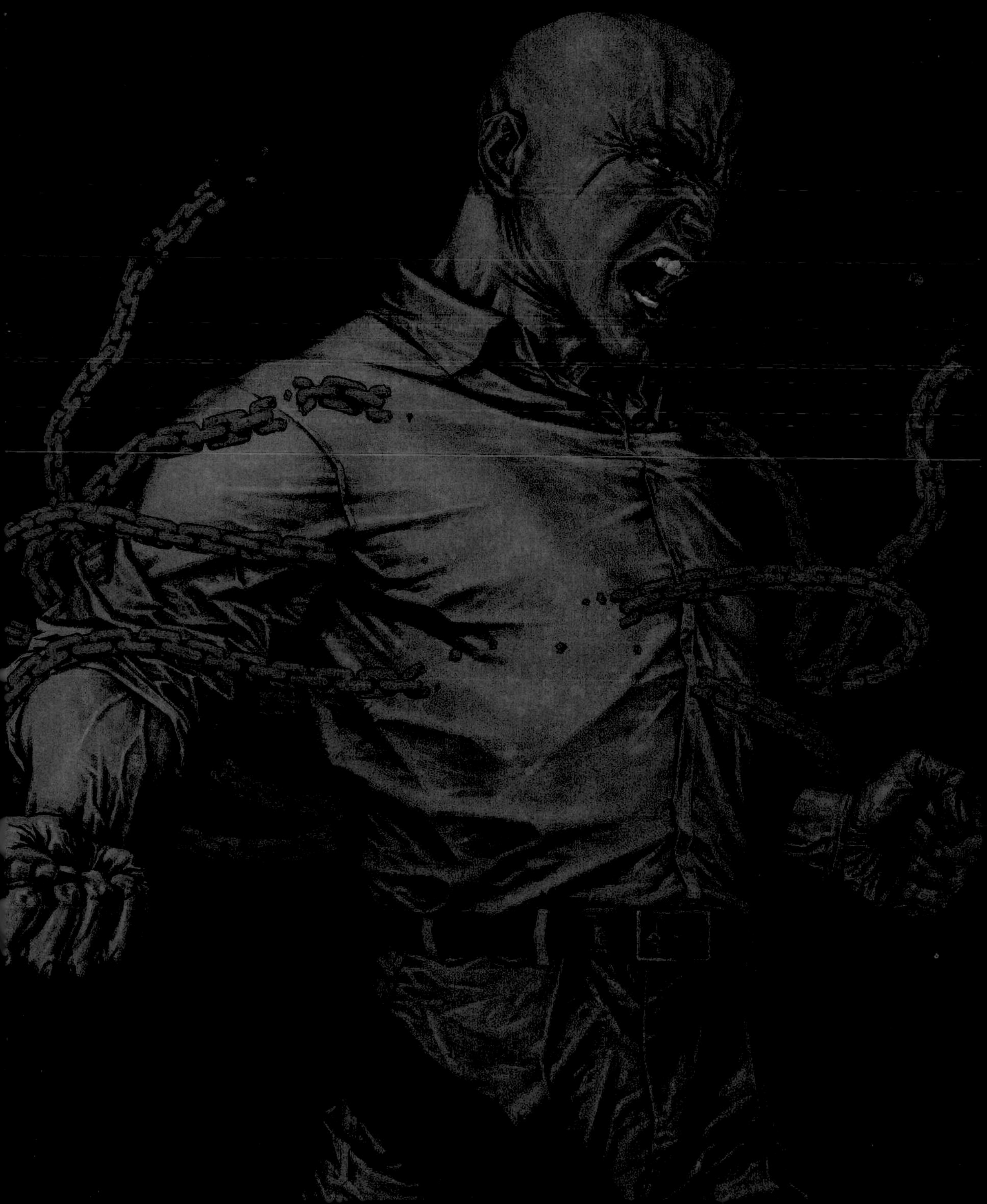

Cover art for issue 2.

Cover art for issue 3.

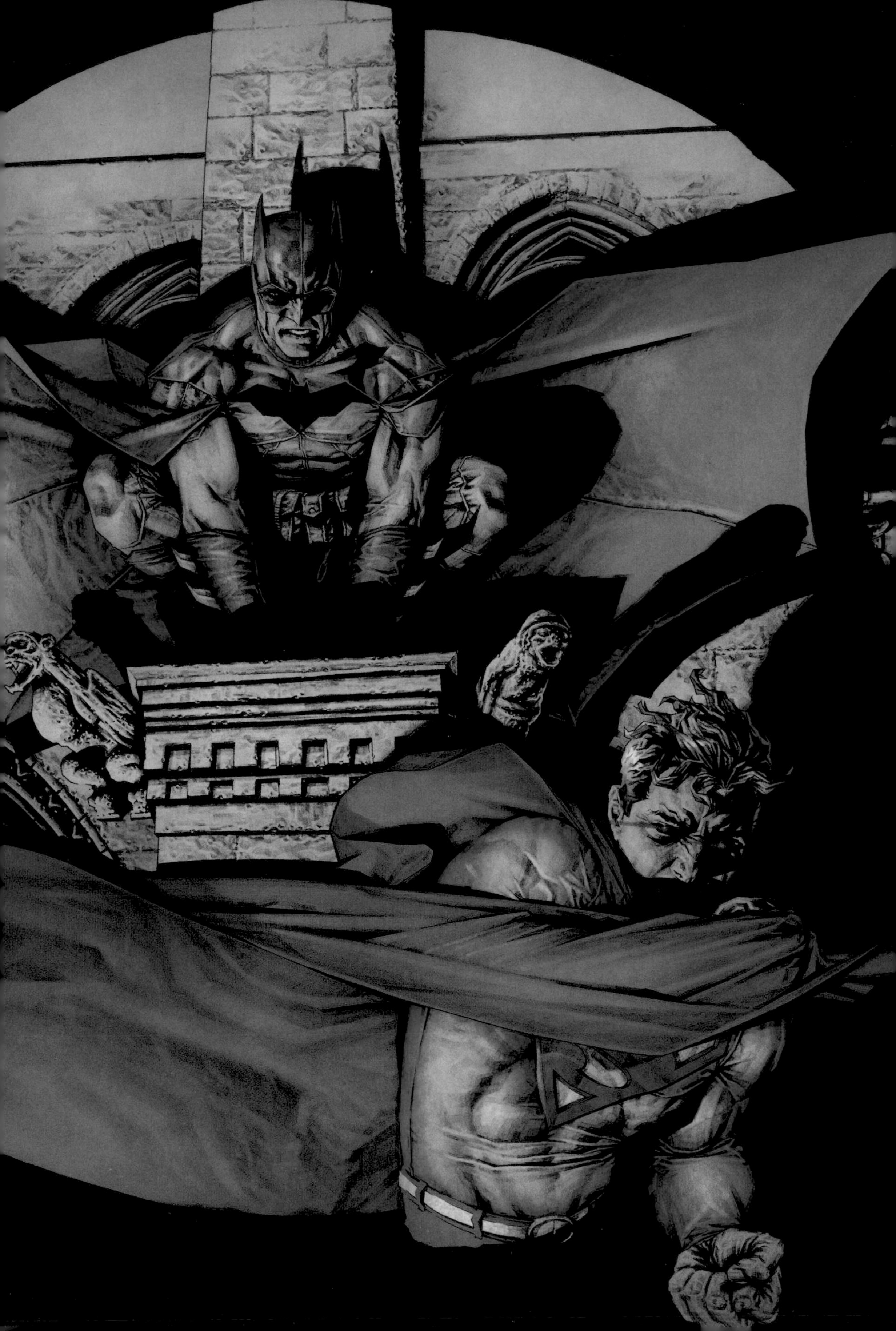

Cover art for issue 4.

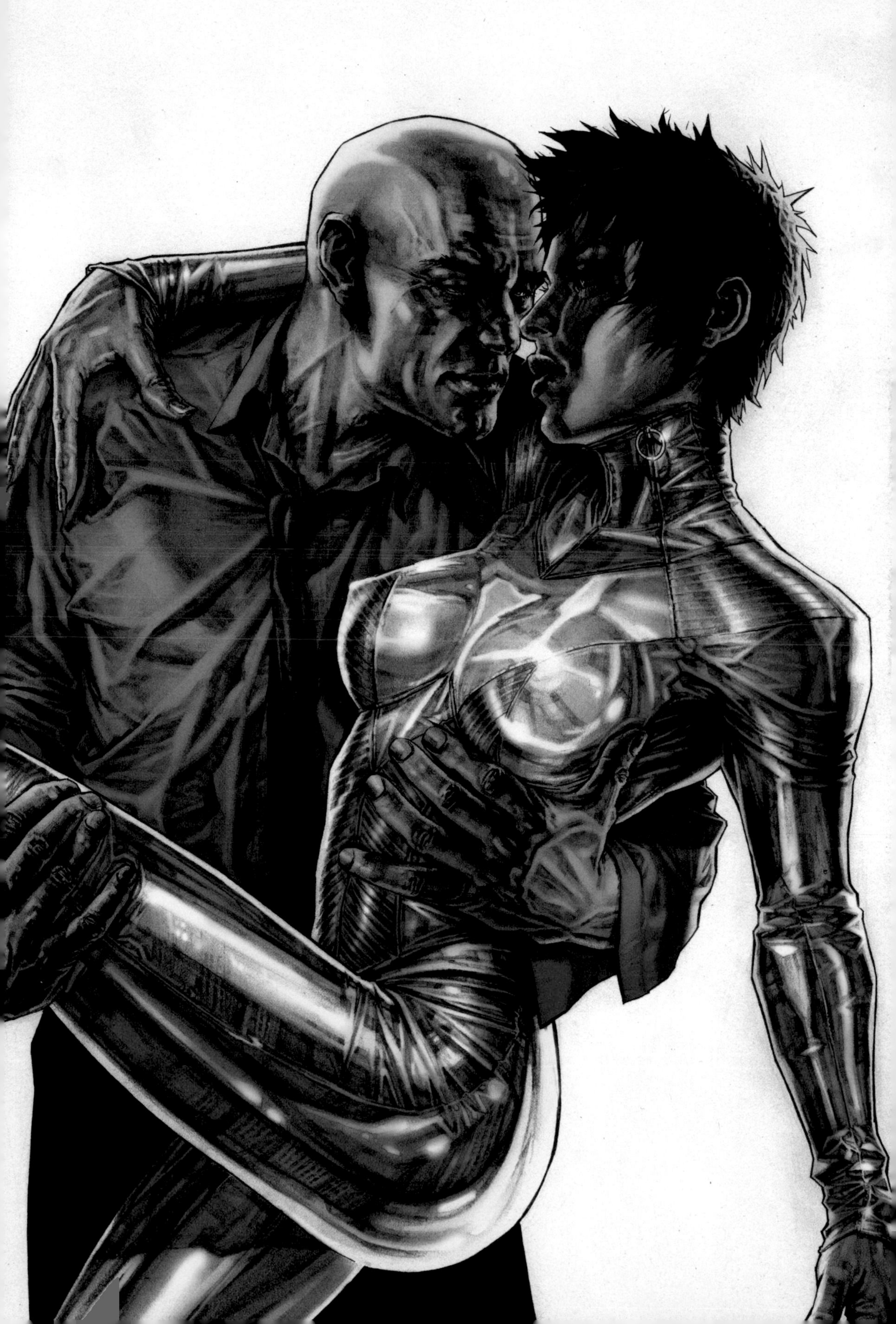

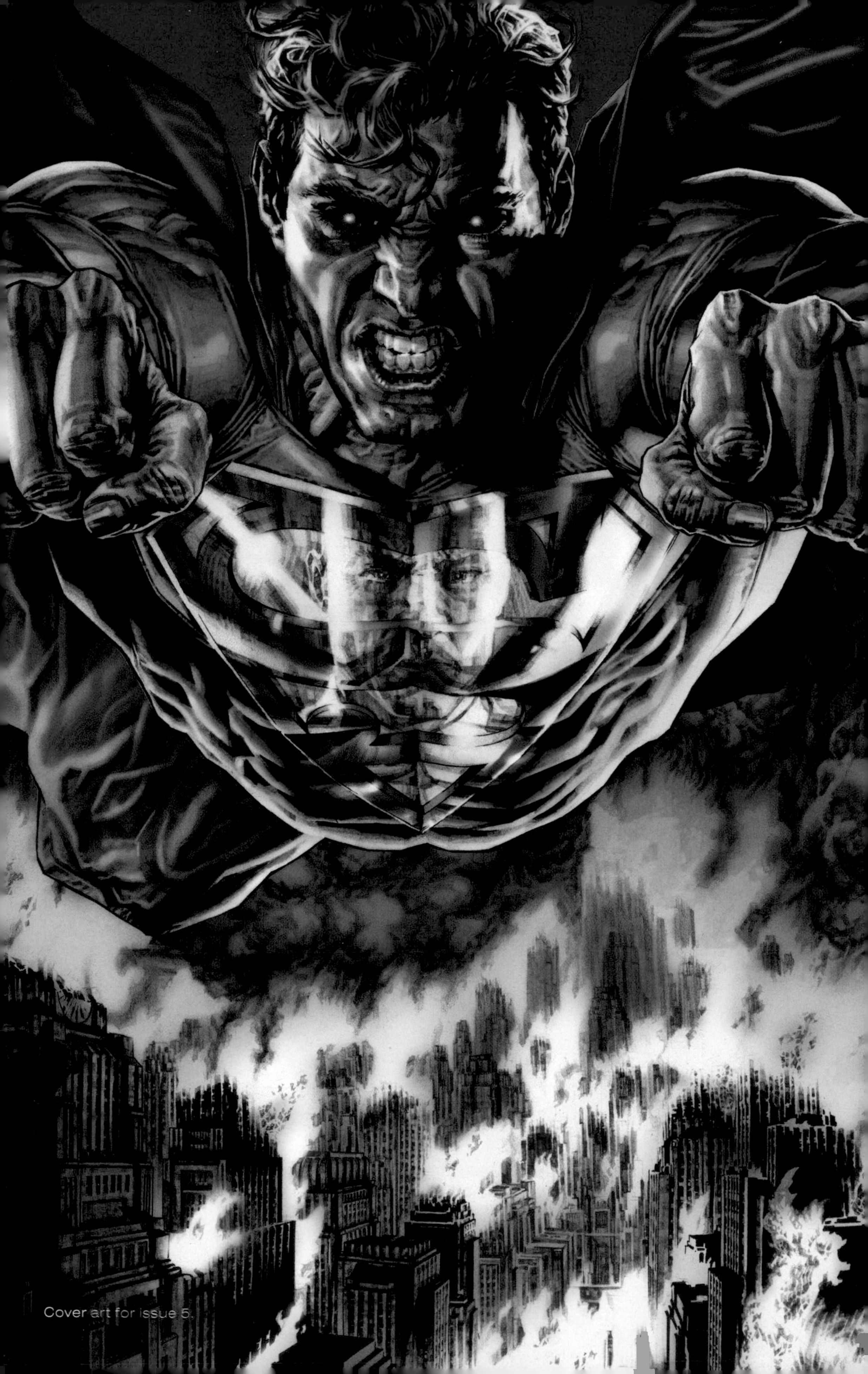

Cover art for issue 5.

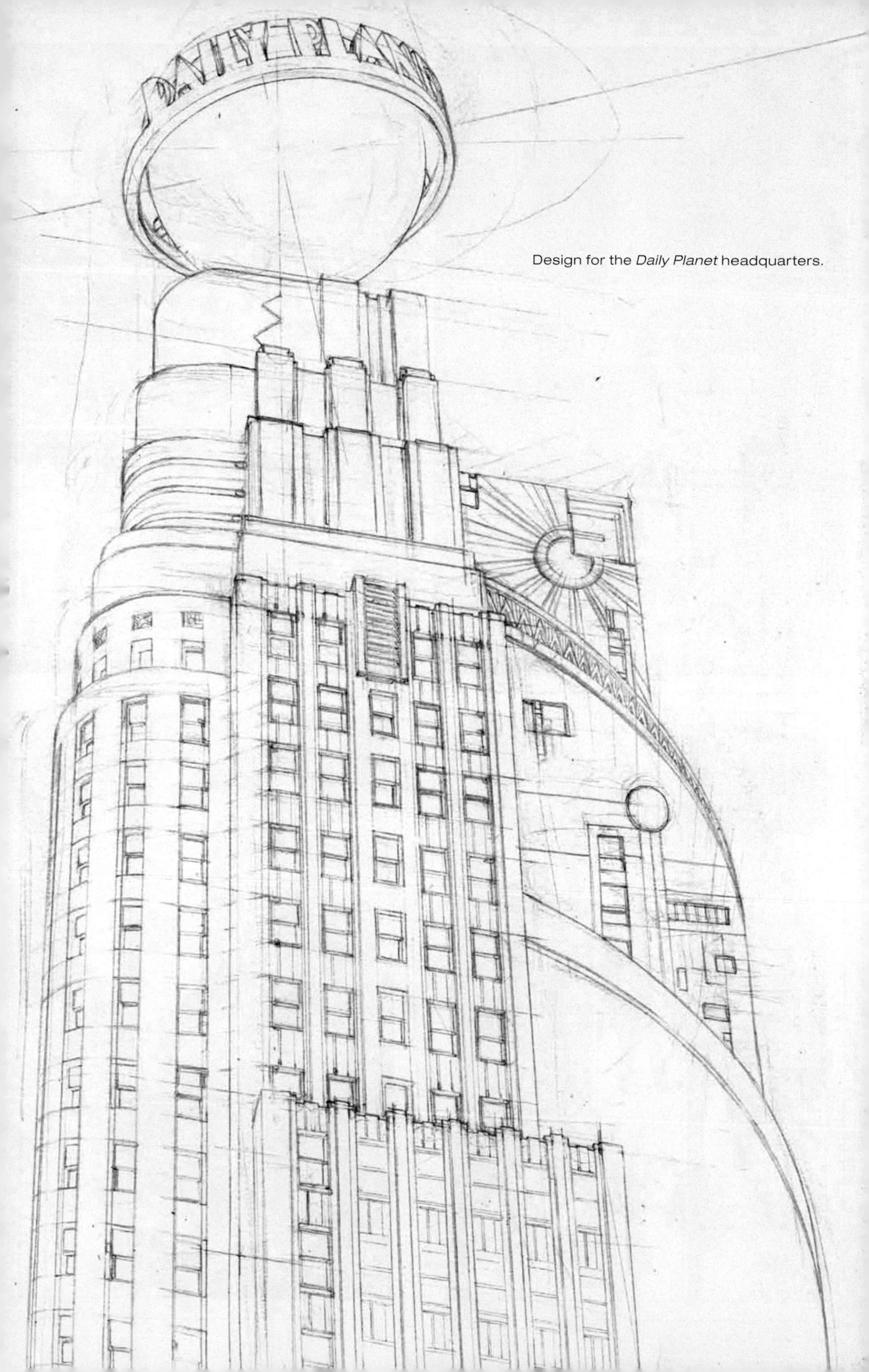

Design for the *Daily Planet* headquarters.

Final uncolored art from issue 3.

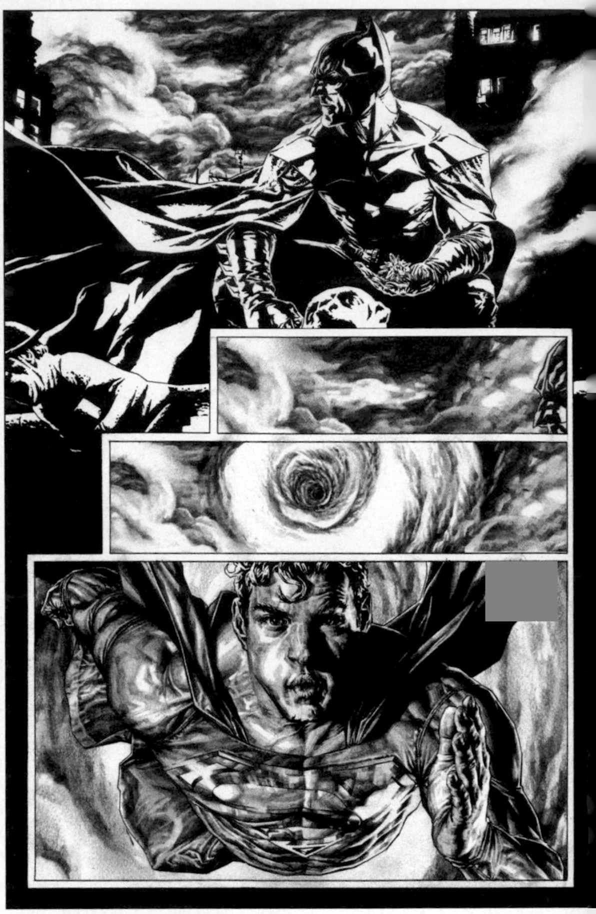

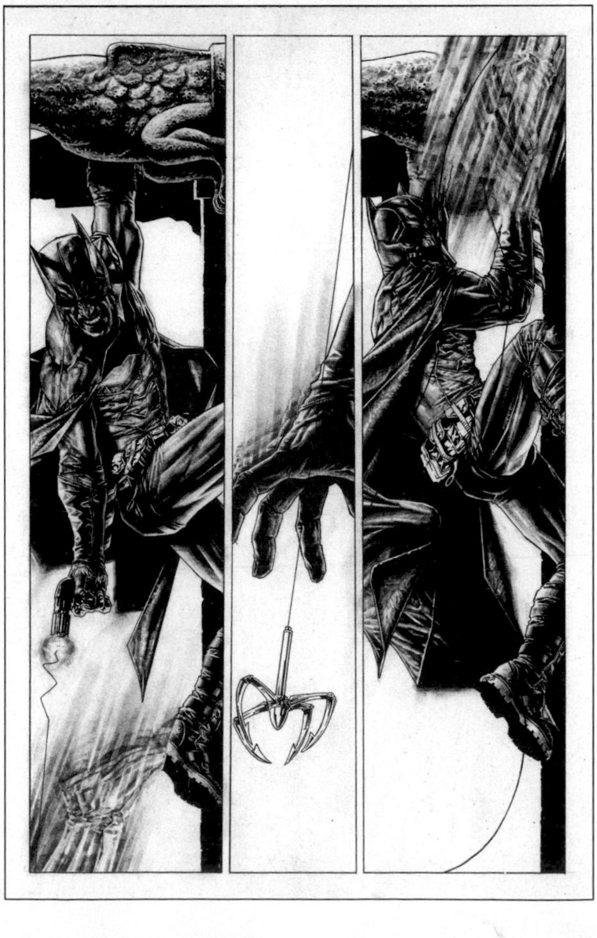

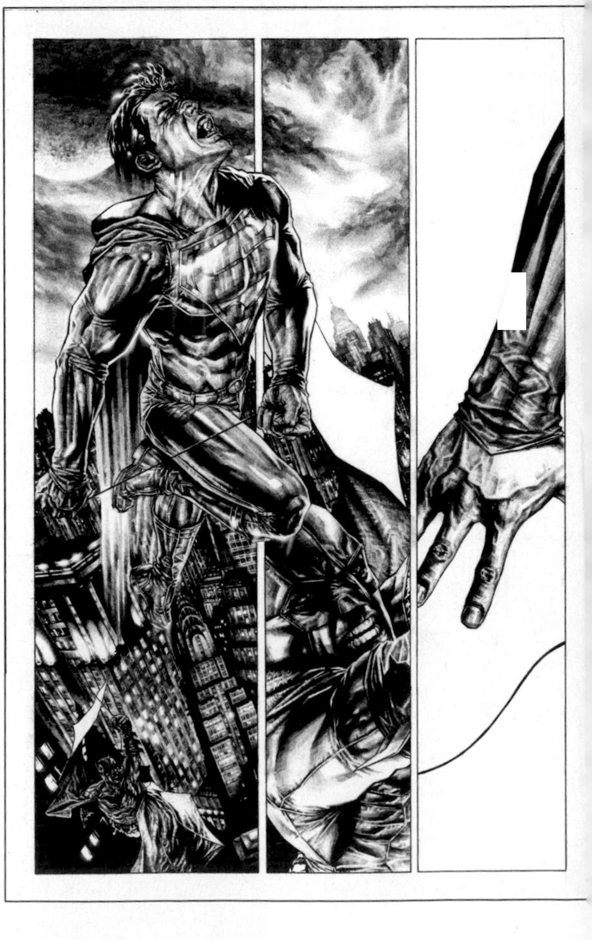

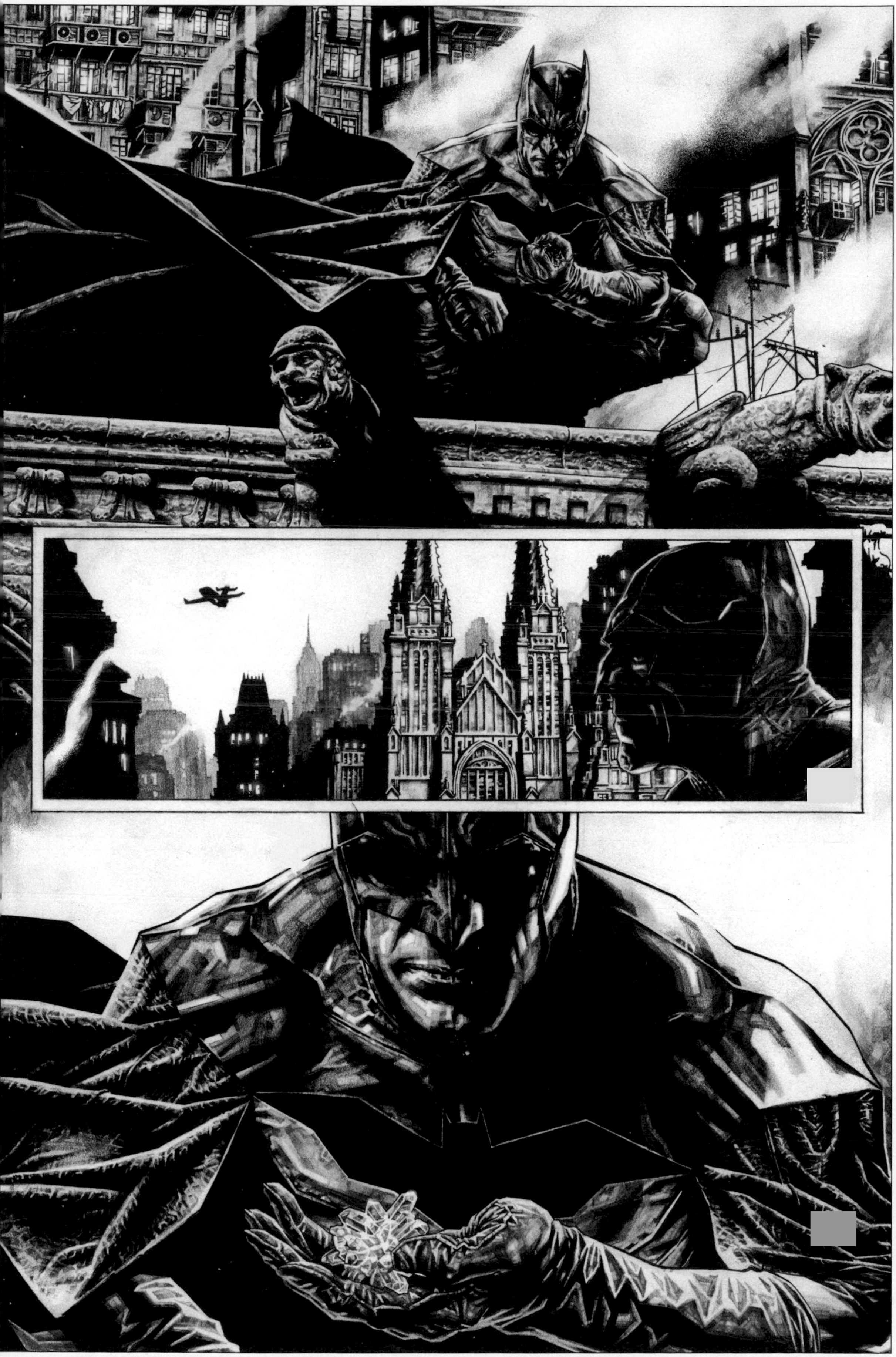

Final uncolored art from issues 3 and 4.

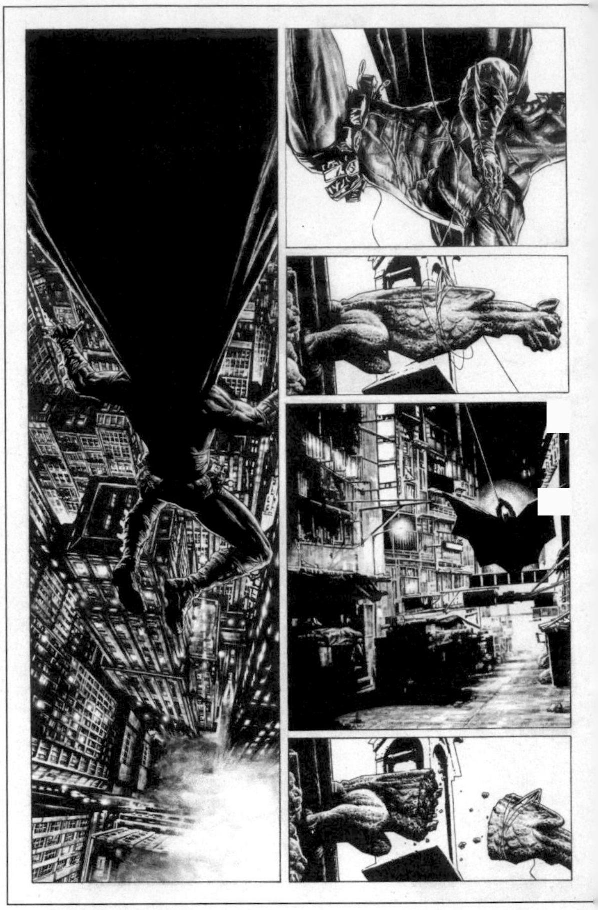

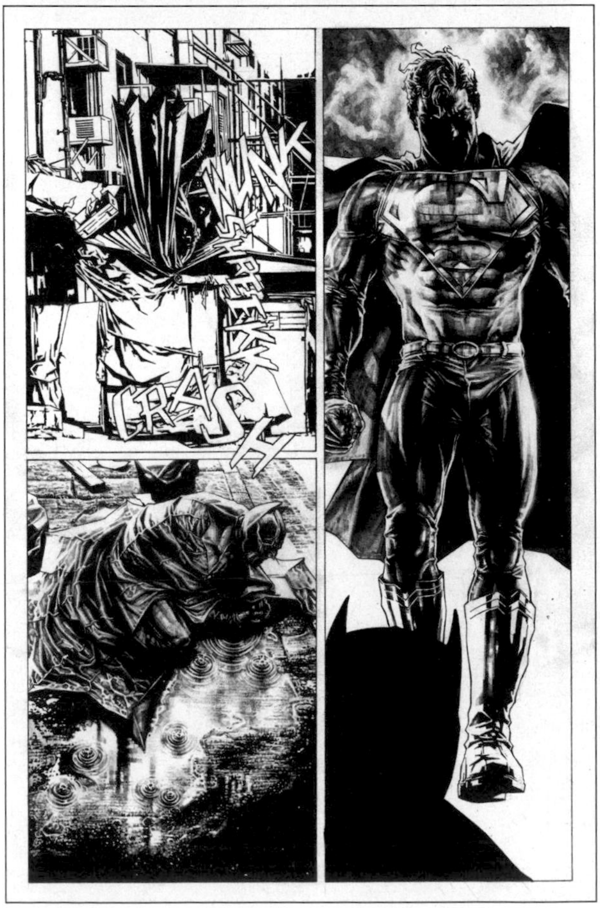
WUNK
CRASH

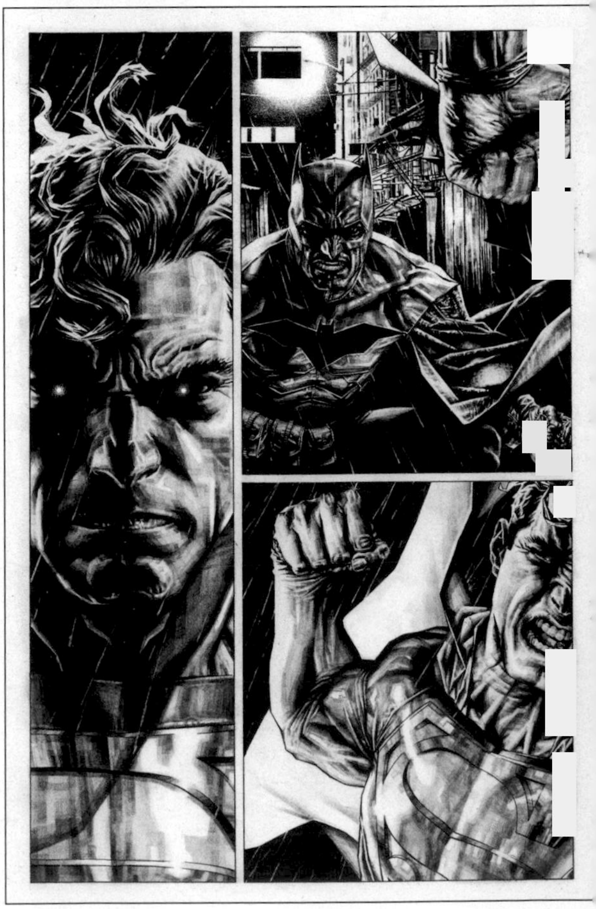

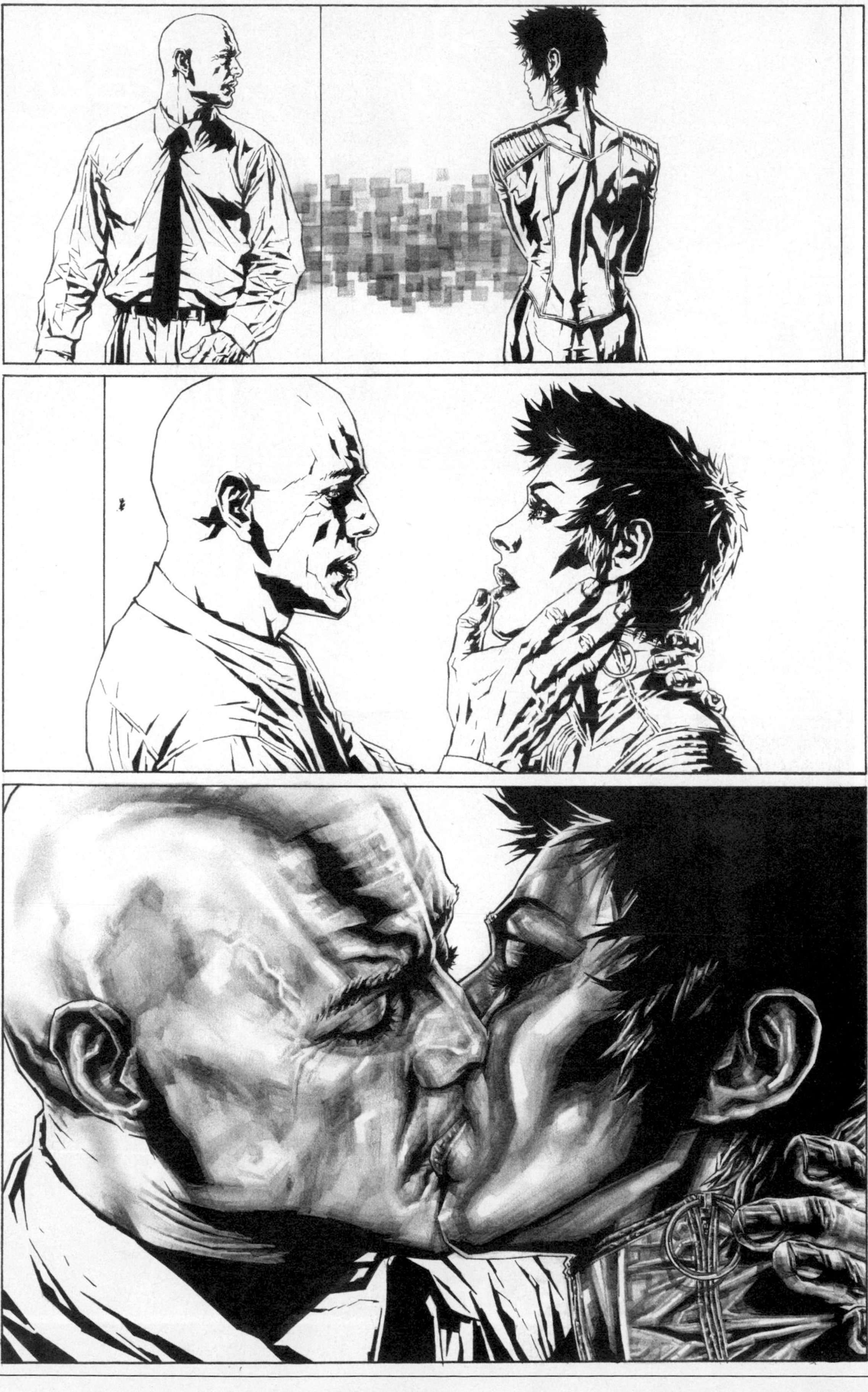

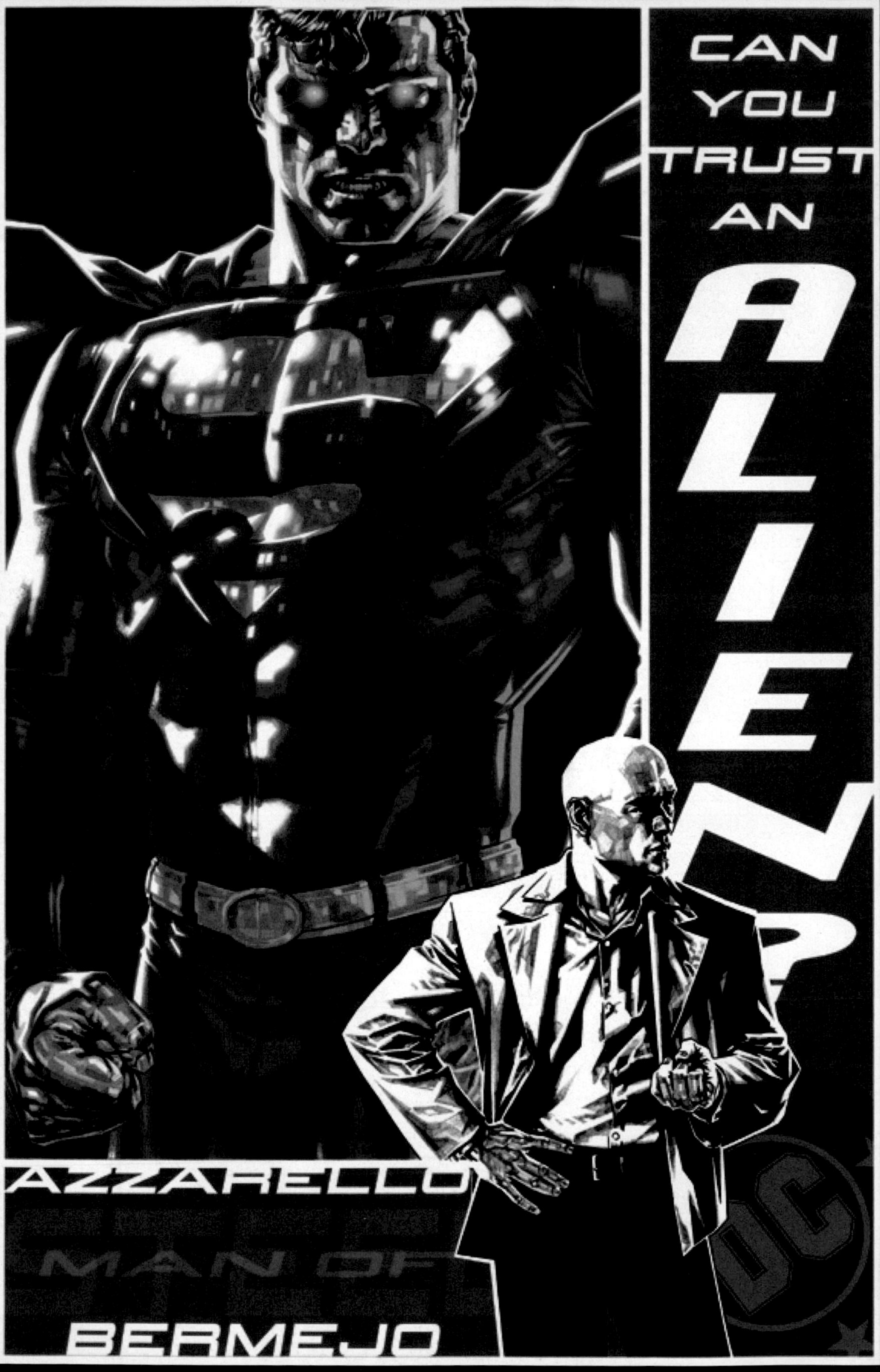
CAN
YOU
TRUST
AN
ALIEN?
AZZARELLO
MAN OF
BERMEJO

Promotional art for the miniseries.

Early cover designs for the expanded hardcover collection of the miniseries.

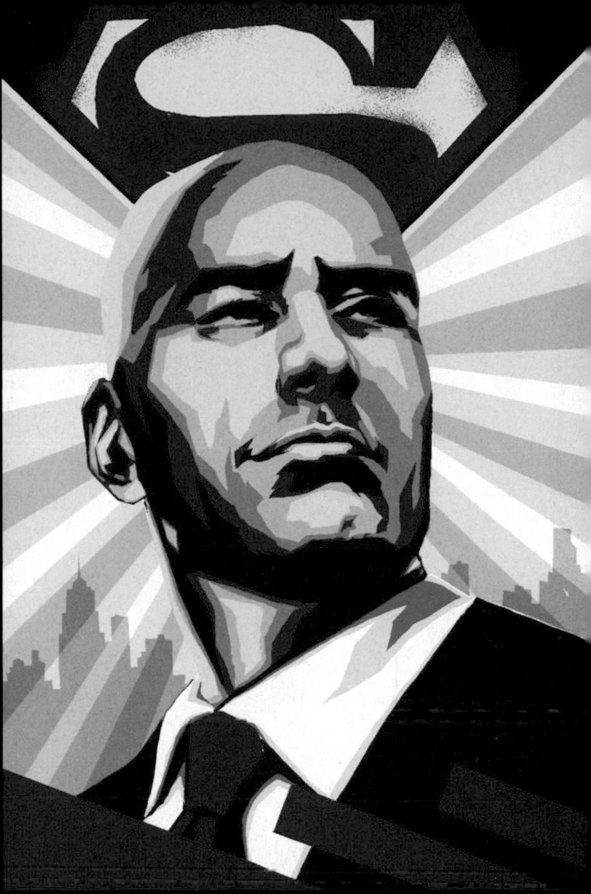

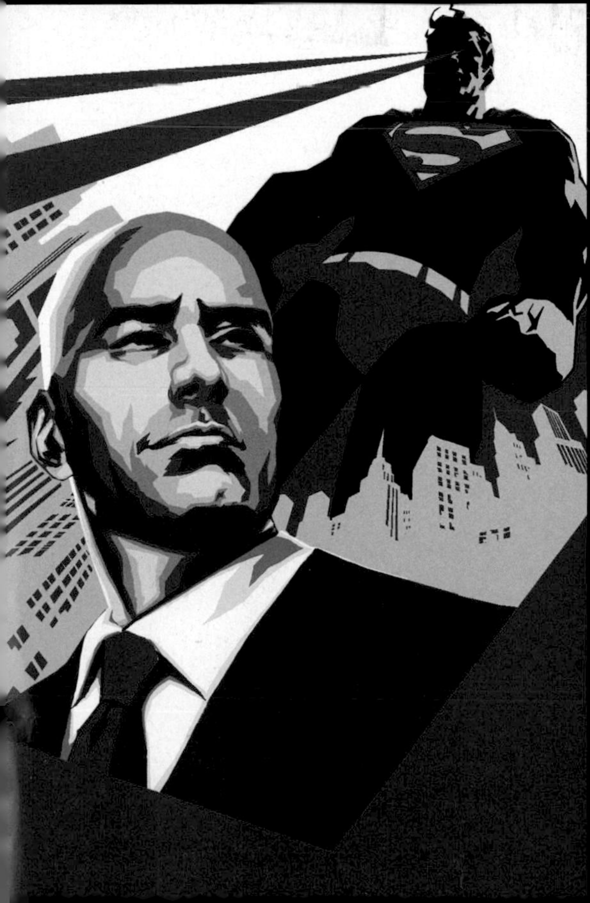

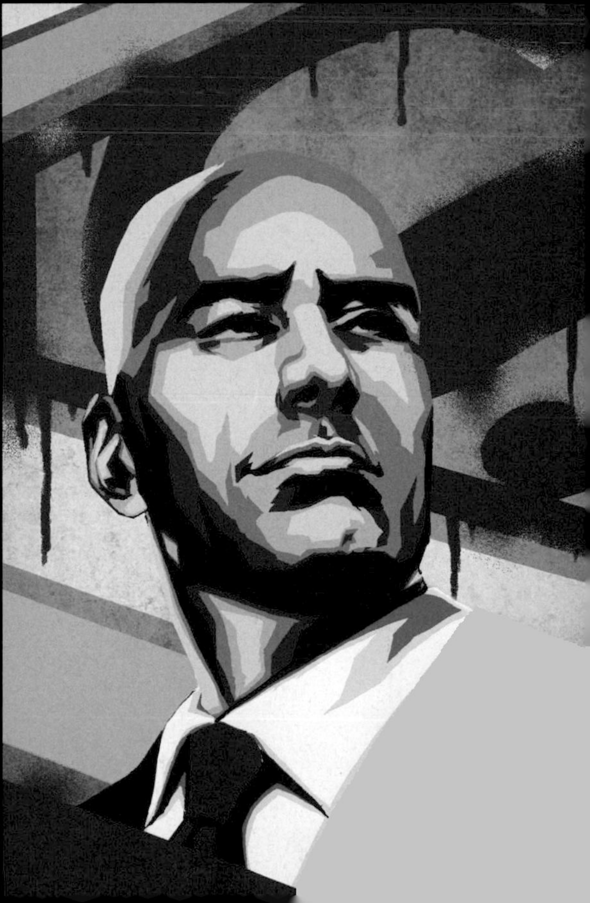

BRIAN AZZARELLO

New York Times best-selling writer Brian Azzarello has been writing comics professionally since the mid-1990s. He is the author of the graphic novels JOKER, LUTHOR, BATMAN/DEATHBLOW: AFTER THE FIRE and BEFORE WATCHMEN: RORSCHACH, all illustrated by artist Lee Bermejo, as well as the Harvey and Eisner Award-winning series 100 BULLETS and the miniseries JONNY DOUBLE and BATMAN: BROKEN CITY, all drawn by Eduardo Risso.

Azzarello's other work for DC includes the titles HELLBLAZER and LOVELESS (both with Marcelo Frusin), SUPERMAN: FOR TOMORROW (with Jim Lee), SGT. ROCK: BETWEEN HELL AND A HARD PLACE (with Joe Kubert), FILTHY RICH (with Victor Santos) and WONDER WOMAN (with Cliff Chiang). He also wrote the Richard Corben-illustrated graphic novels *Cage* and *Banner* for Marvel Comics. You can follow him walking the streets of Chicago, or on Twitter @brianazzarello.

LEE BERMEJO

Award-winning artist Lee Bermejo is the illustrator of the graphic novels BATMAN/ DEATHBLOW, LUTHOR, BEFORE WATCHMEN: RORSCHACH and the *New York Times* best-selling JOKER, all of which were done in collaboration with writer Brian Azzarello.

Bermejo's other work for DC includes the titles GLOBAL FREQUENCY (with Warren Ellis), SUPERMAN/GEN 13 (with Adam Hughes) and HELLBLAZER (with Mike Carey), as well as several dozen painted covers and the best-selling graphic novel BATMAN: NOËL, which he wrote and illustrated. He currently lives with his wife, Sara, in Italy, where he is hard at work on his creator-owned Vertigo series SUICIDERS.